I cannot recommend this book more! It's a heart-warming,
hilarious and honest account of the adventures of
living on a narrowboat. I LOVE it!
Michelle Dockery, actress (*Downton Abbey*, *This Town*)

All Boats Are Sinking is truly uplifting and brilliantly fun. Spending
time with Hannah on her narrowboat is like hanging out with a
good mate. Expect gossip, laughs and insights into her at-times
chaotic love life, and to walk away with a smile on your face.
Elise Downing, author of *Coasting*

If you've ever felt the call of adventure, this book
is for you. Uplifting and witty, a great read.
**Pip Stewart, adventurer and author of
*Life Lessons from the Amazon***

This is a delightful, moving and funny book which will speak to
anyone who has experienced heartbreak or personal crisis, and
in the aftermath sought to forge a fresh path. Just as we follow
the waterways of London and beyond, the reader is taken on a
journey with Hannah as she finds freedom and a sense of purpose.
Interspersed with intriguing vignettes of history and lists cheekily
summarising boat dos and don'ts, Hannah's honest and witty prose
brings to life her experiences, the people who share the waterways
with her and the challenges and joys of life on the canal.
Kat Hill, author of *Bothy*

ALL BOATS ARE SINKING

An Hachette UK Company
www.hachette.co.uk

Summersdale Publishers
Part of Octopus Publishing Group Limited
Carmelite House
50 Victoria Embankment
LONDON
EC4Y 0DZ
UK

This FSC® label means that materials used for the product have been responsibly sourced

MIX
Paper | Supporting responsible forestry
FSC® C104740

www.summersdale.com

Printed and bound by Clays Ltd, Suffolk, NR35 1ED

ISBN: 978-1-83799-401-4

Substantial discounts on bulk quantities of Summersdale books are available to corporations, professional associations and other organizations. For details contact general enquiries: telephone: +44 (0) 1243 771107 or email: enquiries@summersdale.com.

all boats are sinking

hannah
pierce

**Navigating Life,
Love and Locks
on a Narrowboat**

summersdale

all
boats
are
sinking

hannah
pierce

Navigating Life,
Love and Locks
on a Narrowboat

For Mum and Dad

Author's note

Some names and personal details have been
changed to protect people's identities

Contents

Prologue

We sat inside our respective boats, braced for the worst.

It had been an extreme winter, even by West Yorkshire standards, and the snow up at Stoodley Pike would be rapidly melting by now. With rain forecast overnight, the volume of water coming down the hills and entering the River Calder put those of us on the canal at risk. It was cold rain. Hard and loud against the steel. My neighbours' boats were tied onto mooring rings attached to concrete slabs at intervals along the towpath. *Argie Bargie*, my sturdy companion and home these past three and a half years, containing all my worldly possessions, was secured in place with pins I had hammered into the drenched ground myself.

In the afternoon, Dave arrived with several bags of coal. The owner of a local hire fleet, he had been delivering fuel to me these past few months with a cheery disposition and propensity for local gossip. He dropped the 20-kilogram bags onto my roof and recounted a tale from the last known floods on the Rochdale Canal. A boat had become unpinned and been swept downstream and onto the towpath, where it remained as the water levels subsided. I had visions of waking in the night to find I was wedged atop the lock gate below, my home swinging like a seesaw 19 feet above the canal.

That evening, as the downpour intensified and my phone pinged with notifications from FloodAlert about the rising water levels and imminent risk of flooding, my neighbour Jimmy knocked on the side of my boat. Wearing a waxed trench coat, he stood in the lashing rain with a saw in one hand and a large sheet of ply in the other.

"Hi, Jimmy," I said, laughing at the sight of him: a washed-up pirate with his enormous beard and leather boots.

PROLOGUE

He leant forward with the piece of wood and spoke over the rain and wind. "Do you want me to put this across your door?"

"How come?" I said from inside my dry cabin.

"You've not been in a flood before, have you?" His two spaniels were circling him, their brown fur like mopheads that had yet to be wringed out. "When that overflows" – Jimmy pointed to the guillotine lock above – "a tonne of water will come over your deck and in through your doors like a wave."

I looked at my doors and at Jimmy's thin bit of ply. Even if he was right, I wasn't sure it would do much.

"I think I'll leave it, Jimmy. But thank you anyway."

"Not to worry. Are you okay?" he said.

"Yeah, I think so. I just don't really know what to expect."

"Take my number," he said. "You can call or text if you're worried."

Jimmy returned to the other side of the canal. His historic working canal boat *Kyle*, dusty red in colour, was as handsome as any boat I had seen on my journey up here. Moored below the Golden Lion pub, it sat low in the water, wrapped in smoke circles that spun merrily from its iron chimney. The pub above was bright yellow in the rain. Its owners had painted its facade in the spring, in preparation for the Tour de Yorkshire. The race had subsequently been cancelled due to Covid and the new paint job had caused a rift with the council, who demanded they revert the Grade II listed building back to white. To me, this irreverent spirit was the heart and soul of Todmorden, the town I had called home these past two months.

Once Jimmy and his spaniels were safely inside their vessel, I closed up the front doors to my own floating home, a space I had been holed up in since the start of the pandemic, with its rusted and battered exterior, its battle scars. An inside neat but confined, with all my jumbled and eclectic belongings. Plants that hung from hooks and swayed with the movement of the boat. Kitchen appliances on display where no more space could be found in drawers. Piles of books and jars of homemade lockdown jam. Cushions, rugs and blankets of every colour. A black stove in its centre, with patched-up holes in the flue and markings on the floor from sparks and hot ash. An imperfect and muddled home. An extension of me, in every sense.

I sat on my sofa in the comfort and chaos of *Argie Bargie* and waited for the flood to come.

Chapter 1
London 2012

Part 1

~~~~~~~~~~~~~~~~~~~~~~~~~~~~~~~~~~~~~

All Boats Are Sinking

Chapter 1
London 2017

Months of talks and tears had led to this, our final evening together. I can't tell you who said the final sentence: We're breaking up. This relationship is over. But there was only one way we were leaving that flat: decoupled. No one begged or pleaded. No one hyperventilated through shock. There was some blame. Blame wrapped up in fear, guilt, regret. Anger too. Anger at the break-up itself. Anger at the splitting up of friends and untagging of photos. Anger that we had failed. Anger that we felt unheard. Anger that one day we would understand the hows and whys but for now, we couldn't. We sat on the sofa, smaller, lesser versions of the two lovers who had unpacked deeply contrasting books and placed them blithely on a new IKEA shelving unit a year and a half before. Sam had his head in his hands. Bitten nails and a signet ring obscured within his blond hair. We hadn't made eye contact for hours and when it was clear no more could be said, I stood up and left the flat.

The streets were orange with night-time lamps as I walked across the street to my best friend Caz's new home that she shared with her partner Natalie. I had known this moment would come for several weeks. We had done all we could, but our interactions had changed. We were no longer hopeful, and silences had appeared like sinkholes in our living room. The break-up was inevitable and irreversible. While heartbreak is a feeling I am not unfamiliar with, as I walked to Caz's I was heavy with an overwhelming quantity of grief, like I had accumulated all previous heartbreaks into this one. My eyes and their sockets ached, and though I had walked this same short journey many times before, my legs jolted in confusion at what was being asked of them. I made my way to her front door, feeling like an apparition of my usual self, and paused before ringing the bell.

Friends since the age of 11, Caz and I have a well-nurtured and unabating bond that transcends geography, the odd disagreement and seemingly any challenge life will throw our way. We are both able to sniff out underlying issues in each other's worlds and be ready to act with instinctual kindness. We share a humour that only she and I will ever understand, that others will at best find unfunny, or at worst, simply ignore, with knowing smiles across rooms, laughter to the point of tears and a game whereby we send each other screenshots of our internet search histories on the understanding that a refusal to present said screenshot will finally establish who is the weirder of the two.[1]

For the past six months, only a clock tower had stood between our two dwellings in the centre of Crouch End, North London. Caz had lived with Sam and I before she moved to her flat above the butchers with Natalie, where their home had a faint smell of sweet raw meat. She'd seen the relationship unravel quicker than I think we had, but she stood by and watched, ready to scoop me up when the time came.

"Stay as long as you'd like," she said as she was making up the sofa bed.

"Thanks, Caz."

"I mean it." She was grappling with the corners of the sheets. "Whatever you need."

I welled up at her kindness.

Caz stood up and looked at me. "Are you going to be okay?"

"Of course," I said, swallowing the tears down. It was too late at night to be opening up that can of worms.

"Right, okay. Well, we'll see you in the morning for eggs." She handed me a towel and left me to it.

---

1 To date, neither of us has refused to present a search history, though it has been confirmed we share hypochondriac tendencies and terrible spelling.

ALL BOATS ARE SINKING

In their front room, I lay staring at the walls. At pictures of their life together. All smiles and sunglasses. I wanted their home, though not this flat. I wanted a home that reflected me just like theirs reflected them. I had felt alien in my own home, and in theirs, wearing Caz's oversized T-shirt and football shorts, soft with fabric conditioner, I felt comforted, but not comfortable. I was alone again and starting over. No home and no money. I was 31 years old, with an overwhelming sense of failure. This is not how I had imagined my life to be.

With the heavy fatigue of an as-yet sleepless night, I turned my thoughts to the options before me. I would need somewhere to live, and fast. I lay on the sofa bed and searched the internet on my phone. There were one-bedroom studio flats in South-east London for £1,200 a month. Shared houses in Leytonstone. Renting on my own would be financially impossible and house shares provoked memories of a younger Hannah. As tempting as it would be to revert, I could see the slippery slope into behaviours I was just about crawling out of. Untidy bedrooms and passive aggressive texts about whose shelf in the fridge was causing the kitchen to smell like that. I just couldn't picture it.

I didn't have a penny to my name. I have never been good with money and have always lived pay cheque to pay cheque. I'm not a high earner, but I could have been more cautious over the years. I could have put money aside and saved for my future, like Caz had. As I lay in her flat picturing the next phase in my life, I berated myself for my lack of planning and short-termism. I should have spent less money on takeaways and taxis. I have this trait of never looking too far into the future. It's a blessing at times. When I'm standing in a moment of wonder, climbing a hillside or watching flames from a bonfire, I am overcome with emotion and joy, and for that I am so very grateful. But it's a trait that now makes me squirm with my infantile approach to planning.

I'm extremely lucky, though. I know my parents have earmarked just enough for a house deposit for me.[2] Not enough for London but for somewhere outside of the city. So, pondering my future for the first time ever, I searched the internet for properties to buy, checking the commute to work if I headed to Hertfordshire or to Kent. But even with this deposit money, I just couldn't afford it. The mortgage would be too high on my salary.

And then I looked at boats.

I had been intrigued by the London canal community ever since my friend Megan had moved onto a boat. She had left a house-share in East London and with help from her parents had bought a boat from a friend. Megan and I had been introduced eight years ago and had launched a theatre company together. It had since wound down, but our friendship remained. She'd been on board her boat for a year and had not looked back. I regularly visited for wine on her roof, quietly admiring her cocoon-like home. I would return to my rented flat and guiltily daydream, wondering if there would ever be a time when I might follow in her footsteps.

Having lived in London for seven years, I was familiar with the canals that run through its London boroughs. Camden, Kings Cross and Little Venice, places I would otherwise never dream to call home. As I lay in the orange glow from the street, in a flat above a butchers in Crouch End, the idea of joining Megan on the waterways was becoming an attractive prospect.

The boats for sale on the internet were worn but charming, with tiny kitchens and curtains fitted onto brass window frames. Roof gardens with cats hiding amongst miniature wildflower meadows. Painted deck furniture and cast-iron wood-burners. Den-like, they left no room for subtlety or minimalism.

Looking at Caz's living room, I realised a canal boat was probably no bigger than this one room in total. Could I live in a space this small? It was hard to imagine. I'd lived in shared homes my whole

---

2   Or for my wedding day, lol.

life and wasn't sure what being alone should feel like, let alone how much space I might need. There was something comforting in the idea, though, of somewhere I could nest without a care in the world of what anyone else might need or want. Exhausted but curious, I dropped my phone on the floor and closed my eyes. The idea of living on a boat had intrigued me enough to distract me from the insomnia, and I was soon asleep.

I stayed on the sofa bed at Caz and Natalie's until the weekend, visiting the flat once while Sam was at work. Doors remained ajar onto rooms we had once been so intimate in. I kept my head down and gathered a bag of items that would see me through, leaving behind my toothbrush which he had chucked in the bathroom bin, and left.

On my first Saturday alone, I found myself at a Royal Mail sorting office at the end of an industrial estate in North London. I stood in the queue wondering, could these people sense the break-up on me? My hunched posture and furrowed brow; a sure giveaway of my sad state. Would the postal worker ask me how I was today? Would I cry when she did? Did I need to explain that my address is no longer my address?

I reached the desk, mustered a smile and dug out the "sorry we missed you" card stuffed somewhere in my jeans pocket. The postal worker checked my face against its buoyant predecessor on the back page of my passport and disappeared out the back.

My phone buzzed. It was Mum calling me back. I spoke with the phone wedged precariously between ear and shoulder as a shoebox-sized parcel addressed to me was placed on top of the counter.

"It's over, Mum," I said down the phone.

"Oh Hann—"

"It's fine," I said. "I'm thinking about living on a boat."

This wasn't how I intended to raise the idea with the very person who I hoped would be paying for it, but if I knew my mum at all, her reaction to the break-up would spark grave concerns around my future. I needed her to know I had a plan and was in control.

I nodded to the postal worker and walked back past the queue.

"Hannah, you can't even drive," she said.

Tears pinched at the corner of my eyes. "I don't know what else to do, Mum."

I didn't.

"Why don't you move back home?" she said.

Mum has a tendency to go to the extreme. Whether it's a broken dishwasher or a death in the family, her stress reactions are the same. I could hear the panic rising in her voice.

"My work finishes at four some nights." I'd been working as a promoter for late-night music venues, and though I had adapted to my nocturnal schedule, arriving at my parents at sunrise smelling of nightclubs was a memory I felt best left in the past.

"Well then, you can get the six o'clock train that goes from London to Ipswich?" Her regional upward inflection was giving the suggestion a comedic quality. I appreciate it's not uncommon for parents to want to bring their offspring closer in moments of crisis. To look after and console. But this wasn't a crisis. It was sad, sure, but it wasn't a crisis. Besides, I had a plan.

"I'm not sure that's the answer."

There was a momentary silence. I took my opportunity.

"What do you think about this boat idea, then?" I said, soothingly. "Do you remember my friend Megan lives on one?"

"Oh, I don't know, Hannah. It sounds awfully cold."

"Will you think about it?" I said.

"I'll talk to your dad."

I hung up and continued along the winding road back to civilisation. I breathed through the exhaustion and welcomed a new feeling of relief. Telling Mum about the break-up was a milestone, and it hadn't felt as hopeless as I had feared. I knew I would be letting her down, but it seemed that her preoccupation was with my well-being and not with all that I was saying goodbye to. *She wants me to be happy,* I thought, *and in control of my life. And if there is something that can inspire those feelings then I must run with it.* On the bus back to Caz and Natalie's flat, I felt an intense clarity for the first time in months. This was my time to be me. Even if Mum and Dad weren't on board and it meant getting a loan approved, I was buying a boat. I was not commuting from my parents' home in Ipswich.

Chapter 2
Argie Bargie

My first weekend of sofa-surfing coincided with my boat friend Megan taking herself off to Glastonbury Festival. Megan was a circus producer, and she'd landed herself a ticket as a volunteer. Moored alongside Victoria Park, a green sanctuary in the heart of East London, the boat was mine while she made use of the "posh toilet facilities" at the festival.

I stood on the platform at Seven Sisters Overground station, my "stopgap" belongings in two tote bags pressed deep into my shoulders. With a coffee in one hand and my phone in the other, I waited for a train that would take me to Megan's, where I would dump my bags and head straight back out for a ten-hour shift at work. Mum had been messaging. An article in *The Guardian* newspaper titled "Canals offer alternative to London property ladder" had told her all she needed to know about London boat living. Quoting the article, Mum was now more enthused than me.

"It's a solution to the housing crisis, Hannah," she texted. **"An affordable way to live in London."**

Mum had experienced a 180 on the whole affair and this newfound support had led to a stream of text messages about measurements for curtains, mini cookers, washing machines and manual dicers.

"We haven't even found one yet!" I texted, as the screen before me blurred.

Overwhelmed by my parents' willingness to spend their hard-earned money on their youngest in such an unconventional way, I felt a rush of guilt at Mum's texts. Had I given them no option but to support me? *I should be in a position to do this myself*, I thought. It was all happening so quickly, and I didn't know whether to be grateful or angry. Why didn't I have any savings? What if my parents needed this money in the future? Why was London so bloody expensive?

"I've found some lovely green velvet in a charity shop. Perfect for curtains," she texted. **"Shall I buy it?"**

I'd had a panic attack twice before, so I knew what was coming. I dropped the tote bags and squatted down to ground level. The back of my ears were suddenly covered in sweat. Drips slid down my jaw and joined tears at my chin, falling in large salty drops between my knees. I'm not sure how many trains came and went as I sat on the platform in the half shade of the signal mast, not thinking about boats or my parents, or Sam, or my looming ten-hour shift, only breathing.

Once I was able to, I took my phone out of my pocket. My hand was shaking. I called Jim, the manager of the venue I was working at that night.

"Hi, Jim," I said. "I've had a funny turn. I'm sorry, will you be okay tonight without me?"

"It's fine," he said. He was speaking as if to a child, with a softness I'd not heard in him before. "We'll be fine, Hannah, just go home and sleep."

That word. Home.

Moved by his warmth, I thanked Jim and hung up the phone. The sun was strong. I let it dry the tears from my tired skin and stared down the station platform towards the horizon of central London. The track curved round a bend towards the bustle of homes, offices and businesses: a proud view of buildings that sparkled with heat. A still city with its pounding lifeblood. My city. My home.

My breathing slowed.

I peeled myself onto a connecting train and made my way to Megan's boat. I arrived at the mooring spot outside the park's entrance, a scene of boat upon boat along the canal's edge, twinkling with the same city heat. A colourful cutting[3] of water hidden

---

3 The canal network is often referred to as "the cut" by those who use it.

within the London skyline, strong hulls against bottle green water, as waterfowl glided, dipped and skated across their homeland. Megan's grey boat sat under a canopy of trees, tied onto two metal mooring rings on the towpath. I'd watched her tie her boat up before, cautiously adjusting the length and tension of the ropes with such care, her body relaxing when she felt the positioning was just right.

I climbed aboard Megan's boat, closed up her shuttered doors and flopped onto her bed.

~~~~~~~

I awoke with a gentle sway to the sound of chatter on the towpath and sunlight through the curtains, which was making everything red. Megan had recently come back from a trip to Palestine, and her boat smelled faintly of zaatar and dried fruit. I put on a stove-top coffee and turned on the radio, which was tuned into BBC Radio 4.

I opened the parcel I'd picked up from the post office. It was from Syd. Syd and I studied together at drama school, and she was the first person I met during induction week. Back then she had long brunette hair with tight ringlets and the odd straightened segment. She wore leather coats and smoked liquorice rollies. The parcel contained an emergency break-up kit; a penis candle, some chewing gum, a heart-shaped flannel and a handwritten card welcoming me to another period of singledom.

I texted Syd.

"You're so sweet," I said. "Thank you."

"Thinking of you xxx," she replied.

I sat on Megan's small red sofa, my gifts from Syd by my side, and took in the boat. Megan's home was an illusion. Its exterior was light grey in colour but inside the colours pinged like a souk. It had mahogany-stained wood throughout and rainbow-coloured trinkets, sequined clothing draped from curtain poles and an array of scatter cushions, no two the same, flung across the sofa and floor. A disco mirror ball above the kitchen counter moved with the boat, casting white sparks on her walls. A neon ribbon curtain announced the entrance to her bedroom with a playfulness befitting its owner.

I looked over at Megan's bookshelf. There were books about art and books about travel. Novels and feminist literature. On the sofa, an embroidery she had been making – brightly coloured flowers and birds half-finished on a piece of cotton in a wooden ring. I wondered who she was making it for, or whether it was something she just enjoyed doing on the boat. Heavily thumbed cookbooks lay across her kitchen counters. Greetings cards from friends. Candles and pot plants in the windows. Her home was her through and through. Colourful and creative. Cluttered but with such joy and love. It was perfect.

I followed the ribbon and climbed back under Megan's blankets and duvet in the den-like bed at the front of the boat. I lay there for the rest of the morning listening to the birds outside and the voices on the radio. A calmness came over me. The stress from the last few months, culminating in the previous day's panic attack, had left me wiped out, and before I knew it, I was fast asleep again.

～～～～～

Built in the year of my birth, *Argie Bargie* was a 45-foot ex-leisure cruiser in royal blue, currently moored in Teddington, West London. It was a family boat with a sofa and a child's bed at the back by the main entrance and not in any way designed to my taste; it had colourful LED rope lights built into the ceiling, a white and grey tiled kitchen and IKEA-style floating shelves throughout. But there was something about it. Descending the staircase of the boat, I could see a dark wooden floor visible beneath the polyester carpet, and long white walls that evoked childhood memories of beach huts and seaside piers.

Frank was part of the appeal. A German father of two, he'd spent five years doing up a bigger boat and was selling his first project, *Argie*. He gave me a tour inside and out as I asked questions.

"How thick is the hull?" I asked. "Has it been surveyed recently? Does it have a boat safety certificate?"

I had learned from Megan what questions to ask, but in truth, I didn't know what answers I should listen out for. I wished she was with me. This was an important decision. If the boat was a rust bucket, having good zen wasn't going to get me very far. I'm not sure the walls would look so white and long covered in barnacles.

"Have a moment," said Frank after he'd answered all my questions. "I'll be on the towpath once you're done."

Frank left me inside the boat as I wandered up and down the cabin. It didn't feel small with just me in it. Ample kitchen surfaces, a double bed, a sofa, a shower. What more did I need? Frank had put two champagne flutes on the side, set out as props to entice a new homeowner. I instinctively placed my hand at the bottom of the nearest glass. I ran my fingers along the kitchen surfaces and looked across at the silver ripples on the water.

"It's a beautiful boat," I said, climbing the steps to the back deck and looking up at Frank on the towpath.

"We have some more viewings this week," he said, "but if you want her, she's yours."

~~~~~

I headed to Syd's in Brockley, South London for my next temporary stay, clutching the printout of *Argie Bargie*. She answered the door wearing bright Nike trainers and jazzed up leggings. Her now signature jet black hair and undercut marked a significant elevation in style since our drama school days.

"Are you okay?" she said as she hugged me, her hooped earring pressing into my cheek.

Trying to look like a walking break-up but unable to conceal my excitement, I said, "I've found my boat, Syd."

"Yes, Hannah – that's nice, but the break-up?" she said.

I walked past Syd and into the hallway. I handed her the printout.

"I've found my boat," I said again.

ALL BOATS ARE SINKING

Syd is all about embracing adventure, and it wasn't long before she'd joined in with my excitement about *Argie*. We shared a bottle of red and chatted into the night about sacking off love and living in a commune together.

"As long as it has a mooring," I said.

Syd retired for the night, and I lay in my third bed since the break-up. I looked up at another set of walls that reflected a beautiful friend and her unique styles and quirks. Caz and Natalie's home had been all photo collages and mood lighting, the next step on their grown-up ladder to buying a flat and building a family together. Megan's was all cosy corners with disco balls and single-piece crockery items that were more like pieces of artwork than kitchenware. Her hobbies and creativity quite literally shone through sequin costumes and sprawling plants that hung and swayed in the windows. Syd's living room housed an array of vintage glass lamps that stood on 1950s furniture or on the exposed wooden floorboards. Each time I visited, something new had been added. A glass bottle she had mudlarked from the River Thames, her political slogan postcard project, lamps, lamps... and more lamps. My home with Sam wasn't at all like me. How had I let that happen? Where had my personality gone? Our flat was light and airy, with a parquet floor in the kitchen and living room and soft cream carpets in the two bedrooms. Save for the chaos caused by the pigeons above our balcony, it was clean and tidy. But to me, it was grey and sparse. Any belongings of mine seemed scruffy and out of place, stored on shelves with no particular sense of thought or design. I can't blame Sam entirely for my lack of personality in the flat, but it spoke volumes that I hadn't prioritised myself there. Lying on Syd's sofa-bed, I wondered, *What does my future home look like? What even is my style? My personality? I'm a long way from knowing,* I thought. *But I know I now must find it.*

~~~~~~~

The following morning, I called my dad to tell him about *Argie*.

"It's perfect, Dad."

I had thought of little else since I had first seen the boat. The web listing printout was well worn as I pulled it from my pocket like a washing machine tissue accident to show friends, colleagues and (mostly) willing strangers. It had been five days since the break-up, but already so much had changed and my previous life felt like a distant memory. The sofa-bed surfing was an inconvenience as I lugged my limited belongings across London. But it was allowing me to connect to friends and was bringing me a step closer to my new life. *Argie Bargie* was the first boat I'd seen, but I just knew it was the one. I could feel it in my gut.

"Does it have a sound hull?" Dad said. He had been reading up on narrowboats, and along with Mum, was now fully in support of my decision. It was astonishing, really, such openness to their daughter's impulsivity.

"Will you come with me to see it again?" I asked.

Retired and alone at home, he was free to jump on a train to Liverpool Street that day then head out west to meet me.

"I'll see you at Teddington station in a few hours," he said.

As I waited for Dad to arrive, I leaned against the wall of the station and flicked through a 32-page document I'd poached from Megan's about buying a narrowboat. I knew I would do most of my learning as I went but felt I should do some research so I at least looked like I knew what I was talking about. But it was all so complicated. Engines, bilges, weed hatches, anodes.

A text message came in from Sam. WhatsApp had been our mode of communication to date, but there was no "us" anymore and dropping videos and photos and "What would you like for tea?" or "I'll be home in an hour" messages was no longer required or welcomed. Texts had been established as our new relationship status.

Seeing his name pop up on the screen made my heart race. The "distant memory" spell had been broken. I was thrown back into the same sadness and confusion I had felt walking out of the flat five days before. I opened the message. There was no text, just a photo of a water bill and our meter reading. Ever organised, Sam had started the process of working out the remaining payments on the flat.

I believe that break-ups are like hangovers. There's a dull ache. A fuzziness. And just when you feel okay and like you could manage a small piece of toast with some butter and Marmite, you realise it was too much too soon, and back to bed you go. You'll try anything to feel better, and sometimes you will, but it won't last and really only one thing will do it. Time. I put the phone back in my pocket and composed myself just as the train pulled in.

Dad stepped off with arms wide open and gave me one of his all too familiar post-relationship hugs.

Don't cry, don't cry, don't cry.

"Right, where's this boat, then?" he said.

~~~~~~~~~~

My dad had prepared a list of questions he'd compiled from Google searches and through talking to a man from church who once owned a narrowboat. As he stood on the back deck of *Argie* with Frank, he navigated a discussion about the important subjects of boat buying with his trademark attentiveness, while his daughter stared hopelessly at the floor. There was something about how seriously he was taking this that threw me into my first wobble, like my silly idea that I had run away with might actually happen and I had a responsibility to take it seriously too. If my parents were to part with this money, I should understand the complications around being a boat owner, but suddenly all this talk of 240-volt appliances and solar panels felt alien and overwhelming. I hadn't been in the headspace to think about these aspects but surely would now need to. I tried desperately to concentrate on what the two men were saying, as Frank pointed out switches and fuse boxes, pumps, valves and hatches.

"Right. Well, it all looks good to me," Dad said, sounding like an inspector. "Shall we go away and have a chat? Hannah?"

"Yes, let's. Thank you," I said, forcing a smile.

Following the viewing, I sat on the train to central London with Dad, who was still browsing web pages about narrowboats. I looked out of the window. What the hell was I doing? I'd barely been single for two minutes and had dragged my pensioner father into London to look at a boat I was wanting him to buy me. It was a knee-jerk reaction, two fingers up to broken relationships and the housing situation in London.

"You don't have to do this straight away," he said. "How about you take a few weeks to think about it?"

A few weeks meant finding temporary accommodation. I'd been relying on friends to put me up in flats that weren't designed for visitors, popping back to Crouch End while Sam was at work to replenish my belongings.

I looked at my dad's kind face. At a man who had shown me nothing but love my whole life. Who sat with me when I couldn't sleep as a child, who never got angry when I did something stupid and who once skived off work when I broke up with my first boyfriend to drive me to the Shotley Peninsula in Suffolk, where we had sat in the car in silence watching cargo ships leave and enter the port of Harwich.

"No, Dad," I said with a smile. "This boat's great."

Neither Mum nor Dad seemed to have any doubts about this decision. I was so lucky.

"If you're sure," said Dad.

"I always have been a sucker for a snap decision," I said, attempting to give him a chance to back out.

"Don't I know it," he said with a smile.

It's true, though, I am impulsive. I love a last-minute trip, a sudden career change or signing up for new projects that I like the sound of, and this was no different. If I sit on things for too long, they just don't happen.

"Let's do it," I said.

Off the train, Dad called Frank and put in an offer.

~~~~~

ALL BOATS ARE SINKING

I was at Syd's the following morning, googling away in bed. I wanted to see what the realities of living on a narrowboat looked like. Not the Scandinavian style, hanging pot plant, fairy light versions; I was looking for the knee-deep-in-exploding-toilet account of living on a narrowboat.

I didn't have to look far for either version.

While Pinterest covered the former with alpaca fur rugs, yellow and pink furnishings, spider plants and never worn before Hunter boots, the grittier format of YouTube showed buckets for toilets and holes in hulls. I went into a vlog rabbit hole. There was the jewellery maker living on a mooring who'd never taken her boat out for a spin, the three art students sharing a 50-foot narrowboat with no toilet, and the young couple and their "do up" project.

I thought of all my camping holidays, the love I have for trawling through mud at festivals and my recently discovered diary from year six in which my New Year's resolutions read...

Try harder at school

Wash more

I was destined for a more feral existence, though I knew from Megan that it wouldn't have to be like that. She's glamorous, and clean, and has a job and everything.

I headed over to Amazon and lined up an order of kitchenware, an ornamental bucket, stool, a hose and more besides. I was about to complete the biggest order of my life when I got a call from Mum.

"What do you need on the boat? We're having a clear out," she said, full steam ahead with my new life choices.

Mum was always "having a clear out", though her penchant for charity shopping will far outweigh any ability to actually clear. I ran through all that was in my Amazon basket. She had everything. Pots, pans, cheese grater – retro ware from the 1970s and 80s.

"This is all perfect, Mum."

"Never go on Amazon before you've spoken to me," she said.

The phone call was interrupted by Frank.

"The boat is yours," he said, "and you can pick it up next week."

I texted Mum the good news, and she replied, "Fantastic. We'll bring the stuff up in the car. Looking forward to seeing this boat. And you, of course. xxx"

I smiled at the text and let a tear fall down my face. I couldn't believe it. I had a home, and a beautiful one at that. I felt nervous flutters in my stomach. The kind you get when embarking on something new. The best kind of flutters. Those that spell adventure.

Chapter 3
Downsizing

They say that our relationship to smoking derives from our earliest memories of it. My grandfather smoked, and I would watch with curiosity as his yellow fingers rolled thin papers packed with tobacco at our kitchen table. Then he would sneak off for a moment of calm at the bottom of the garden. As an adult, I was now rather fond of the disgusting habit.[4]

I feel the same may have happened with my relationship to boats. Boarding a boat was a treat as a child. We would take day trips on a boating lake in Suffolk. The 60-acre Thorpeness Meare has islands with model dragons and forts built into them, inspired and named by J. M. Barrie, the creator of Peter Pan. My three brothers and I would jump on two boats and race across the lake, hopping off to explore each of the magical islands before coming back for fish and chips on the beach in Aldeburgh. Later on, I had a stint working on cruise ships. I loved being at sea. Night or day, I would grab any opportunity to stand out on deck looking at the waves, breathing in the smell of engine oil and fresh deck paint as droplets of salty water splashed onto my cheeks. I remember the transatlantic crossing particularly well. The journey from Southampton to Barbados, with a stopover in Madeira, took nearly a week, and on those "sea days", where the air and light softened as we moved closer to warmer climes, with no sight of land for days at a time, my love of gliding through water was firmly established. I've always found comfort in being on water and so the decision to call a boat

---

4 At time of writing, I am not a smoker.

my home did not feel foreign. From the break-up on Monday to viewing *Argie* on the Thursday, I had packed up all my belongings ready to move on the following weekend.

Sam was in the flat on the day I moved out, sitting on the sofa in his blue Spurs tracksuit. It was the first time I'd seen him since the break-up. He looked spent.

"Where exactly are you going?" he said, flicking through channels on the TV.

"I'm moving onto a boat," I said without looking up.

I knew this news wouldn't sit well with him. Sam's office overlooked the canal in East London. The view would serve as a reminder of someone he now potentially loathed. He turned off the TV, laughed and headed to his spot on the balcony.

"And this is why you and I would never have worked out, Hannah," he said, sliding the door behind him.

I wanted to follow him out onto the balcony. To say that this wasn't how I planned for it to go. That this wasn't all my doing. That I had felt stifled and wasn't allowed to be me in this relationship. That he never asked me how my day was, or what I thought of something. That the time he screamed at me when I bought a Christmas tree as a surprise wasn't kind. But I didn't. I carried on sorting through my belongings, keen to get out of the flat before his distaste turned to anger. I loaded four bin liners into the lift for the charity shop. My life looked small, with everything able to fit on the double bed in the spare room. I looked around one last time. Sam was still out on the balcony looking out over the Waitrose car park. We'd only been there 18 months, but we'd made memories together there. The small living room where we'd slow danced to Van Morrison's "Sweet Thing" on the record player. The balcony I'd filled with more chilli plants than one household needs and the large windows where Sam would hang his pastel-coloured shirts every Sunday evening before the working week. Though more recently it had been a suffocating environment, a place reserved for arguments and tears and sleeping in separate bedrooms.

ALL BOATS ARE SINKING

To begin with, I had liked living somewhere posh, where famous faces could be spotted browsing in book shops and where streets of semi-detached houses were pink with cherry blossom in the spring. Crouch End was as homely a community as one could hope for in London. It should have been a dream to live in. With an abundance of coffee shops and several global cuisines in a five-minute radius of our home, we could, and did, eat out several times a week, bemoaning when management changeovers affected the speed of service, and we were always familiar with at least four people in any establishment at a given time. He ordered predictably. I ordered expensively.

We lived in the heart of the village, with bakeries selling giant croissants, and pop-up Christmas tree sellers, kitchenware shops and a well-stocked fishmongers. I liked having a GP nearby. I liked the quality of the produce in the shops. I liked midweek visits to the Lido to avoid the crowds. But I had become restless and depressed, withdrawn and resentful of my life there. I would stare at the bus stop announcement screen on the way into the city and watch the minutes count down at an unbelievably slow rate. Bored of the mundanity of it all.

My colleague Tanya arrived with her van and Sam helped us carry boxes to the lift. After we'd finished loading, he stood in the doorway and offered me a fist bump, which I accepted.

"Have a nice life," he said.

And that was that.

I sat in the front seat of the van looking up at the flat.

"Are you okay?" Tanya said.

"Yeah," I said. "Let's go."

As Tanya drove us from Crouch End I said goodbye to the clocktower that stood between mine and Caz's homes, and the town hall, with its huge regeneration plans and even bigger list of signatures of opposition. The restaurant I used to wait tables in, where property developers and their lunchtime drug habits would prop up the bar, the pub I used to be manager of and practically live at, the queue of commuters at the W7 bus stop and Dunn's, the best bakery in London. Leaving in Tanya's van, looking down at the buggies and cockapoos, I realised that the compact community of Crouch End wasn't mine anymore, and it instantly felt as such.

I love being the passenger in a white transit van. They're scruffy with coffee cups and crisp packets under foot. You shouldn't put your leg up on the dashboard of a car, but in a white van you can. Driving through Central London with Tanya in her paint-splattered jeans, her tattooed fingers on the wheel, we talked about our respective homes. She and her van conversion, me and my new boat. Things were shifting. I was a solo woman now, a boater. It felt good to talk about it with someone who understood. It was a warm July day, and my cork keyring, designed to float should I drop my keys in the canal, lay on the dashboard as a symbol of my new life. Tanya cranked up the radio and drove us west out of London to pick up *Argie Bargie* from Teddington.

The boat was sitting low in the water with its blue and white roof almost level with the concrete bank. I gave Tanya a tour and we loaded my belongings inside. We ordered a roast dinner from the Anglers waterside pub, which stood proud at the edge of the Thames 65 feet from *Argie*. We ate our meal on the roof, washing it down with warm prosecco in enamel mugs.

"Thanks for today, Tanya," I said.

"To your new life, Hannah." She raised her mug. "I couldn't be more jealous."

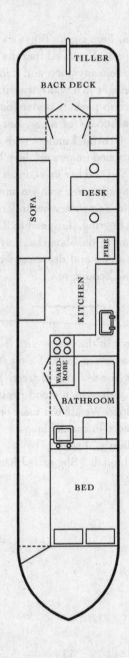

TILLER

BACK DECK

SOFA

DESK

FIRE

KITCHEN

WARD-
ROBE

BATHROOM

BED

Chapter 4
Alone Time

Hampton Court to Walthamstow Marshes

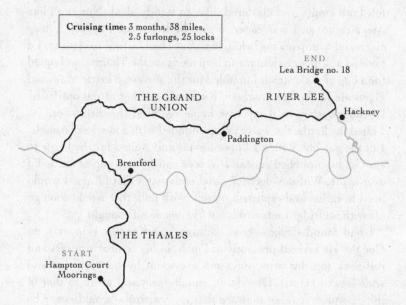

Cruising time: 3 months, 38 miles,
2.5 furlongs, 25 locks

THE GRAND
UNION

RIVER LEE

END
Lea Bridge no. 18

Hackney

Paddington

Brentford

THE THAMES

START
Hampton Court
Moorings

With Tanya and her van gone, I pulled the curtain across the open doorway and stood for the first time alone inside my boat. I had this feeling like I was being watched, though on one side of the boat I could see only cigarette butts and the occasional pair of feet. Maybe it was the proximity I was feeling. I was inside my boat but only a few metres from members of the public. I felt weirdly exposed. On the other side, the River Thames was my view, with swans, coots and fervent rowers. The water was silver, with shards of white dancing in the early evening sun. I hoisted myself on top of the kitchen counter and let out a short laugh. I couldn't quite believe it. This boat moored up on the River Thames was now home. It didn't feel like home yet, of course, with my boxes of belongings piled high along the narrow passageway and a smell of wet metal that I didn't recognise.

I looked at my fingertips. They were grey with dust. The cabin felt both empty and cluttered, like an untidy shed. Not at all like Megan's home. I was eager to give both me and the boat a deep clean and to unpack my belongings, but I had no time to settle in; I'd booked a skipper to join me to help navigate the Thames, so I opted for a cup of tea instead. I fumbled for the stove-top kettle Mum had given me in the box marked "Kitchen", scoffing at my optimistic labelling system as if my new home required the distinction. As I filled the kettle, the water pump sounded with a low-level rumble. I lit the gas hob with a Clipper lighter and waited for the kettle to emit its high-pitched squeal. It was as satisfying a cup of tea as I'd ever made. Without electricity and with water that I knew I would need to ration and replenish myself, with milk that would soon go off with no fridge on board.[5] *Just like camping*, I thought.

I had found Craig – boat enthusiast and expert skipper – on Google. He arrived promptly at 7 p.m. in his combat trousers and roll-neck top, his army days made evident by his crew cut and wide-legged stance. Dressed in equally practical attire to that of the ex-squaddie, and unaware that my wardrobe would never be the same again, I climbed back past the boxes and out of the boat to greet him. I stepped on the handrail and pulled myself up to the concrete above.

"Hi, Craig, is it?" I said, dusting myself down.

---

5 I'd soon give up on milk.

"Good to meet you." He shook my hand and lowered himself onto the boat with greater ease than I had demonstrated. He poked his round face inside my control cupboard by the entrance and peered at the board of dials, switches and lights. He was obviously familiar with the set-up.

"How many leisure batteries do you have?" he said.

"Erm, three, I think?" I said, recalling the trio of black boxes strapped in next to the engine that Frank had said would power my internal electrics.

"And you have gas for your hot water and cooker?"

"Yes."

He pressed a few buttons, muttered some more acknowledgements and headed back out on deck. I climbed down to join him.

"Would you like a cup of tea?" I asked.

"No, I'm fine," he said. "First, I'll show you how to start your engine."

Straight to it, then.

"Pull out this handle so the engine is in neutral, push it forward and hold down the starter plug for fifteen seconds." I was trying my hardest to concentrate on every movement he made.

"Now turn the key until the engine kicks in," he said.

He started up the engine.

"It'll need longer in winter."

I nodded.

He cut the engine by pulling on a handle attached to a black cable near the floor.

"Now your turn," he said.

I stepped forward and repeated his movements. Push handle. Hold down button. Turn key. And with a bellow of white smoke and a loud whooooosh, the engine started. Craig pulled the lever back into its neutral position as the sound settled into a regular put-put-put beat. I was conscious of people nearby. The lunch service at the pub was over and the beer garden had all but emptied, but the engine wasn't quiet for anyone still around to listen, and more importantly, to watch.

"Right, first lesson," he said. "Take everything slowly." He was softly spoken and I strained to hear him over the engine. "There's no rushing in boat life."

Craig climbed back off and walked along the towpath to the front of the boat. He lifted the rope that was attached to the front of the boat from a bollard and held it.

"Now you do the same at the back," he said.

The front of the boat began drifting away from the bank.

Back on the concrete, I untied the back rope from the bollard and jumped down onto the deck with a thud. I couldn't remember Megan's boat being this low. Craig was walking down the side again, holding on to the white handrails along the roof. I wondered how long it would take me to move as confidently around the outside of my boat.

"Okay, put the rope down," he said.

I placed the bundle on the floor by my feet.

"You won't need those until you moor up. So for now —"

The boat was moving further away from the concrete bank.

"Take this." Craig grabbed the rope that was attached to the middle of the roof and passed it to me. "It's called the centre line," he said, "and it stays with you at all times."

"Okay," I said, placing the rope on the roof nearest the back door.

"This is your throttle, or speed lever." He put his hand back on the plastic gear stick thing attached to the side of the railing.

"Now, move the tiller[6] in the opposite direction to the way you want to go and push this forward."

Trying to remain calm about the gap that was growing between us and the bank, I thought for a second, put my hand on the bronzed bar near my hip, moved it in the opposite direction to the way I wanted us to go and carefully pushed forward on the throttle. The propeller turned under us, kicking up water behind, as the boat shook and moved further towards the centre of the Thames.

---

6 The pole that engages the rudder.

ALONE TIME

I couldn't believe it… we were moving.

"Okay, straighten up," he said.

I brought the tiller to the middle and the boat levelled off, with the front and back now several yards from the bank. We were off. My knuckles were white as I held on tightly to the tiller. The ropes that had tethered my new home to land lay limp on the roof and back deck as the engine propelled us forward. We powered through flowing water like scissors through velvet, cruising with intention to reach the London canal network. Using the tiller, I aimed for the centre of the channel, but the boat had other ideas. I zig zagged along trying to adjust the direction of travel this way and that.

Craig explained that we needed to pass oncoming boats to the right.

"Maybe you could take the tiller if that happens?" I said.

He looked at me and smiled. *Of course*, I thought, *I need to get good at this*.

"Try thinking about the middle of the boat as the pivot point," he said. "If you think you're veering off there, gently move the tiller to the other side and the boat should stay straight."

Easy for you to say, I thought.

"Not too much. Go gently," he said.

Craig grabbed the tiller and nudged it. I looked to see what he was doing.

"Concentrate on where you're going."

I turned back. The boat was veering again. Again, he grabbed the tiller. I felt like a child learning to ride a bike, but the longer we cruised, the less he held on to the tiller. It was getting easier, and as we moved through the water, I began to take in my surroundings and relax a little. There were swans everywhere and other boats, bigger boats, moored on jetties to the left[7] of me.

---

7 Portside

ALL BOATS ARE SINKING

"That's it. See, you're getting better," Craig said, as I let out a small laugh.

Before I knew it, Craig was leaning against the railing and watching. I was steering my boat alone, and it felt wonderful.

"So, what's your biggest advice to me as a new boater?" I was getting confident enough to converse.

"Don't become a 'crusty'," he said.

"What do you mean? I was thinking of more practical advice."

"It is practical," said Craig. "You know... hair where there shouldn't be, dirty nails. Just watch out for it... it can creep up on you. Particularly for women."

I wished I hadn't asked.

We'd been cruising for a few hours. It was late and the sun was dipping. Craig looked at his watch and explained the plan. We would moor up in Hampton, and in the morning come off the tidal Thames and onto the canal network. Being on the tidal Thames meant we had limited time to get to the canal before the river became too low to travel through.

"Pass me the tiller," he said.

I was relieved to hand the driving over and watched as Craig manoeuvred the boat to the river's edge in Hampton. He angled the nose of the boat in, straightened up with ease and clambered ashore with the centre line in his hand.

"Can I help?" I asked.

"You can cut the engine," Craig said. I pulled on the plastic toggle under the throttle. The sound of seagulls and traffic returned.

"Well done," he said, climbing back on board. He descended the stairs into the boat's cabin. "I'll sleep here, then?" He put his bag on the child's bed at the back. It was 9 p.m., a weird time for a nap, I thought.

"Excuse me?" I said.

He looked at me.

"You're sleeping?"

"Yes, here," he said, sounding slightly annoyed.

"We need to leave at four a.m. to catch high tide," he said.

ALONE TIME

I was stunned. At no point in the booking process had Craig said he would be staying on my boat, which wasn't fancy or large enough to have separate bedrooms. I'd been reading a lot about the boating community and wondered whether this was something I'd need to get used to, people crashing willy nilly. I couldn't get my head around the idea of spending the evening together on the boat, so I suggested we headed to a nearby curry house for dinner. I texted Tanya en route to say where I was. We walked in near silence to the restaurant. Since I now knew he'd be my cabin mate, I was conscious of our interactions. This stranger would be sleeping in my new home, and it didn't sit well at all. I thought over the booking process. I suppose it was plausible that I'd missed this detail in our emails. I'm not the most thorough person at the best of times,[8] let alone in a strange and unknown world like this. After an awkward dinner, when we got back to the boat, I was too exhausted to be concerned by his presence, so I climbed up into my bed and set my alarm for 4 a.m.

Like Megan's, my bed was tucked in the bow[9] of the boat, though unlike hers, mine was built at height to accommodate storage underneath. To climb into it, I'd need to step on to the radiator cover with one leg and lift myself up. Not very graceful, but once there, it turned out to be as cosy as anything.

In bed, with Craig the other end of the boat, I checked my phone. Caz had messaged.

"Where are you?" she said.

"On the Thames out west!" I replied.

"How's it going? Are you doing it alone?!"

I couldn't tell Caz about my cabin mate. She would take the next train to Hampton and drag me out of bed.

---

8 I once printed out a job reference that my colleague Will had written for me, in which he stated: "Hannah has good attention to detail." Not so good, however, as to notice the "PS: she's also a c*nt" that he'd written at the bottom.

9 Front

41

ALL BOATS ARE SINKING

"A few early hitches but getting there. Learning lots quickly," I said.

〜〜〜〜〜〜

I awoke to my 4-a.m. alarm, and for a moment forgot I wasn't alone. The sound of seagulls filled my ears, as shadows of moving water danced between the gap in my curtains on the white panelling above. Was I really here? My sleeping quarters raised up like a child's cabin-bed had proved to be as comfortable as it looked, and even though the night had been short, I'd slept through, tucked away safely in the bow of my new home. The boat didn't rock as I thought it might, but as I jumped out of bed, it bounced against the fenders and bank; a sign that I was indeed on water.

I passed Craig, who was asleep on the child's bed, and saw an empty bottle of wine that he'd polished off while I was asleep. As he emerged, I saw that his lips and teeth were stained red. I reluctantly made him some tea. Out on deck I started the engine, this time without being asked to.

Craig untied the ropes and we set off, cruising at speed through the fast-flowing river: Kingston, Twickenham, Richmond. I was gaining confidence with every bend of the spectacular river and marvelling at everything. We journeyed through wealth. My little blue boat passed the seventeenth-century National Trust property Ham House and its immaculate surroundings, family homes along the water's edge with gardens and boat houses that sloped into the river as if descending into another world. *Gloriana*, the Queen's 90-foot rowing barge, was moored up against a bank of grass. The water was moving quicker than we were, but we seemed to be gliding along at quite a speed. I smiled and waved at anyone I saw, though they were few, and I was delighted to show off my new navigational skills.

"Ah, it's a little later than I had hoped," said Craig, looking at his marine-style watch.

"What does that mean?" I said, eyes still ahead of me.

"It means we won't make it to Limehouse."

We had planned to cruise through London, its iconic centre, passing the National Theatre and under Tower Bridge, and entering the canal network to the east. But this part of the Thames was tidal and time was running out.

"We'll need to turn off at Brentford and get on to the Grand Union Canal there," said Craig.

I was a little disappointed to miss the opportunity to cruise through the *Eastenders* opening credits. As the water level began to drop, the newly exposed edges of the river gave off an oily and sulfuric smell, with herons and muntjac deer now trudging through its silty bed. Craig assessed the levels below us. The riverbed moved closer to the bottom of *Argie* the nearer we got to Brentford. I could feel the boat struggling in the shallow water.

"Okay, we need to move quickly." Craig took the tiller and I stepped aside.

"I wanted you to moor up, but this is a little tricky," he said.

Craig cruised the boat alongside a jetty at the junction of the Grand Union. It was 8.30 a.m. and we had just made it before the tide dropped entirely.

"High tide is at three p.m.," he said.

"What does that mean?" I was tired and groggy.

"We're still on tidal waters, though safer here than out there." He pointed to the middle of the river, where we had just cruised through. "But it means that we need to wait."

Craig disappeared and I climbed back into bed, grateful to be alone.

I awoke from my nap with a start. My body was stuck to the wall, and cleaning products and boxes were strewn across the floor. The boat was well and truly on the huh,[10] with the tide so low that the boat was stuck in mud at the bottom of the riverbed. I was annoyed that Craig seemingly didn't know the tidal activity for the

---

10 A Suffolk expression meaning lopsided.

day and frustrated that he would soon be coming back to the boat when all I wanted to do was make this new place, which was now looking like the end of a bowling lane, my home. I climbed out of bed and wrestled between boxes that were now precariously stacked at an angle, threw on a jumper and climbed out of the boat. I couldn't get off. It was too far from the jetty.

Back inside the boat, I sat on my leaning sofa looking at the boxes. *I might as well try to get some sorting done while I wait for the tide*, I thought. There was one small wardrobe between the bathroom and kitchen. I was keen to find out if my clothes would all fit. As I hung my shirts up, familiar smells of my previous life replaced the smell of hot engine oil. The clothes, like the boat, were hanging at an angle. I stuffed them inside the wardrobe and shut them in. They did fit inside – just. Unpacking with the boat like this wasn't going to be much fun, though, so I climbed back into bed and waited.

By the afternoon the water level had returned to normal, and the boat was buoyant again. Craig was back from his brunch at the café, and we were able to cruise. We set off and turned to join the slender canal network that I was to call home. It was magical leaving the Thames for the Grand Union. The water was no longer tidal, but narrow and winding and bottle green. Seagulls became ducks and the eggy mud was now vibrant weeds.

Craig hopped off the boat to tackle the Hanwell flight of six adjoining locks, opening and closing the gates as I cruised in and out of each of the enormous canal features. The boat bumped against gates and walls as if communicating morse code. I had reached my limit of learning and engaging in social interactions with a stranger. I was exhausted, and nothing Craig was saying about the locks was going in. He was talking about things called paddles and sluices. I counted down the six locks, desperate to drop him off at the top of the flight.

Five

The idea was to start this new life alone, and in the lock as I watched my skipper do something with a metal hammer-thing

that made my boat rise up to the next step on this canal ladder,
I realised...

Four

... I'd been rushing around solidly since the break-up...

Three

... and I was desperate to be independent...

Two

... to be still.

One.

I dropped Craig off on a bend near Southall with a short sharp
goodbye. As I cruised the boat back off the towpath and into the
middle of the canal I looked around and saw I was now alone,
casually driving my boat through London, for the first time. I let out
a deep sigh of relief. This was my time now, to enjoy my inaugural
solo move and my first adventure of many.

Meandering through the waters of West London with not
another boat or soul on the towpath for several miles, I cruised
from Southall to Northolt to Greenford. I was euphoric. Just me
and my boat, gliding through the unfamiliar landscape. My hand
clasped around the tiller, right to go left, left to go right.

I pulled the boat alongside the towpath to practise mooring up
away from watchful eyes. It was simple enough. Nose of the boat
in, then straighten up with the back. Slowly, slowly, and then off
again. I sang the Spice Girls back catalogue from my back deck.
There was something about being alone and on my boat that made
me feel like a child again. I don't know what it was, maybe the
playfulness of being in command of a vehicle. I don't drive, so this
feeling was entirely new. I felt safe and secure in the middle of the
channel, where no one could get to me.

As I approached Alperton in West London, just south of Wembley,
I looked for a suitable place to tie up. There were other boats about
now and my childlike joy dissolved as I became self-conscious once
more. I found some mooring rings on the concrete near a block of
flats. I pointed the nose of the boat towards the bank a little too
sharply and it bumped the side. This was a wider section of the canal

and the back end of the boat, where I was standing, swung out into the centre and I became caught in a current. Why was there a current on the canal?[11] I panicked. Unsure what to do, I wiggled the tiller in any direction, gave the throttle some bursts of power and through a combination of my incompetence, the wind and sheer momentum somehow managed to turn my boat around so it was facing the other way. I laughed nervously to myself and to anyone who might be peering through their curtains at the drama unfolding. My confidence had dissolved and just like that, I felt like a stranger to the boat again. The back end was at the water's edge, so I hopped off with my centre line in my hand and pulled the boat in straight. I was in position, albeit the wrong way round. I tied the rope to the rings with a dubious knot and hoped that no one had seen my accidental three-point turn (this would not be the last time I'd do this).

I cut the engine, took the tiller handle off[12] and shut myself inside the boat. I giggled at the incredulity of the past few days, and of the excitement in mooring up (semi) successfully on my own. I was in no way confident in my ability but delighted to learn and to forge a life like this. Not reliant on a partner or anyone else but me. Able to become someone new. I couldn't wait to be a boater.

—〰〰〰—

Caz was visiting for the first time, and I was nervous as anything. She had been my best friend for 20 years, and her approval meant the world to me. In my eyes, she hasn't aged a jot – she is as playful and absurd as the 11-year-old I met as I walked up the alley to start secondary school. We have different memories about our first meeting. Mine is that she called across the street "Did your mum dress you?" with her friends jeering along with the commentary. She resolutely denies this encounter, and I've got to be honest, while I defend my memory, it

---

11 There wasn't a current. Just a bit of wind and gentle water flow.
12 Megan had taught me to keep the tiller inside, so it doesn't get nicked.

doesn't sound like a very Caz thing to have done. I'm not sure she's ever said anything cruel to me (since). Perhaps it's her wicked laugh that made me link up that memory to her. A laugh that escalates into palpable joy as her limbs stiffen and tears stream down from her eyes. Her emotions sit close to the surface, though the beauty is that Caz doesn't know that. It's this openness that I was nervous of. I knew she'd find my reaction to the break-up a little extreme and I didn't relish the prospect of her inadvertently highlighting the flaws in my plan. She really had her shit together now: a successful career in TV, and primed to get on the housing ladder with her partner, Natalie, with whom she enjoyed a balanced and wholesome life.

Caz announced her arrival in Alperton by knocking on my window and clambered on to the back deck, wearing ankle boots and an off-the-shoulder flowing top. She crouched down to enter the boat with caution.

"Is this the bathroom?" she said, squealing in her delightful way at the quirky corners of my new home. "And that's where you sleep? It's so cute, Hannah."

I was relieved by her positive reaction. After the tour, we sat together on my sofa with a cup of tea.

"How are you feeling?" Her blue eyes were wet.

The question threw me. I hadn't realised it, but I was very sad. Here comes a hangover wave again.

"I miss him."

"Yeah," she said.

"I'm scared I'll always be alone."

It was a cliché. But I meant it.

"You won't be, Hannah." She was shaking her head, her yellow hair brushing against my white walls. "There'll be a point," she said, "a fair bit away, mind, but a point in time where you'll look back and realise this was the best thing that happened to you."

She turned, rejigging the cushions underneath her; cushions we'd shared in two houses before. I knew this break-up was affecting her too, just as hers had affected me, and I found myself wanting to console her. But she wasn't done. Uncharacteristically, she grabbed my hand.

"You are very loved, Hannah," she said. "And you're not doing this alone."

She took in *Argie*.

"What you've done here is great, but you've got a lot of change going on. Please, please take care."

I smiled through tears at the very best of friends. As usual, she'd nailed it. Warning heeded. Though things were looking up, we both knew I wasn't out of the woods.

Chapter 5
My First Summer

The annual "continuous cruising" licence for me to live on the water with *Argie* stipulates that the boat must be moved every 14 days to a new location. The boat also must travel in one direction for 20 miles before being turned around. My plan was to stay in a mooring spot for two weeks, then pootle on to the next, and roughly speaking move from West London to North-east London and back again over the course of a year. For the Canal and River Trust these rules ensure the network remains free flowing and boaters don't all gravitate to their favourite spots and "drop anchor".[13]

Some boaters have been accused of creating environments for birds to build nests on board boats, like tires strategically placed at the waterline. If a bird were to use said tire, the boater is legally prohibited from disturbing the nests, thus rendering themselves unable to move from their favourite locations. I don't know a boater who would do this, though. It's a right old pain being stuck in one location, not being able to move to get water when you run out and sharing a boat with a family of birds.[14]

Boat movements are monitored by staff and volunteers working for the Canal and River Trust, like parking attendants of the waterways. If this requirement is not observed, licences may not be renewed the following year, which would leave me a bit stumped. My plan was to cruise the boat around my working week, which

---

13 Anchors are not needed on the canals. I do have one, though. It's a licence requirement when navigating tidal rivers like the Thames.

14 More on this in book two, in chapter titled "three months barricaded out of home in peak boating season due to moorhens nesting on back deck".

for me, meant leisurely moves on quiet weekdays away from watchful eyes.

Becoming accustomed to my home was a joy. I'm a master at pottering and I took great care in unpacking and arranging my belongings, stopping to enjoy a cup of tea out on deck, or to reposition my chilli plants in order to receive the most light in the ever-changing position of the stern.[15] Coming home to a new location after a long shift at work was something I looked forward to immensely, as I discovered new areas of London and their Tube and Overground stops. I would chuckle to myself at the brief ownership I felt over a new neighbourhood, even if it was only mine for a few days. I would spot other boaters on the trains, casual creatures amongst the hordes of city workers and night-time revellers. They were instantly recognisable with their grubby fingernails, fantastic tans, worn boots, loose shirts and a cork keyring hanging from their frayed pockets.

I moved the boat a lot in those first few weeks; short moves, occasionally with friends and more often than not with Megan's assistance. My aim initially was to head east, where I could enjoy the remaining summer months near my work and Megan's boat. From Alperton in West London, I journeyed through Kensal Rise and Little Venice, delighting every time I managed to complete a move without incident, and filling up on water with a hose trailing from a tap on the towpath to the bow of my boat where the tank is stored. With Megan on board, we tackled the Maida Vale and Islington tunnels, cruised through London Zoo and Regent's Park and scaled the trio of iconic locks at Camden flanked by footbridges and hundreds of tourists and sunshine seekers. We travelled through the trendy neighbourhoods of Haggerston and Broadway Market and I took mental notes of all the places I wanted to stop for longer next time I passed, whenever that might be.

---

15 Back of boat

MY FIRST SUMMER

I would stand at the tiller with my support bubble of friends, chatting about everything and anything. We'd start the cruises with tea and biscuits, and end with a barbecue and beers on the roof, bringing candles out to keep the mozzies away and wrapping up in blankets as the sun set on another beautiful day on the canal network of London. When my friends were gone, I closed up the doors to the world outside and embraced being alone inside the boat. I had become used to being in close proximity with towpath users. No longer self-conscious, I felt comfortably hidden within my home and enjoyed overhearing snippets of conversation from those who didn't know I was so close.

I was forever repositioning my belongings. It had become clear that everything I owned would have to be on display and the careful placement of kitchen utensils and books, toiletries and tinned food was key to creating the boat's warm ambience. There was no room for untidiness. I bought pot plants from Mare Street florists to fill every spare surface. My personality couldn't hide on *Argie*, and I was enjoying discovering how both the boat and I were evolving in that regard.

Sleep had never been so peaceful. The evenings would turn in as the canal-side activity calmed. Boats stopped moving through, and the birdsong quietened. With limited electrical appliances at home to distract me, I was going to bed earlier and sleeping deeper. The boat's movement rocked me into my slumber. It was humbling to wake up in bed, so close to the water and canal wildlife.

This was not only my first boat, but my first time living alone, and I was enjoying every minute of it.

~~~~~~

I met Sarah while we were waitressing in Crouch End. She'd moved from Canada and had set herself up as a yoga teacher. Sarah has an enviable quality of being positive and driven, but with a wild side. I call her Prosecco Sarah after a Sunday session that ended in the early hours on a Monday, after which she still managed to teach a yoga class in central London at 9 a.m.

I was moored in Victoria Park, East London, when Prosecco Sarah came to visit. I had a sweet location by the entrance of the park and was only a week into my stay when the toilet tank filled. I planned to cruise to the toilet pump-out facility in Broadway Market and with Sarah's help would return to my spot for another week. Sarah and her partner Jamie lived close by, and she was beyond excited to see the boat, and me, moored up in her neighbourhood.

"Oh my God, Hannah," she said in her Canadian staccato.

I poked my head out of the boat as Sarah appeared, wearing her signature frayed denim skirt over leggings, a black hoodie and, though it was a summer's afternoon, a purple scarf wrapped tightly around her neck. She feels the cold like no one I know, which surprises me for someone who was brought up in Ontario. Sarah was filming her approach on her phone, her brown hair in a high ponytail swinging side to side.

"This is so freaking cool," she said, climbing onto the boat.

"Don't drop your phone in," I said. A month into my new life, I was still a nervous boater.

I let Sarah and her camera explore inside while I prepared the boat for the move, placing my centre ropes neatly on the roof at the back of the boat and attaching the tiller handle.

"Okay, so I need to leave in a few hours for a class," said Sarah. "That's okay, right?"

"Sure." I started the engine.

"Where will we be by then?" she said.

"Oh, I've no idea. Not far, though. Canal time – you can't plan."

This move would see us cruise to a turning point at the south-west corner of Victoria Park, to the pump-out toilet facility at Broadway Market and back again. Not much distance, but a few niggly manoeuvres, two locks and a fair bit of summer bustle on the canal.

We cruised through Sarah's neighbourhood. As she filmed from the back deck, I feigned confidence on the tiller. We scaled the first lock with another boat, turned around at the turning point[16] and travelled back through the lock and the next one at Broadway Market.

It was busy on the towpath and on the water.

"Okay, here's the pump-out," I said, noticing it for the first time myself. It was tucked in behind the lock landing.[17] I needed to turn the boat around again, either before or after the pump-out. I eyed up the width of the canal.

"The next turning point isn't until Angel, but it looks wide enough here," I said semi-confidently. "I might as well do it now." Sarah continued documenting the move on her phone.

I was very wrong. As I attempted the manoeuvre, it became apparent that the space wasn't wide enough. I ploughed on with the turn as the boat slowed and came to a halt. We were wedged across the canal between the bank and a wide beam.[18] Thankfully, my front and back fenders were positioned to protect the paintwork both on my hull and the wide beam's.

"Erm, Hannah, I'm really sorry but I'm going to have to go?" said Sarah. The question mark was at odds with the certainty of the statement, but the sentiment was confirmed as she hopped over the wide beam and onto the towpath.

"Oh, that's totally fine," I said without an ounce of fine-ness. "I'll see you soon."

I tried to dislodge the boat, which was blocking the canal width ways. First, I tried to turn the boat in the direction I was aiming for, then I attempted to spin it back round the way I came. The boat was stuck; my heart began to race and my face became hot. I put some revs into the engine in an attempt to force it free. Nothing.

---

16 Generally speaking, canals aren't wide enough to turn a 45-foot boat around in (with a few exceptions). There are turning points built into the canals that are marked on maps and signs as "winding holes".

17 A lock landing is a section of the towpath either above or below the lock for boats to moor up before or after using the lock.

18 A wide beam is the Land Rover of the canal boat world.

After a minute, a boater emerged from a nearby cabin and started slipping on her trainers.

"Hey," she said, squinting in the sunshine.

"Sorry," I said, relieved to have someone to soundboard with. "I'm totally stuck."

"It's okay, I'll help. I'm hungover, though, so bear with," she said. The boater climbed onto my back deck and walked along the gunwales.[19]

"I'm Hannah," I said as she passed.

"Hey," she said, focusing on her narrow journey down the side of my boat. She looked like she'd done this before. She sat down at the front and pushed with her legs against the wall, while I gave the engine some revs. Eventually, the nose of my boat scraped itself free.

"Oh my God, you're an angel," I said as she walked back along the boat.

"No problem." She spoke few words, which I attributed to the hangover. She looked rough as anything, with last night's make-up smeared across her eyes and a permanent squint.

I reversed the short distance to the pump-out point and dropped off the hungover helper.

"I take it you're not moving today?" I said.

She shook her head.

"I'll pop by later and say a proper thank you."

"Take my number," she said. "It's good to know people all over the network." I entered her number into my phone and said goodbye. How lovely to have the number of a new friend on the canal. I loved her willingness to help. I couldn't remember any conversations with my neighbours in Crouch End, beyond the odd parcel collection.

It was only my second time emptying the toilet tank. Much like a petrol fuel cap on a car, the access point sits on one side of the boat. Fatigued and a little embarrassed post-wedging, I made the

---

19 Pronounced "gun-alls". This is the edge either side of a boat to walk along.

hasty decision to throw the hose over the top of my boat to reach the location of the cap. The pump-out hose is long and heavy with a metal attachment and plastic lever at the end. Its function is to suck the toilet waste from a pump-out toilet. I threw the hose and heard my kitchen window smash into several pieces, falling with a plop into the canal. I rushed to grab my net which I kept out on the back deck to retrieve any items that had dropped into the water, but it was too late. The shards had hit the bottom of the canal.

Could this move get any worse?

Yes. Yes, it could.

Toilet pumped out, I cruised to Angel and down another lock with another boat. I turned around at the actual turning point and headed back through the Angel and Broadway Market locks again. I was grateful to be sharing the locks on my return alongside another, more experienced boater. This move had taken far longer than I had imagined, and I was losing energy and, clearly, focus.

"Where are you off to?" said the driver of the boat in the lock with me, at Broadway Market again.

"Just round the corner here," I said. "I was there earlier today."

"Okay, I'll let you go first, then. We're going further."

Turning out of the lock to moor up at the entrance of the park, I eyed up the same spot I'd left earlier in the afternoon. It had been taken. I had not double moored before, but I knew I could pull up against the boat in its place and tie on to it, a common necessity on the busy London Waterways. My legs were tired. The adrenaline from my mishaps with the broken window and wedged boat had left me weak and I was desperate to tie up and inspect the damage.

In theory, double mooring is much the same as a normal mooring but with a boat between mine and the bank. I'd seen Megan do it before and it looked easy enough.

I could hear Craig's voice in my head: "Take your time, Hannah."

I cruised alongside the boat that had beaten me to the spot I had been in before and parallel parked, stepping on to the gunwales with the centre line in my hand. This boat had a fibreglass roof and no handrail, and as mine began to drift with the natural momentum

I had not yet become accustomed to, I attempted to grip on to the shiny roof with the pads of my sweaty fingers.

The sensible thing to do here would be to calmly hop across the back of the neighbouring boat and pull mine in from a firm footing on the towpath. Instead, I put one foot on the six-inch rim of the neighbouring boat and watched as my legs slowly pulled apart like a retro cartoon, until I had no option but to fall in. I heard several gasps from the towpath as I splashed into the canal. I desperately tried not to swallow the eggy water that had entered my mouth on impact. Kicking the water behind me, I resurfaced and spurted out air and water like a breathless whale.

Time stopped. The water was warmer than I had imagined, and there was something peaceful about being in the canal. Fully dressed in jeans and Dr. Martens, I was ten years old again, getting ready to swim to the bottom of a pool in my pyjamas to retrieve a brick, to the applause of my classmates. As I moved through the water, I thought of Sam and how he loves to swim in the sea. My engine was still running, and I turned and swam back to the ladder attached to my back deck, installed for precisely this eventuality.

"I saw that in slow motion," said a boater who had climbed out of his cabin nearby.

I scaled the ladder as someone from the towpath captured the scene with his long lens camera. My denim shirt was stuck to my chest. I reached into my pocket to check on my phone. It had gone, fallen silently into the water below. I'd never get it back. Lost amongst the weeds.

"Throw me your rope," said the boater.

"I'm such an idiot," I said.

"Don't worry," he said. "We've all done it." He caught my ropes and pulled the boat in. "Go and have a shower. I'll tie you up and we'll have a beer and a laugh when you're ready."

I showered, and sure enough the neighbour had a tinnie ready when I emerged ten minutes later.

"Cheers." He passed me the cold beer. "Was that your first dip?"

"It was. And the last, I hope." I didn't tell him I had been stuck width ways across the canal, or that I had smashed my kitchen window with the pump-out hose on the same afternoon.

~~~~~~

It was a busy few months, adjusting to life as a boater and enjoying my first summer on the London canal network.

I ripped out the child's bed at the back and filled the space with rugs and an old shell of a radio from my late granny; the only piece of furniture I owned, it would store my shoes. I separated my wardrobe and put all my winter clothes in sealed bags under my bed. I continued to downsize as the weeks went by, discovering more and more things I just didn't need.

The summer air had the sweet smell of nettle bushes, elderflower trees and warm dog piss. I would enjoy my morning coffee out on deck, listening to birdsong and staring into the water, mesmerised at the stillness to be found in the centre of London. The ever-changing landscape of boats moving through would mean there was always something new to take in. The waterways in London are bustling with activity. Calm and slow to those that live there, but constant and vibrant with the sound of music and bicycles. Drunken chats from a neighbour's roof would soothe me to sleep, a comforting reminder of the warmth of my new community.

Boaters in London live in close quarters to each other and clambering over each other's boats is the norm. We'd have chats in our PJs about good mooring spots, toilets and the best laundrettes to go to. Of course, some boaters choose this life because it allows them to be alone, unbothered. But I was finding that the majority of boaters seemed to embrace the community aspect.

I was astonished by the curiosity of towpath users. It was forever busy, and I would be questioned by dog walkers, tourists and large families taking their weekly strolls.

"Is it cold in winter?"

ALL BOATS ARE SINKING

"How much was your boat?"[20]

"Do you have a shower?"

"Where does your post go?"

And I had to get used to the cameras too. I had no idea about this side of being a boater. It was novel and I was happy to oblige... the questions, that is, not so much the photographs.

Boat moves were getting easier. I would take my time, and on arrival into a new mooring spot would say, "Sorry... I'm a new boater," as I clumsily pulled in alongside, wondering how long I could get away with saying this. If someone was aboard, they'd pop out, catch my rope and welcome me to the new spot.

"It's a contact sport," they'd say. "There'll always be little bumps here and there."

~~~~~~~

"Can you smell that?" I said to Megan one day.

We had been moored in Clapton on the River Lee for a few days, Megan's boat towpath side and mine tied along the length of hers closest to the middle of the river. Our grey and blue boats were buddied up on a bend with moorings enough for a dozen or so boats, 24 if double moored like ours, which invariably they are. Rain was lashing down and we were enjoying one of our wine nights in Megan's home and unwinding after a day at work. Lizzo's first album was playing from Megan's Bluetooth radio (I know, all the mod cons).

"I can't smell anything," said Megan as she pulled apart some chicory leaves.[21]

Megan and I were growing closer by the day. I loved having her as a boat buddy. A neighbour I could call on and someone to plan my post-relationship social life with. I was inspired by her

---

20 I find this one really odd. Do people do this with houses?

21 We may be boaters, but we still like good produce.

conscientious work ethic and brilliant sense of humour. Megan knows exactly who she is and what she is capable of.

"It's really bad, Meg," I said, referring to the smell.

She joined me at the back of the cabin, still pulling apart the leaves, and sniffed the air.

"Oh, yeah. Maybe it's the drains?" She turned up the volume on Lizzo and returned to assemble the salad.

I wouldn't tell her until after we had eaten. I'd spent enough time in London flats and pubs to recognise the smell of a dead rodent and there was most certainly one on Megan's boat. We ate our meal, but before her final bite, Megan piped up, "Oh my God. What the hell *is* that smell?"

"I think you might have a dead rodent on board, Meg," I said. "I'm sorry."

"Gross." She downed her wine and opened the doors, which most certainly did not help matters.

I climbed outside and the smell of sweet dead mammal intensified.

"Fucking hell, Megan. That stinks."

I turned on my phone's torch and pointed it towards Megan's bow. Strawberries that were nearly ready to be picked were growing from a terracotta plant pot. Two empty and corked wine bottles were tucked under a seat, and an ash bucket and hose was under her built-in seating. No dead rodents. But the smell was worse than ever. I shone the torch at my boat. Nothing but wet chilli plants and a cool box.

"Don't tell me it's coming from under the floorboards?" I said.

"How would it get under there?"

"Oh, they can get anywhere," I said, remembering conversations I'd had with pest control companies over the years about "eyes of needles" and "2-metre radius". I turned the torch towards the gap between mine and Megan's boat. And there it was. Not a rodent, something bigger.

"I think I've found it." I covered my mouth and nose with my arm and with one foot on either gunwale, approached the smell.

"Is it a cat?" asked Megan.

"Hmm, not sure." It was lashing down with rain as I strained to see what was going on between our two boats. "But it's wedged."

The creature was jammed between our two boats. Orange in colour. Bigger than a cat.

"I think it's a fox," I said, looking down at the bloated corpse.

"Oh no!" said Megan. "What are we going to do?" I could sense from her tone, that "we" meant "me". I was closer, after all. It was my corpse now. The smell was too much for both of us. Megan was gagging, looking out towards the river. I started retreating back down the edge of our boats to join her, when a voice called out from the towpath.

"Hey, Hannah. How's it going?"

It was Scott, an actor from Sheffield who had once lodged at my parents' house while on tour. He had since moved on to a narrowboat with his partner. I'd bumped into him a few times already. We clearly had similar boat movements.

"We're moored a few boats down. Should have you both over for a dri— Woah, what's that smell?" Scott took a step back from the edge of the river.

"We've got a dead fox wedged between our two boats," I said.

"Oh no, poor thing." There was an air of Heathcliffe about Scott as he lifted a leg onto a bollard on the towpath and rolled up his damp shirt.

Megan was in the doorway, her wine miraculously topped up. I could tell we were both thinking the same thing. I wasn't going to de-wedge the corpse. And nor was she.

"Scott, are you squeamish at all?" I said.

Before it was necessary to plead, he had read my mind and was jumping down onto the back deck of my boat.

"Do you have a barge pole?" he said.

I reached over and located the pole from my roof and gave it to Scott. His hair, heavy with raindrops, was slicked across his forehead. He leant down and untied my ropes so that the fox could be released. I couldn't watch and stood in Megan's doorway as she refilled my glass too.

"Lucky I came along," said Scott as he poked the pole into the water and gently teased the fox from between the gap and into the flow of the river.

I turned to face Megan and gave her a look that said, "I think he's enjoying his rescue mission."

"That should do it," said Scott as the fox drifted away. Together we tied up the boats again.

"Good timing," I said, "you appearing like that. Thank you."

"No worries," he said. "Come round for dinner soon, yeah?"

I returned to join Megan inside the boat and shut the doors. She lit a scented candle.

"That was good of him," she said, clearing away our plates.

"Very." I sat down on the sofa. The smell had begun to dissipate.

"Do you ever just want a fella around to help with stuff like that?" said Megan.

I thought for a moment.

"That was hardly an everyday occurrence," I said.

"I know, but sometimes you just want that little bit of extra muscle."

"We would have sorted it," I said.

I could feel the contradiction in what I was saying versus my actions. I was right that we would have sorted it eventually, but my willingness to let Scott take charge and get his hands dirty spoke volumes. Megan and I were doing this perfectly well alone. She had been on her boat for a few years and was competent at boat maintenance, engine servicing and operating locks; all single-handedly. She didn't need a fella to assist. But when Scott came along, it was impossible to ignore that we were relieved and willing to step aside.

I took a sip from my wine.

"Well, I am more than happy to have some fella come and de-wedge a mammal corpse from time to time," said Megan.

Chapter 6
An Introduction
to Locks

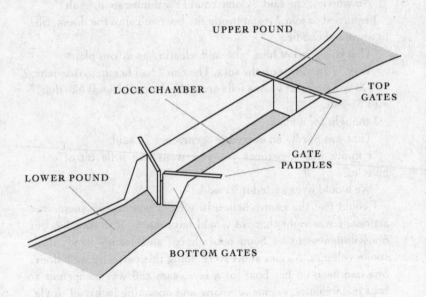

UPPER POUND

LOCK CHAMBER

TOP
GATES

GATE
PADDLES

LOWER POUND

BOTTOM GATES

Travelling on the canal network consists largely of one of two things: cruising or going through a lock. Locks occur whenever the land is hilly. Though there are many different types, they all work on the same basic principle. The locks act like stairs for boats. In order to raise or lower a boat up or down these stairs, the water level must be raised or lowered inside them. This is done by users filling or emptying the lock chambers with water

AN INTRODUCTION TO LOCKS

from above or below. By using a windlass[22] to open or close underwater paddles or sluices,[23] the user enables water to gush in and out of the locks, thus changing the water level so that boats like mine can cruise in and out of them and up or down to the next pound[24] of water.[25]

There are 1,569 locks on the British rivers and canals. They're a significant part of a boater's life and there's a lot to be said about them.

When travelling with another person, or more, the lock duties will be shared, with someone generally staying with the boat, while the other(s) prepare and operate the lock. Locks require concentration and physical exertion. If there's a momentary lapse of judgement, it can be dangerous for both boat and owner. The danger of a boat sinking is increased when in a lock where there's a cill and gates upon which the boat can get caught, and the rapid rush of water can bash the boat about too. When doing them alone, it's a slower process and the solo boat owner will do the following steps:

* Cruise up to the lock
* Tie the boat onto the lock landing, which will have a couple of black and white bollards on
* Prepare the lock using the paddle gear and windlass[26]
* Walk back to the boat
* Cruise into the lock
* Climb the ladder of the lock or step off onto the land (depending on whether the boat is ascending/descending)

---

22 A windlass is a lock key. A big metal L-shaped handle with holes for lock mechanisms to fit in.
23 Kind of like mini underwater gates and channels.
24 Section of water
25 Are you still with me?
26 Or occasionally a standard Yale-style key if it's an electric lock.

* Lay the rope on the floor (descending) or loosely tie the boat on to the bollard inside the lock (ascending)[27]
* Operate the lock using the paddle gear and a windlass, all the while monitoring and adjusting speed of water flow and position of the boat within the lock
* Get back onto the boat by jumping (ascended) or climbing the ladder (descended)
* Cruise out
* Tie up onto the lock landing on the other side
* Close the gates behind[28] (unless someone else is coming in)
* Cruise off

Every lock is different in depth, speed and capacity. The whole process can take up to 30–40 minutes, particularly if they're not set "in your favour" when you arrive.

They're hard work, but they're great. Beautiful archaic structures that have barely changed for hundreds of years. They serve an excellent purpose, and watching the boats go up and down, the water flowing in and out, is all part of the slow-paced life of boating. You'll often find pubs near locks, and they can feel like the centre of a community. On a summer's day, they're a hub of activity, with everyone watching, asking questions and getting involved. Locks used to fill me with dread, but now I love them.

---

27 This is debated within the boating community. I like to wrap the rope around once, loosely, so I don't lose it, but the emphasis here is on the word "loosely". Tight wraparounds can be an invitation to get a boat caught in a lock and sunk pretty quickly.

28 This is best practice, and I'm pretty diligent about it myself. It regulates water levels and helps the next boater who uses the lock.

Chapter 7
Needs Must

Ryan and I had never found ourselves single at the same time. He was the tall centre-half in our sixth-form football team. Caz and I would cheer him on as he stood positioned at the back of the field with his floppy hair and big smile. He had moved to London and the three of us had kept in contact. He's a great guy, with a heart of gold and a sunny disposition. Over the years, Caz would catch us flirting with one another, telling us to "behave" like we were naughty school children again.

Since the break-up, Ryan and I had been together at the pub a few times. Pints flowing, our hugs would linger a little longer and he'd kiss the top of my head with his hand stroking the small of my back. The flirtation had been bubbling away under the surface for years and it had reached a point of no return. One Sunday Ryan dropped me a text.

"So, when can I come and see this boat?" he said.

"What for?" I replied playfully.

"A boaty call," he said, followed by, "Sorry about that."

I replied, "Haha," and then, "How about now?"

And within 20 minutes, he was there. Giggling like... well, Ryan. It wasn't long before we were snogging. Ryan led us to the bedroom, his long limbs striding across the boat in just a few steps. I gave him a massage with oil I'd given Sam that he'd placed back with my belongings. The smell of sweet rosehip took me right back to our flat in Crouch End, but I wasn't going to let that get in the way. Ryan was lovely, and I needed this. After the massage, he turned around to face me. It took some manoeuvring to work out the best position. Because my bed's raised, there was little room between us and the ceiling, and so I had to bend to one side with a crick in my neck. Not the sexiest of sights, but Ryan didn't seem to mind.

The height restriction did also provide us with a surface upon which to push against, which caused Ryan to leave a Rose-from-*Titanic*-style handprint that stayed for several weeks. It was hot up there in the raised bed, with a kind of dangerous excitement knowing we were just inches away from the towpath and any potential late-night dog walkers.

What I soon discovered is that getting intimate with a friend is quite odd. Where I'd been used to looking deep into partners' eyes and feeling that intensity of love between us, with Ryan, I had this familiar, dare I say, brotherly face and enormous smile beaming back at me.

"This is fun," I said.

"It is!" he said through laughter.

"Stop laughing."

"Sorry," he said.

"Long time coming." I was just filling the silence with words now. "All those years…"

Ryan was newly single too, so we were much in the same boat.[29]

"Well, you know, Hannah… needs must."

"Excuse me?" I stopped what I was doing.

"Oh shit, no I didn't mean that."

"You did," I said with faux outrage.

We were both laughing now, lying against the mattress side by side and staring at the handprint above.

"What a ridiculous thing to say," I said.

But he was on the money. It *was* kind of ridiculous. Two newly single friends bonking on a boat.

I had been nervous about my next foray into the world of sex and dating, terrified to fall in love or to put myself through heartbreak again. But being with Ryan was easy and enjoyable. We were on

---

29 Stop it, Hannah.

an equal footing, with no expectation or confusion between us. We made it clear to one another that it was simply a fun thing to do. After a few weeks it fizzled out and we reverted to being friends that flirted in the pub sometimes.

Chapter 8
Things I've Lost to the Canal

- Ray-Ban sunglasses
- Phone (then the net used to try to retrieve it)
- Phone again
- Silver fork from a vintage cutlery set given to my parents as a wedding gift
- Cap from water tank
- Myself
- Engine stop T-handle
- Parasol (could have been nicked – we'll never know)
- Plant pot
- One Samsung Galaxy earbud
- Chimney brush
- Paint brush
- Chimney hat [30] x 2
- Bit of steel from side of boat (called rubbing strakes) [31]

---

30 These go on top of a chimney to protect the fire from rain or wind.
31 I'm aware these are all terrible of me. I must stress that I often fish out items I see in the canal as they pass. Many more than I've dropped in.

Chapter 9
The Breakdown

Before setting off on a move, I'll do the following checks to my engine:

Oil, water and diesel levels

Check the alternator belt[32] isn't too loose and isn't too tight

Check the weed hatch[33] is securely fastened

The weed hatch is where I can access my propeller (also known as a "prop") should something get caught. This happens during boat moves, more frequently in the summer, when there's significant growth down there. Cruising in a city, it can pick up all sorts along the way. If there's something caught, the tiller will become stiff and the engine will start to overwork. If ignored, more will gather on the prop and I won't be able to steer. I soon learned that if I could feel something was caught on the prop during a move, I had to either pull over, cut the engine, and use my hand or a knife to remove the detritus – or ignore it, hope for the best for the rest of the move and deal with it at a later date. It can be gross going down there and it really kills the serene boat-move vibe. And in the winter, sticking a hand in the canal is brutal.

The first thing you're taught at Canal Boat Purchasing School[34] is: if the weed hatch isn't secured tightly enough, the propeller will

---

32 The alternator belt is designed to transfer power from the starter battery to the leisure batteries, so I can charge my phone and the like.

33 The weed hatch is a steel trap door to the canal below.

34 This doesn't exist. But if it did, I would be booked as a guest speaker. A bit like when people who had been incarcerated came in to give a talk in assembly and to say, "Don't make the same mistakes I did."

violently draw water into the engine bay and sink the boat as fast as you can say "Is there anyone alive out there?" The fable of a boat sinking in 30 seconds because of an unsecured weed hatch is told gravely and regularly within the boating community. It is true, though… it can and does happen.

The fear of a narrowboat sinking may seem a little over the top when the canal is shallow and speed is rarely an issue, but it is a possibility. Boats can be lifted out and dried off, but with all my worldly possessions on board, it was not an experience I particularly wanted to add to the repertoire. Boat sinking nightmares are as prevalent as the "actor going on stage without learning their lines" dream, and happen to every boater, I promise. If I leave a party early during a storm, I'm only behaving as any sane home-loving boater would.

So, I'll do these checks every time I cruise. The checks themselves, though, are not enough if what then follows is a poor sequence of decision making.

~~~~~~

It was August Bank Holiday and I was squeezing in a boat move with Megan before heading to Notting Hill Carnival. I'd never been before but this was a summer of new adventures and I couldn't wait to see what all the fuss was about. Had I been moored out west, I would have wandered up to join the festivities on foot, an ideal scenario. But being moored out in East London, I'd planned to do a move with Megan, tie up the boat and jump on the Tube to Warwick Avenue.

I cruised the boat while dressed all fancy in my festival attire – a highly impractical flowing skirt that I tied into a knot on one thigh. A boat-move in convoy with Megan in the sunshine, followed by dancing in the streets. Was there a better summer's day in the capital?

Before I set off, I noticed my oil level was weirdly low.

THE BREAKDOWN

"Hmm, Meg… come and look at this?" I said. "The oil has dripped out of my engine and it's all in the sump."[35]

"Oh yeah, weird," she said. "I've got some oil if you want to top it up?" Megan retrieved the bottle of engine oil and I poured all four litres into the engine.

We cruised. Megan up front, me following behind. A little apprehensive about the oil situation, I kept an ear out for any unusual noises coming from below deck. All seemed fine. We'd travelled about a mile when my engine cut out. Silence.

I let the boat drift to the towpath, hopped off and signalled to Megan, who was now a hundred yards ahead of me.

I lifted my deck boards and checked the oil levels. Sure enough, they were low again. In fact, there was no oil left in my engine at all. This hadn't happened before, but then nothing looked burst, snapped or overheated. I wasn't panicking, though. I guessed that I could call an engineer, hand over an annoying (though not back-breaking) £80 call-out fee and be on my way. Megan brought her boat back to join mine. We sat and waited for an engineer in the midday heat.

"You've got oil on your face," said Megan.

"Standard," I said.

An engineer called Alan arrived within an hour and worked in silence, straddling my engine in his mucky jeans. Megan and I sat waiting on the towpath grass, contemplating beers to get us in the mood for Carnival.

Alan poked his head out of the engine bay.

"So," he said, drying his hands on a rag, "that oil in the sump has leaked out of your engine somehow. You should have stopped cruising as soon as you noticed. I'm afraid the engine has seized up."

I didn't know what this meant, but it sounded expensive.

---

35 The sump is the area below the engine that collects oil, diesel and any other fluid not welcome for disposal in the canal.

"We'll need to crane it out, give it a look over and likely replace some parts. It will set you back a fair whack," he said.

I felt nauseous.

"How much?" I said.

"I wouldn't like to say." Alan looked at me. I sensed he wasn't finished. He tapped the rust beneath his posterior. "Can I ask, did you get this boat surveyed?" he said.

"Yeah…" I said.

"May I see it?"

Megan lifted herself up onto her elbows. I looked at her then back at Alan.

"Sure."

I went inside to retrieve the printed survey and returned, handing it over to Alan. He flicked through and stopped at the page with the hull measurements.

"Hmn," he said.

Hmn didn't sound good.

The document was a pre-purchase survey, though in truth, Dad and I had parted with the bulk of the cash before getting it done. The most important detail to look out for in these surveys is the thickness of the hull. It can be a beautiful boat, but if the hull is too thin, you're in trouble. Alan shook his head…

"You see this N/A written at the back section here?" he said.

"Yeah, not applicable," I said.

"No." His no was drawn out. "In this instance, it means not available." He looked up as I looked down at the N/As.

"The steel on this part of the boat at the back is so thin that a reading couldn't be taken," he said, pointing at the diagram of *Argie*.

I took the survey from Alan and stared blankly at the N/A, N/A, N/A written on the back section of the boat.

"I don't understand. N/A means not applicable," I said. Everyone knows that.

There was silence as both Megan and Alan allowed for the information to sink in. I could feel panic start to rise in my chest and wanted so much to ask them both to kindly leave now.

THE BREAKDOWN

Megan, who had been busying herself with her pot plants, walked over.

"Hannah, there's nothing we can do right now," she said. "Let's just take it one step at a time."

"Now, because of the seized up engine," Alan said, "you'll need to get the boat towed to Lee Valley Marina in Stanstead Abbotts, which is further up the River Lee. It'll take a day. There's a guy I know who can do it for you. Give me a call in the week and I'll hook you up."

"Will it sink, though?" I said. "With the hull so thin?"

"It shouldn't. But it needs sorting before you get a hole... or several."

Alan tidied away his tools and left.

I flicked through the survey, wishing for the pages to say something different. Megan made us both a cup of tea. She started talking about the need for further investigation, over-plating,[36] welding.

I wanted her to stop talking.

"I don't understand," I said. "Why didn't the surveyor say that this is what N/A had meant? Surely N/A is universally Not Applicable?"

I think Megan knew not to answer this. Two rowing boats of teenagers passed as we stood in silence. I was devastated, with a sinking feeling of regret knotted in my stomach. How could I tell Mum and Dad that I had made such a terrible mistake? Why did I rush into buying the first boat I saw? Why didn't the surveyor explain the N/As to us?

Megan was right. I needed to take it one step at a time. But I knew, whatever the findings from the marina, that I had a job on my hands with this boat, and that all the work I had done to feel strong and capable in my new life was precarious and it could

---

36 Over-plating refers to the welding of patches/sections over the top of steel, as a secondary layer. A bit like a permanent boat plaster.

dissolve in a moment. And this was the moment. I was right back at the beginning. In that flat again in Crouch End, incapable and lost.

"I think I'll give Carnival a miss, Meg," I said, putting my boards back down on the back deck.

"Don't be silly, Hannah. Let's just go have a nice day," she said.

We left our boats where mine had stopped alongside Walthamstow Marshes and walked to the nearest Tube. I was embarrassed and anxious, but there wasn't much I could do until I was able to book in the tow later in the week. Instead, for now, I was determined to enjoy Carnival, and to forget about my N/A hull.

Chapter 10
Things I've Cut
From My Propeller

- Weeds
- Weeds with leeches in
- Bits of rope
- My own rope
- Tarpaulin
- Fishing line
- Wire
- Nondescript rubbery stuff I'd rather not think about
- A decapitated Barbie doll head
- Fishnet tights
- An anchor and barbecue (at the same time)
- A kazillion plastic bags

Chapter 11
Toilet Chronicles
(Part I)

The first question I'm asked about living on a boat is often, "Where does your poo go?" From my six-year-old niece to my friend's elderly parents, it tops the chart of necessary intel. Most folk will launch straight in, as if it's been burning a hole in their minds ever since they took a walk along the scenic towpath. They are not satisfied with witnessing the beauty of newly hatched ducklings, inhaling the smell of burning wood rising from our postcard chimneys or seeing a keen gardener harvesting his latest crop from an impressive roof garden – these really are superfluous observations when the most important question is and forever will be to all flush-toilet-owning land dwellers…

Where does your poo go? How do you deal with morning poos, sickness poos and other people's poos on that small, poorly ventilated boat?

So, let's just clear it up now.

There are three types of toilet on a boat: a pump-out toilet, a compost toilet and a cassette toilet.

A pump-out toilet is one with a plastic tank that lives below deck, often underneath your bed. It will fill with a mix of wee, poo and Elsan fluid (the smelly blue stuff that stings your nostrils at festivals) over several weeks and maybe months, depending on the tank size. The boat will start to feel heavier in the location of the tank when it reaches capacity, at which point you will drive your perfect little poo boat to a pump-out station to have its contents sucked out with a suction hose for a small fee. I assume your poo then mixes with any other landlubber human poo in the populus cesspool of toilet waste.

A compost toilet is a nifty little standalone unit, often decorated, but essentially containing a bucket for poo and a bottle for wee. The wee can be chucked into a nearby bush, doing no harm to the natural surroundings, though some harm to your own natural odour if any of it inadvertently splashes back on to your legs/shoes/face. As for the poo part – if you're an excellent eco-boater, it will be carefully loved over time and mixed with sawdust, paper, coffee granules and food waste and turned into delicious, non-stinky compost. For the rest of us, it can (much to the annoyance of the Canal and River Trust and general waste services) be bagged and binned.[37] Which is… well, bagged and binned.

A cassette toilet operates much like a pump-out, though it is smaller, more compact and can be carried by hand to the nearest Elsan point on the canal network, which is a big drain for you to empty your slosh into.

What do I have? (Maybe skip this part if you're squeamish/know me/want to know me.)

When I first moved on to the boat, all decorated canal buckets and pot plant green, I'd inherited a pump-out toilet. I was liberal with its usage in the first six weeks, with several visitors using it also.

Since I had been enjoying the novelty of a flush on a boat, the toilet tank filled up quite quickly. A few days after the Notting Hill Carnival and hull bombshell, and before I'd managed to pin the elusive tow man down to a date, I discovered it was full. More than full, and I think there may have been a suction issue or a blockage. On its final flush at capacity, the toilet started to do a strange fill-up thing in the bowl. The toilet was backing up.

Twenty-four hours later, the full-to-bursting contents of the tank under my bed were now rapidly rising up and out of the tank and into the toilet basin. Specifically (and yes, I will be specific here,

---

37 More recently, the Canal and River Trust and waste services have tried to put a stop to this practice.

for it is firmly etched on my mind as the most horrendous of boat experiences), the toilet bowl filled up every 45 minutes with an indescribably coloured toilet swill.

This being the time when my engine had seized up, I couldn't cruise my boat to have the tank emptied the normal way, and I resorted to syphoning the fluid out with a TK Maxx hand-held pump. Given the size of my tank, this took some time. I set my alarm every 45 minutes for 24 hours to continue pumping into bottles, food containers, my newly purchased cool box and anything with a lid.

After little sleep I called my friend Lauryn the following morning.

"Alright love." Whether she's performing on stage or offering advice down the phone to a friend in need, her warmth and charisma is palpable. She's cool under pressure and has seen all sides of me over the years... perfect for poo-gate.

"I've
Been
Syphoning
Shit
Out
Of
My
Toilet
For
Over
Twenty
Four
Hours."

I was hyperventilating down the phone.

"Oh, Hannah," said Lauryn.

"Hey, Hannah," came a voice I didn't recognise.

"Bex, meet Hannah." I was on loudspeaker.

"Hi, Bex," I said to Lauryn's new partner.

"Don't worry," said Lauryn. "Bex has worked on boats, she's not fazed by this."

"Nice to meet you, Bex," I said.

"What can we do?" asked Lauryn.

"The situation is beyond help, but I do appreciate the support, women."

I put down the phone and returned to the bathroom, where I stared into the toilet, laughing/crying at the state of it all. Bottles of toilet waste stood in the shower. Destroyed towels. Specks of green on the tiles. I thought of Sam and the memory of my old life, which felt like an old postcard washed away at sea. What would he think of me? I felt completely alone but couldn't imagine the possibility of sharing this experience with another human. This was something I quite rightly had to do alone.

The tank was finally empty. I gathered up the towels and chucked them in the nearest towpath bin, ordered a new glitter-lined compost toilet to be delivered to the marina I was going to be towed to and set up two buckets to improvise in the meantime. Interestingly, no plumber wanted the job of removing the faulty unit, so following some YouTube instructions, I capped it off myself, cleaned out the tank and ripped out the toilet.

That evening Lauryn called. "How's it going?" she said.

"Better, thank you," I said. "Capped it off, and have just done a run to the skip, with the toilet strapped onto a trolley."

"Your first plumbing job, hey? You are so badass nowadays, Hannah."

I smiled down the phone. I suppose it was a bit badass.

"I didn't have a choice, Lauryn," I said.

This was the new way now. Anything broken, I must fix myself. I cleaned the boat from bow to stern, showered the smell from my skin and hair, and lit some incense. My home had transformed from an overflowing sewer to a floating example of hygge. The boat was beautiful once more.[38]

---

38 At the time of publication, I now fully compost my waste... poo, food and all. Let me know if you want some.

Chapter 12
A Brief History
of Canals

Romans were thought to have built the first canal in the UK, though the modern British system was largely built during the late eighteenth and early nineteenth centuries as part of the industrial revolution. These artificial inland waterways (spanning 4,000 miles) were cut through the land and fed by rivers, reservoirs and rainwater. Boats transporting the nation's goods were drawn by horses, which gave the path to the side of the canal the name towpath. Evidence of the use of horses can still be seen today where ramps can be found at the water's edge. These were built into the towpath so horses could access the canal to rehydrate. There are also indentations on some canal bridges where ropes attaching boats to horses have rubbed against the stone.

The canals were built to transport cargo efficiently across the country and were commissioned by wealthy individuals with a business interest in transporting cargo. You'll find this in the canal names; for instance, the Duke of Bridgewater commissioned the Bridgewater Canal.

At 137 miles long, the Grand Union Canal is the longest on the UK network. It starts in London and ends in Birmingham and is thought to take 72 hours to navigate.[39] The shortest UK canal is the Wardle in Cheshire, which connects the Trent and Mersey

---

39 Source: Canal and River Trust website. They have some great articles about our canals and rivers.

and the Shropshire canals. It is 72 feet in length and has one lock.[40] Wide canals like the Grand Union can fit two narrowboats side by side in a lock, and narrow canals, like the Oxford and Coventry canals, can fit only one boat in a lock at any given time. These narrower canals were designed to be cheaper to build and quicker to navigate through.

The British canals were the main mode of transportation of goods before the rail network came to prominence at the end of the nineteenth century and the waterways were eclipsed in a short space of time. By the twentieth century, motorways had been developed and the canal network was basically left abandoned until the mid-twentieth century, when it was nationalised and began to be used for leisure and tourism purposes, and by the likes of me.

40 Bless

Chapter 13
Sam

I was the general manager of a pub in North London when we met. The venue hosted gigs, ale festivals and comedy nights, and a legendary bluegrass promoter, Ralph, held a twice-weekly residency, spinning his extensive collection of vinyl on top of a vintage football table. The pub was a beloved haunt of locals. Tobacco smell from years of old clung to the ceiling tiles, and toilets that hadn't been touched since the 1970s required constant maintenance. Weekends, it would transform. Buggies, family board games and tables piled high with roast dinners. I'd get used to cleaning baby food off wooden high chairs and fishing out Scrabble pieces from the back of shabby sofas. I was certain I'd find the love of my life working there. A creative type I could win over with my managerial confidence. I soon learned that every left hand bore a wedding ring. This community was a young family hot spot.

It was a busy Friday night in November when a man with sky-blue eyes and a shy smile came to the bar and ordered a stout from my assistant. Niamh, a devoted Spurs fan and a crucial addition to the pub, was excellent with the customers. They hit it off and within minutes were bouncing around song suggestions and new club signings. He was drunk but functioning. Wearing a knitted jumper and sporting a tash (Movember), his look wasn't uncommon in the pub. Unlike the usual customer, though, this one wasn't wearing a wedding ring, and he was catching my eye. A lot.

Running out of reasons to busy myself behind the bar, I took the till drawers to cash up and disappeared into the office, watching him finish his pint on CCTV and shaking hands with the door staff on his way out.

SAM

Niamh poked her head around the office door.

"Whatcha looking at?" she said.

"Go away," I said with a smile.

The next night, he returned.

"How's it going?" He was drunk again, but less so than before.

"Not bad," I said. "What can I get you?"

"Your number."

"Very smooth," I said, picking up a glass to pour his stout.

Niamh came round the corner with a knowing smile.

"Oh, hello again," she said.

And that was that. Niamh gave him my number, and the following week we were on our first date at a nearby Thai restaurant. Neither of us played it cool after that. He would frequently come in to work and stand at the bar, developing a bond with the staff, and with me. He'd help me lift up chairs onto tables at the end of the night and walk me home, or back to his. He'd bring me hot dinners and introduce me to his friends over the bar. I stayed at his flat more and more, and when it came to renewing the contract on my shared flat, we moved into a new build together with Caz in Crouch End. It was, for a year, a perfect arrangement. There was a familiar domesticity in our weekend rituals. Saturday afternoon football from a flatscreen of unnecessary proportion would reverberate in our living room. We'd lie half on, half off the grey IKEA sofa, legs slumped across one another's, my legs swinging restlessly, his strong and unmoving. Sam would react to the ref's decisions with a vocabulary that didn't quite fit with memories of those same afternoons from my childhood, while he sipped on bright yellow orange squash, which did.

Early evening would roll around. I'd head to work, as he took to his usual night-time spots with a local group of friends. We'd reconvene in the early hours. He'd arrive with a drunken earnestness, sit on a stool and watch as I finished up my shift. Looping arms, we'd return to our flat together, sharing local gossip from the events of the evening, and with the anticipation of our guilt-free lie-in would flop into bed. In the morning would come a fry-up, more football and another pub visit, for good measure.

ALL BOATS ARE SINKING

In that flat, my solo hobbies ceased to exist. I'd stopped reading; it didn't go with the relationship and would interfere with our time together. And our time was precious. He worked weekdays, a 9–5 overseeing business deals for a large corporation. I was working nights and weekends, forever cancelling plans when a chef didn't turn up, or heading to the pub in the middle of the night when the intruder alarm sounded. CCTV for the pub was installed on my phone, and at dinner, I'd check it to see how busy we were. Sam hated that. He despised his job but had the ability to leave it at the office. I loved mine, but it came home with me.

I think I knew he wasn't the one, but as I straddled entry into my fourth decade, with single friends dropping off and into a world of couples' holidays and mortgages, I believed we were content enough. We enjoyed the benefits of our grown-up relationship: getting away whenever we could, joint wedding invitations and Christmas cards, and our combined friendship group, which was a constant source of stimulation. We didn't have a huge amount in common, but, having been an actor before joining the pub trade, I had previously only ever dated people in the arts whose conversations revolved around facial hair or the detailed mechanics of a bunraku puppet. I was revelling in a different type of conversation. Cars, football, jobs that required a shirt and tie – a throwback to my childhood. I got on with his friends, he with mine. My family liked him. He would fill the silence at home with hip hop records, computer games and football. He was a breath of fresh air and I adored him.

But it wasn't enough.

I behaved in a cowardly way as the relationship unfurled. I should have walked away sooner, we both should. But we didn't. And instead, when the relationship was on its knees, I cheated. A kiss with an actor. I decided not to confess while I worked out what I wanted and two days later suggested we had a break. I moved out and sofa-surfed for a week. I was confused as to what the kiss had been. Had I checked out of my relationship entirely? I still loved Sam, and I missed him. The Sam who used to bring me hot food to work in a Tupperware.

SAM

I moved back home after the week-long break apart. We agreed to try again, and I was certain it would be too hurtful to admit the truth about the kiss. But my conscience had other ideas, and the morning after I moved back home, I awoke to a tense Sam lying next to me.

"Who's Felix?" he said.

"What?" I turned to face him.

"You said his name in your sleep last night."

Sam saw it in my face. He rose up and out of bed, punching holes into our flimsy new-build walls. *There goes our deposit*, I thought. We tried to patch it up, a dream holiday in Thailand should do the trick. It didn't. And six months after I kissed the actor, we separated for good.

Chapter 14
Towing

Walthamstow Marshes to Stanstead Abbotts

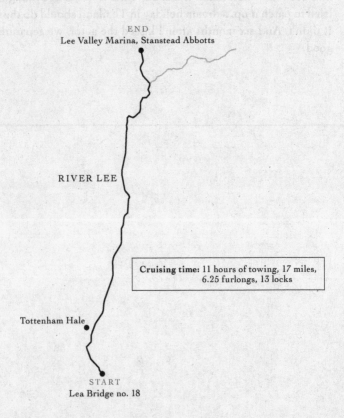

END
Lee Valley Marina, Stanstead Abbotts

RIVER LEE

Cruising time: 11 hours of towing, 17 miles, 6.25 furlongs, 13 locks

Tottenham Hale

START
Lea Bridge no. 18

TOWING

I was moored (or marooned) on the River Lee, exactly where I had broken down a week before. Ray was coming to tow me and the boat to the boatyard so I could get my engine fixed and the new over-plating welded onto the hull. Ray pulled his own boat in alongside mine and stepped onto my gunwales.

"Course it's raining," he said, pointing to the clouds. I picked up the East Anglian accent straight away.

Ray was a gruff-looking boater with shoulder-length black and grey peppered hair.

"Hello, I'm Hannah," I said, climbing out of the boat.

"Hello, Hannah. Right, where are we going?" he said.

"Lee Valley Marina in Stanstead Abbotts, please," I said.

"No problem." He looped his ropes on to the bow and stern of *Argie*. "One for luck," he said, attaching the centre line to the middle. "Now, I've got a bit of a leg infection, so we'll share doing the locks, if that's alright?"

"No problem," I said. "Can I make you a tea?"

"That's okay. I brought supplies," he said.

He pointed to a four pack of cider on his back deck. At this juncture I didn't care if my driver was half cut or not. After the seized-up engine fiasco and the exploding toilet, the bar for narrowboating (generally) was pretty low, and I could do with a drink myself to be honest.

"No judgement from me," I said.

Ray looked at me as if to say he didn't care if I judged him or not. I liked Ray.

"That's all tied up," he said. "Now, in order to tow your boat" – he was leaning on his tiller facing me – "I need to drive mine from here, and it will make my life a hell of a lot easier if you stand at your tiller and mirror my movements. That way the boats are working in tandem. Make sense?"

"So, I just do the same as you, even though my engine won't be on?" I said.

"Correct," he said.

ALL BOATS ARE SINKING

"Sounds good." I put on a rain mac and got into position on the back deck.

We set off. Because we were tied together, we were able to talk to one another from our respective back decks. I moved my tiller in sync with Ray's as we cruised north and out of the bustle of East London. We nattered about Suffolk and his expert knowledge of trees and boats. I'd not travelled this far north so was enjoying seeing what the River Lee had to offer.

The River Lee (or "Lea" if you're talking about the whole section up until its source in Luton) is the second largest river in London. The Lee Navigation (the bit that's navigable) starts in Hertford and meanders down rural Hertfordshire, alongside East London and eventually joins the Thames at Leamouth (get it?) in Tower Hamlets. Ray and I were heading out of London towards pockets of green marshland, reservoirs and ancient trees, with clusters of industrial units and breweries. We cruised along the winding river, with power lines and the M25 motorway passing overhead, on our way to the Essex and Hertfordshire border. It felt good to get out of the city.

Despite having asked me to share the locks, Ray did most of them alone.

"It's alright. You go and make a cuppa. It's nice to loosen up my leg a bit," he said.

It was raining heavily for most of the day. We passed through Enfield, the landscape becoming more rural as we cruised further north. Ray, who had sunk all his cider and was now a little wobbly, misjudged a low-hanging tree as he turned a corner on the river near Cheshunt. In slow motion the tree pulled several items from his roof into the water below, including his bike.

He seemed unaffected by the mishap.

"It's alright, I'll come back later with a magnet," he said.

Ray must have been tired. We had been cruising for hours in the rain. By late afternoon, we arrived at the marina, to be greeted by all and sundry who had heard about my thin hull and bone-dry engine. I thanked Ray and paid him in cash for the tow.

TOWING

Argie (and I) would be stuck in the boatyard for the next six months.

Chapter 15
The Boatyard
(Part I)

Staying on the yard was a strange though not entirely awful experience. While I waited for my boat to be craned out, *Argie* was tied to another boat by the marina entrance. The neighbouring vessel was drying out after sinking earlier in the summer. The staff gave me a key to enter and leave the yard via a big metal gate so I could live on board *Argie*, but with access to a shower block, washing machine and shoreline power. Given that mine was a last-minute booking, they'd see to me when they could. Six weeks after I arrived, *Argie* was lifted up by four straps attached to a crane and put on hard standing (railway sleepers). The craning happened while I was at work, and when I returned, the boat was in position. It was the first time I had seen the bottom, the propeller, the shape of the hull. A thick layer of fresh-water mussels had attached to the base plate. In the wind they sounded a siren. Hundreds of natural windchimes.

The workmen on the yard were jolly and easy to talk to, with a deprecating nature and just enough piss-taking to suit me, affectionately renaming my boat *Argie Bodgie* after a few weeks – though they were sympathetic on the whole.

I had a phone call one day while at work.

"Hannah, it's Joe from Stanstead Abbotts. What was the name of the dodgy boat surveyor you had?"

I told him.

"Thought so," said Joe. "Okay, thanks."

"Why do you ask?" I said before he hung up.

THE BOATYARD (PART I)

"Oh, the toe-rag is trying to get on the marina to survey someone's boat," he said. "I'm telling him to turn around."

"Oh, right," I said, surprised by Joe's support.

"Oh, and Hannah," he said. "Those mussels on the bottom of your boat. They're starting to smell real fishy."

It meant a lot to me that Joe had called. I had felt stupid and embarrassed since the day I discovered my boat's hull was not as it seemed and was encouraged that the boat experts could see the fault was down to the surveyor for "not doing his job properly", as Joe put it. I arrived home later (smelling the not so fresh mussels from the entrance of the car park), to find Paul the welder had started on my boat. He talked through what he was going to be doing. A whole new base plate would be welded on and a new drainage system installed inside the engine bay. *Argie* would get a new prop shaft, new weed hatch, new decking and a new diesel tank. It was a big job, and with winter approaching, I felt guilty that my boat appeared to be the only one getting any work done outside.

"Ah, it's nothing," said Paul. "And don't feel silly."

"Is this a bad one, though?" I asked.

"No," he said. "They're all projects, Hannah. Every last one of them."

He pointed at the vessels around us, in different states of repair. Some with layers of rust. Others with pitting and punctures like bullet holes. Older boats, remnants of their former selves. Timber roofs that had half rotted away. Boats with tarpaulin flapping in the wind, covering open cabins. Hulls rough and bumpy like metal cellulite.

"All boats are sinking, Hannah, just at different rates," he said.

I smiled and climbed the ladder onto my boat. It was solid on its raised structure, like public art on a plinth. Not at all as it was designed to feel. Paul loaded his van and drove off. There was something reassuring in his comment. The inevitability of decline. That only so much can be done. Things go wrong, windows leak, rust returns. Jobs take longer than you think they will. But it was all fixable. The sun had set. I sat on the railing on my back deck and

ALL BOATS ARE SINKING

looked around the yard. It was beautiful with the light of the moon casting dramatic shadows. All these boats, with their own histories. Hundreds of owners and stories of how they came to be. And my little boat, *Argie Bargie*, in the middle of it all.

Chapter 16
About the Job

I was sitting in one of those old pubs with mahogany panelled walls and a curved saloon bar near Tottenham Court Road. Bottles of ketchup and plastic menus were stark evidence of the now generic pub owners. Earlier that day I'd given my notice at work. The role I'd been promoted to, away from pubs and into the events side, wasn't as I'd hoped. I felt ignored and the stress had become too much to bear. I didn't have a job to go to, but with a broad CV from over the years with jobs in theatre, pub management, events, children's entertainment and now as a fledgling mermaid, I wasn't too worried. But here I was sitting in this pub waiting for Jonathan, a senior colleague, and the one who had put me forward for the role, to show. His response to the resignation was to suggest we meet and discuss the issues I was having over a beer. I frowned at the email on the screen. Jonathan was a friendly enough man, though his reputation as a Lothario was well known. He was much older than me and had asked me out for dinner plenty of times over the years, to which I'd often blushed and politely declined.

I said I'd meet him, yes.

He walked up the stairs of the pub, holding a copy of the *Evening Standard* under his arm. The tight ringlets behind his ears bounced with each ascending step. As he approached the table, I felt a flutter in my stomach given his previous advances. I'd dressed a little smarter than usual, and in an attempt to cover up the smell of diesel and engine oil that had become a constant feature since being in the boatyard, I reeked of perfume. As he approached the table with a big smile, it felt like this set-up may be perceived to be a little less innocent than "work chat". For both of us.

He dropped his paper.

"Top up?" he said.

I'd been waiting half an hour and my shandy had gone down rather quickly.

"Please."

As he walked away, I looked at this person I'd come to know well as my colleague and saw an attractive man in a pub buying me a drink.

"Come on then, what's going on?" he said upon his return.

I fumbled through a nervous monologue about how I felt my role wasn't as relevant as I'd hoped. That I was confused by some of the direction I'd been given and that I felt the results weren't being seen. He listened, brilliantly, apologised for his part in allowing me to feel this way and said he'd ensure I was more included in decision making.

"But Hannah, you must put yourself out there a bit more. We need you to really lead on this," he said. "No more loitering around in the background, yes?"

Oh God, he'd read my deepest insecurities. Growing up in a big family, the youngest of four, the only girl, feeling overwhelmed and unheard.

"Would you like another drink?" he said.

"Sure."

Soon we were chatting about our lives, our upbringings and, unexpectedly, the death of loved ones.

"Gosh, I'm so sorry," I said.

"Oh, it's fine," he said. "It's certainly made me appreciate the fragility of life."

He took a swig from his drink, keeping eye contact with me throughout.

"We're quite similar, Hannah," he said.

Bloody hell, we're not, I thought. But sure, if he wanted to tell me that he understood how I was feeling, then fine.

He asked about the boat and laughed at all the mistakes I'd made with the hull, the engine.

ABOUT THE JOB

"Another drink?" he said.

"Sure. Why not," I said.

He told me about his early career. He seemed sad to talk about those years, full of regret and longing. I don't know, maybe it was the beer, but his eyes were softening. He said he didn't like this pub, so we moved to another one. The second was bustling with city workers and we sat on a high table in the middle. All work chat had long since wound up, and we were in a rhythm. Theatre, travel, music, relationships.

"I'm a bit pissed, sir," I said.

He looked at his watch.

"Right, well the last train is in ten minutes. Come back to mine."

I thought this might have been coming, but I wasn't prepared with an answer. I laughed, then stared into his eyes. He smiled and repeated the request.

"I'm not sure. Let's have another half," I said.

He rolled his eyes, ordered another round and paid up. Knowing what was about to come, the flirting ramped up. We'd missed the train and so he ordered us a cab. In the taxi, we were snogging like teenagers. I couldn't quite believe what was happening.

I stayed the night. Our bodies seemed to melt into each other's. The next morning, he lay on my stomach as I ran my fingers through his ringletted hair.. We were comfortable in the silence but able to pick up any subject easily and learn a little more about each other. The irony was that I had felt like my voice wasn't being listened to at work, but on that night and on that morning with that man, I felt heard.

By mid-afternoon, I was showered and saying goodbye, with the enormous elephant poking its head round the door.

"About the job..." I said.

"Well, I think you're staying, don't you?" he said, kissing me one final time.

I walked back to the Tube station with a smile and an expression of disbelief across my face.

I messaged Syd, "FFFFFUUUCCCCCCCCCKKKKK".

Chapter 17
The Boatyard
(Part II)

Stanstead Abbotts to nowhere for six months

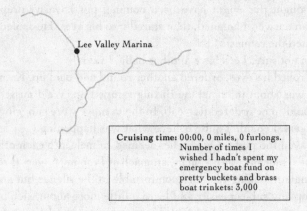

Lee Valley Marina

Cruising time: 00:00, 0 miles, 0 furlongs.
Number of times I
wished I hadn't spent my
emergency boat fund on
pretty buckets and brass
boat trinkets: 3,000

My friend and colleague Will used the term "Silly Season" to describe the partying that takes place in December. He'd drop me a daily text with an update on the previous night's antics and his plan for the rest of the week. Will's an Oxford graduate who I totally misjudged when we first met. His blond youthful hair, rugby shirt and foppish accent give him a particular vibe. I was very wrong. He's grounded, emotionally intelligent and a farm boy at heart.

THE BOATYARD (PART II)

Silly Season was in full force for me too and I was burning my candle down to its wick. Being stuck out of town in the boatyard, I'd get the train into London for work, attend a social engagement in the evening and take my often tipsy self back on the train to Stanstead Abbotts Marina, where my boat remained on hard standing. I would climb up and down the ladder in my Christmas party clothes, concentrating hard on the rungs made visible only by moonlight. When I arrived home, the boat would be freezing. I'd build a quick fire and climb into bed with two hot water bottles.

The men on site started early, and I would awake to the sound of their power tools seemingly right by my skull. The boat was dusty in the yard, inside and out, and there was little point in doing much about it. By the time January came round, I gave up on cleaning altogether and spent any free time I had in my engine bay chipping away at rust.

In deepest winter, the Marina quietened, with only a few people staying on their boats. Visits from friends had long since stopped and the weather had turned. In February, The Beast from the East – a cold snap from Siberia – arrived, and with it inches of snow and sub-zero temperatures. Trains to London stopped running and for a week I was stuck working from home. I would take my laptop to the pub nearby and return to the boat after dinner. I hadn't quite got the knack of the fire and was prone to filling the boat with smoke. In the mornings and evenings, I would sit on the floor beside it, coaxing the kindling with a poker, and slowly build up the layers of seasoned wood and briquettes. But it never stayed alight. I would awake in the middle of the night shivering with every part of my body, unable[41] to rise and start the fire over. My skin was suffering. I stopped wearing make-up to try to clear up the spots and dry patches caused by the harsh conditions.

---

41 Unwilling

97

ALL BOATS ARE SINKING

A vicious cough set in and got progressively worse. The cough had started in my throat, before bedding deep into my lungs. Fits of coughing would have me leant over the kitchen units in agony as I stood clutching my chest. My head felt light and my body fatigued. I slathered on vapour serum and cream for muscle relief. I steamed over a bowl of hot water nightly. It did nothing.

At week three of the illness I awoke in a cold sweat, delirious and struggling to breathe.

I called Dad.

"I think I might need you to pick me up," I said down the phone.

"Oh Hannah, you sound awful," he said.

"I'm sorry," I said to Dad, feeling like a teenager again.

He picked me up and drove me to Ipswich Hospital, where I was diagnosed with the early stages of pneumonia and a broken rib caused by coughing. My body ached and all strength seemed to have left me, in body and in mind. I went to my parents' house to recover. The week-long trip was like visiting a five-star resort after a weekend at a festival. I continued working, but I took it easy, answering a few emails then napping on the sofa wrapped in Mum's blankets, to be woken up by her bringing me a cup of tea and a slice of her homemade fruit cake. Unlike visits at Christmas time or Easter, we didn't discuss my life choices. She merely brought me food and drink and commented each day on how the colour was returning to my cheeks. Their home was clean and bright, not at all like the boatyard. It made me realise how inhospitable it was to be living there on the boat, where the air was filled with welding fumes and dust was caked on everything. I took long baths at my parents' house to heal my body and vowed to return to my own home restored and to frankly start taking better care of myself.

When I arrived back at Stanstead Abbotts, I was greeted with worried smiles from the staff. The boat was in a bit of a state. I hadn't realised how poorly I'd got and had clearly struggled to keep my home in order. Feeling considerably better after a course of antibiotics and Mum's tomato and lentil soup, I climbed onto the roof to clean out my chimney. Sure enough, it was completely blocked. A thick tar had lined the inner circle of the flue, and it took all my strength to dislodge the lumps with a chimney brush I had purchased at the boatyard chandlery.[42]

The next day, my engine was finally returned and craned back in.

Alan the engineer had come to the marina to reposition and refit the engine into the boat.

"So do we know how the oil drained out of the engine?" I asked Alan. He was looking over Paul's welding while sat in my engine bay.

"Oh," he said, "either it was the wrong type of filter or it was affixed too loosely. The oil had no chance."

I'd had the engine serviced back in the summer. It must have happened then.

"All fixed now, though, and it should run beautifully," he said. "Bet you'll be pleased to get back on the network?"

"I'm nervous to be honest, Alan," I said.

"Why's that?"

"I'd barely been on it five minutes before the boat was craned out. I've been here for six months. What if I can't remember how to drive it?"

"You'll be alright," said Alan with an elbow nudge and a smile.

I was nervous, but I also couldn't wait to get on the move again. To travel back down the River Lee not being towed by someone, with a toilet that worked and a hull that was solid. The week at my parents had done wonders for my energy levels, and despite the nerves, I was feeling positive and raring to go. It was March by the time the boat was lifted back into the water, and spring was on its way.

---

42 Much like a sweet shop, but for boat gubbins. Some of them also sell sweets. They can be found mostly in marinas and boatyards, though there used to be a fancy one in central London, right on Shaftesbury Avenue. This sadly shut down after the pandemic.

Part 2

Adventures on *Argie*

Chapter 18
VV

A year after leaving sixth form, Caz and I would find our friendship facing its first test. She'd gone to university and had become a funnier, fuller version of the already hilarious friend I'd known for years. She'd got into the female football team, and it seemed to take up her life in and out of term time. Weekly dress-up nights out on the lash in Lincoln, and holidays to Kos.

I'd stayed in Ipswich while my parents quietly seethed at my lack of conventional aspiration. I wanted to be an actor, but I was living in a perpetual state of self-doubt, and those two things don't sit well together. While Caz was in her first year at university, I'd spent my winter attending an acting course in the hope of gaining some confidence.

Between the acting course, waitressing in a fish restaurant and drama school auditions, I landed a job working on cruise ships as a kids' club host. The trips varied from a four-night mini cruise to Amsterdam to a two-month stint cruising the Baltics, Mediterranean or my favourite, the Norwegian fjords. I would keep this job over ten years, during drama school – in the holidays, and the subsequent "jobbing actor" years, when I'd rope in an actor friend to join me for a stint. It was a strange temping job, where time on board seemed to stand still. The ships were old fashioned, with pomp and ceremony laid on every night for the elderly passengers. The décor and entertainment programming was dated, and even the smoking ban that had come into force in the UK was bypassed by flexible sea laws for some time after. As staff, we would converse with passengers over dinner as part of our duties, hearing about grandchildren, long and varied careers, wars. But mostly, the talk was about ships.

ALL BOATS ARE SINKING

The stresses and uncertainty from back home didn't exist on board. It was a bubble away from politics, career choices, family. Waking up in the mornings I'd jump out of bed to see the new view out of my porthole. Copenhagen, Antigua, St Petersburg, Guernsey. At night I'd dress up in Monsoon gowns that I'd bought off Ebay, ascending grand staircases in kitten heels to enjoy enormous buffets in the dining room.

I would post pictures of the cruises on my Facebook account, while Caz posted another night out with her football team dressed as sailors, or as Bob the Builder. She returned home after her first year with a beer gut and a whole new set of words to describe "good times". She was settling into her new life with an irreverence that I wouldn't find for several years yet. I envied it, and though I had met Caz's new friends on a visit to see her, and took kindly to them, I knew that university life wasn't for me. I was too earnest.

"How's it going at uni?" We sat in Costa on my lunch break from my waitressing job.

"Well, you know. Same old." She took a sip from her vanilla latte. "How's the cruise life? Photos look amazing."

"Yeah, it's been fun to do a bit of travelling. And to get paid for it."

"Sure sure sure," she said.

I looked at my oldest friend. We were drifting apart.

"Hey, have you heard about this festival happening?" I said.

"Yeah, Mum was telling me about it. Looks good."

"Shall we go?" I chanced it.

"Sure, why not. I have some student loan left."

We bought tickets for the first ever Latitude Festival over the counter at HMV in Ipswich. In the festival fields, excited and mesmerised, we walked around like we owned the place, with a swagger that is so unique to people who choose to let loose at a festival. In our combat trousers and cowboy hats, we were carbon copies of each other once more, like the past year hadn't happened. We cared nothing for how we looked and soaked in every beautiful moment.

Snow Patrol headlined and we, in the height of our "Chasing Cars" obsession, stood towards the back of the crowd of the main stage surrounded by young families and inflatable furniture, and with our arms on each other's shoulders, sang our hearts out into the Suffolk skies above. My skin tingled with excitement as the feeling of being at one with a large crowd took over my body. Even those unfamiliar with the new releases had picked up the riffs and joined in with the hardcore fans. A vast sea of people, arms in the air, singing along together. It wasn't my first gig, but it was a moment and the beginning of my real love for live music.

Caz and I let our differences go that weekend. And I realised that we didn't need to be in each other's circles or at the same life stage to know how strong our friendship was. I knew it when we danced together watching Snow Patrol. We would always be the best of friends.

With an impressive music and arts programme, Latitude has grown over the years from a small posh festival in Suffolk into a larger posh festival in Suffolk. The festival site now spans over several rolling fields that are transformed into a playground for adults who used to rave and their children. Colours pop, with rainbow-coloured sheep and a neon light display over the central lake. I would return to the festival every year (bar one), sometimes as a punter and sometimes as a theatre maker.

Caz never went back to Latitude after the first year. She returned to life at uni and got her head down. She carried on enjoying being part of the football team and graduated with a 1st degree before embarking on a career in TV that would grow and grow. I was (am) so proud of her.

Over the years of attending the festival I had developed a routine for the weekend: I would stop off at my family home on the way, see Mum and Dad, decant my chosen alcohol into plastic water bottles (they have a strict no glass policy) and get a lift from Mum to the festival site.

ALL BOATS ARE SINKING

In 2011, two years after graduating from drama school, I had encouraged an energetic crowd of hopeful actors to join me on my annual trip to the festival.

"It better be good." Mark was one of the best actors in our year and is far too nice for the industry. He's a natural listener and had become like a brother since we'd spent time working together on the ships.

Suede and Paulo Nutini headlined. Our chosen tipple was vodka from Lidl. I journeyed via Ipswich in the usual fashion, Mum topping up the booze order with her homemade sloe gin, much to the delight of Mark and the group.

Back then I would take pride in avoiding the showers at the festival. The queues were long and there seemed little point when I was likely to get mucky again straight after. I would leave it until absolutely necessary and have a cat bath in the tent. On the Saturday morning of this particular trip, I decided it was time for a freshen up. I removed my clothing inside my two-man tent, poured water into a mess tin and unwrapped a new soap for the occasion. I washed my face and pits, then went for my soft bits. What followed was an excruciating pain, a burning sensation like I'd never felt. Most of our group hadn't emerged from their tents yet, so I clenched my teeth and breathed away the pain. I concluded that I must have been allergic to the soap and poured on more of the water to wash it away. The pain worsened. I was sweating. Grabbing some nearby baby wipes, I held them against the affected area. Eventually the pain subsided and I rolled out of the tent to crack on with the day's festivities, not telling a soul about what had happened inside.

It was a boozy weekend. Cider for breakfast, beer for lunch and spirits in the evening. The sloe gin had gone down a treat on the first two nights and at 5 p.m. that afternoon Mark said, "Right, let's crack open that vodka. Hannah, it's in your tent, I think."

"Oh my God," I said.

I laughed for several minutes before I could speak, tears cascading down my once again grubby face. Mark joined in as he awaited the punchline.

"I used that two-litre bottle of vodka to wash this morning."

"Bbbbaaaaaaaaaahhhh!" Mark was doing circles round the tent. "VV!"

Vodka Vagina remains my proudest nickname.

Chapter 19
Things I Wish I'd Bought Sooner

- A waterproof floating phone case
- Phone insurance
- An angle grinder
- A compost toilet
- Manual food processor
- Fridge
- Cheap sunglasses
- A foldaway table
- A boat

Chapter 20
Fair Weather

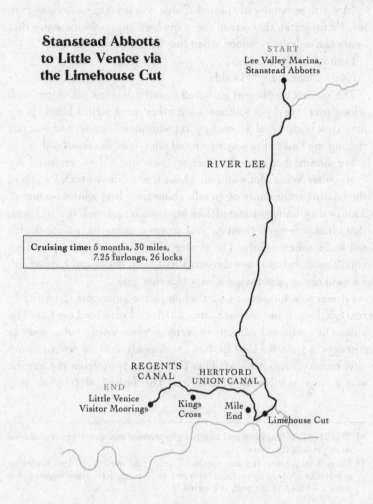

**Stanstead Abbotts
to Little Venice via
the Limehouse Cut**

START
Lee Valley Marina,
Stanstead Abbotts

RIVER LEE

Cruising time: 5 months, 30 miles,
7.25 furlongs, 26 locks

REGENTS
CANAL

HERTFORD
UNION CANAL

END
Little Venice
Visitor Moorings

Kings
Cross

Mile
End

Limehouse Cut

ALL BOATS ARE SINKING

I watched in fear as my boat was lifted high into the air by four engineers and a crane perched on the bank of the River Lee at the marina in Stanstead Abbotts. Now canal and river worthy, it had been fixed up, patched up, with a reconditioned engine and my new glittery gold compost toilet, and painted with a thick shiny layer of epoxy along the bottom side of the hull.[43]

"Are you renaming it, Hannah?" Joe was smoking a rollie next to me. I'd forgotten that one of the many boat superstitions states that boats can only be renamed when they're out of the water.

I thought for a moment.

"Nah. I like *Argie*,"[44] I said.

The marina employees gathered round to see me off. After such a long time, we'd got to know each other quite well. I filled up my new tank with diesel, started my reconditioned engine and was off, ringing my bell to the waving crowd who lined the riverbank.

Six months had gone by, half my boat life. I'd experienced my first winter living alone and on a boat (out of the water). People in the boating community often talk about their first winter on board. Things they underestimated, like how much fuel each fire requires, that chimneys need cleaning and stoves require maintenance. It's not to be taken lightly. The winter of 2017 had extreme weather conditions, and as a new boater, I had been naive and haphazard. I would never approach a winter like that again.

I'd learnt a lot about boats while in the boatyard (specifically rust) and – just in time for spring 2018 – I'd mastered my fire. The village of Stanstead Abbotts is pretty… some lovely pubs, rows of cottages, a friendly Co-Op, but I was ready now to return to my city, renewed and revived. That first move away from the marina was a huge out-breath of emotion. The feeling of freedom was

---

43 This is called blacking and needs to be carried out every three years or so to protect the metal.

44 Most boats have female names. I find this weird, if I'm honest… gendering a piece of metal. Don't get me wrong, I love my boat as if it were a human… but still, it's weird.

incredible as I retraced the journey back down the Lee. But this time, I wasn't being towed. I was driving.

~~~~~~~

After a few lengthy boat moves down, I arrived in Tottenham, North London. Tottenham is one of my favourite London mooring spots. It's close to green and pleasant Hertfordshire, has a retail park near the river and the station is the best in London, hands down.

The Beast from the East had brought us six inches of snow, biting winds and the city to a standstill. Two weeks later, in Tottenham, daffodils were out. I had planted spring bulbs while in the boatyard – pots containing tulips and daffodils on my back deck and on the roof – and they were out too. I'd never known such a dramatic change of season. I opened my back door and held my wintered features up to the sun. I pulled my table and chairs off the roof, still caked in boatyard dust. As I did so, I noticed other boaters were peeling their doors open and emerging from their cocoons too, leaning over roof gardens to inspect newly softened soil, smoke petering out from their chimneys as the sun brought instant colour to pale faces. It was all the spring cliches on that morning in Tottenham. A fresh start, a new beginning. I breathed in the air, the perfume of new buds and the musty scent of hurriedly built birds' nests.

I'd made it. My first winter.

I finished my morning coffee and went inside.

My phone lit up with messages coming through. Not one, not two, but three...

"Hey, Hannah, whatcha up to?"

"Where you moored?"

"Got any plans this arvo?"

I paused and briefly reflected.

Where

The

Chuff

Had

ALL BOATS ARE SINKING

These
Fuckers
Been
For
The
Past
Six
Months?
I drafted a reply....
"Oh hi. Yes, you can come round. Yes, we can have a barbecue on the
roof. But the next time I'm tucking a hot water bottle into my pants
under several jumpers in minus six degrees you'll be there, right?"

But I thought against it.
"Come round. Bring ice!"

Chapter 21
Two "I Do"s

Jonathan's name flashed up on my screen. Communication with my senior colleague (away from work) was only ever via WhatsApp, so I was jolted by his call.

"Hello, Hannah." His words were delivered with such delicacy. His voice was the same whomever he spoke to, and in moments of intimacy, hearing words or phrases whispered in my ear in Queen's English only added to the fanciful nature of our affair. It wasn't an affair in the sense of betrayal. He wasn't married or in a relationship. But he was many years my senior and in a position of power within the company where I worked. I'd told a few friends (including Caz, obviously) but no one at work knew about it. He was responsible for my recent promotion and a line manager to many of my friends, all of whom I was keeping this a secret from. We had been seeing each other semi-regularly over the past six months. Every few weeks he would send me a message out of the blue, inviting me out for dinner, trips to the theatre, or for evenings at his home. He'd even been to the boat.

"I'm afraid I've made a scheduling error," he said.

At the weekend we were due to travel the length of the country to attend two weddings. Matt, an ex-boyfriend and still a good friend, was getting married on the Saturday in the north-east, and another friend's wedding was in Warwickshire over the Sunday and Monday.

"What does that mean?" I said down the phone. "That you now can't come?"

"I can," he said. "But I'm out on Friday night with some of the accounts team. It's okay, we can drive up early on Saturday morning. We'll set off at five a.m. and still get there on time, I promise."

I had booked a hotel for Friday so was a little irritated by the slip up.

"Okay," I said. "I'll come to yours on Friday night. What time will you be done?"

He had a habit of being late for our engagements. If we had plans to go to the theatre, he would turn up just as it was starting. I would have found our seats and he would scoot along the row as the lights dimmed, making eye contact with each and every audience member that he squeezed past and saying sorry in his oh so familiar way. He never missed a show, but he always nearly did.

"Ten p.m. at the latest. I promise," he said.

"Okay, I'll come to yours for ten p.m.," I said.

It was a weekend requiring three outfits, with the second wedding spanning two days, and though I like dressing up fancy, I don't like shopping. Two weeks before the big weekend I was out for lunch with my friend Jo and her sisters, Michelle and Lou. These women are elegant, playful and stunning. When I'm in their company, I want to be them, or at the very least adopted as a fourth sister.

"Do you have your outfits sorted for these weddings?" Lou, the eldest, asked.

"I'm going to Westfield shopping centre this weekend," I said.

Michelle, who was in a separate conversation with Jo, turned round.

"No, I'm not having that," she said. "You're coming to mine after lunch and borrowing some bits."

Michelle is a regular at red carpet events.

"No way, Michelle. I won't fit into your dresses," I said.

"Of course you will," said Jo, and they bundled me into a taxi like a scene from *Sex and the City* as we headed to Michelle's pad in East London to raid her walk-in wardrobe. They dressed me up like a toy doll, pulling me this way and that into Michelle's various bespoke designer outfits. I was right, I didn't fit into many. But

TWO "I DO"S

I did squeeze into a few. I walked down the towpath to my little blue boat with a Burberry dress bag containing three unique outfits and a handbag Michelle had designed herself. I couldn't wait to turn up to my ex-boyfriend's wedding with Jonathan on my arm dressed in one of these.

Friday night came round and I texted Jonathan a few times to recap the plan. At 8 p.m., he called.

"Hellllllooooooo." He was drunk. "So sorry, Hannah, I'll be a bit later, and my phone battery is about to die."

"Right," I said. I was still at work, hiding in a storeroom to take his call. "What time shall I be at yours, then?"

Jonathan was laughing at something someone was saying.

"Jonathan," I said.

"Sorry. I'll be home at eleven p.m. I'm very sorry," he said before hanging up.

I arrived at Jonathan's with my outfits from Michelle and a weekend suitcase. It was 11.15 p.m. and his lights were off. I stood on the driveway waiting, and with each minute that went by saw the weekend and our relationship drift further and further away. A sense of panic began to rise as I thought about the prospect of attending tomorrow's wedding alone. Matt had remained a good friend after our break-up five years earlier. I knew his partner and I was very happy for them both and looking forward to their big day, but with all Matt's friends and family there, I was not relishing the idea of going alone.

I phoned Jonathan, but the call wouldn't connect.

I sat down on the doorstep and tried not to move. His security light was sensitive. I watched as a fox weaved in and out of view, between lamp-posts and cars. On the prowl.

The arrangement between Jonathan and me these past six months had provoked a strange mix of fear and empowerment in me. At times I felt in control and framed it as simply a matter of choice on my part. That I was having a casual thing with a colleague. That when I was with him, I felt heard. And there was nothing wrong with that. But recently it had begun to feel like love, and I was terrified. He'd told me early on that he had never been in love, that he didn't think he had the capacity. Despite his age and obvious experience, this news hadn't shocked me.

Thirty minutes passed. I stood up again and brushed myself down. "I'm ready now," I said out loud to no one. *This is exactly what I needed to happen*, I thought. To gain the perspective on this arrangement I so desperately needed. This relationship wasn't right. It wasn't equal. I would attend the weddings alone, return to work on Tuesday, quit my job (again) and put the whole thing behind me.

I ordered an Uber to take me back to the boat.

As I stood on his driveway waiting for my taxi, I was not angry, but relieved that my assumptions had been correct. He didn't see a future with me. It was midnight when the taxi turned onto the road.

I approached the driver as Jonathan came around the corner.

"Sorrryy-y," he said. "My phone battery died."

He was hammered.

"What the hell, Jonathan?" I said.

He walked up to the taxi driver and slurred, "It's okay, you can go."

I paused and watched him walk past me to his front door.

I followed him inside.

"I'm going to have a bath," I said.

In the bath, I wondered if I would have had the strength to turn up to the wedding alone. Jonathan entered the bathroom carrying a bowl of buttered asparagus, some crumpets and a cup of tea. I wasn't hungry, but it was impossible not to find the gesture both sweet and funny. Again, I couldn't believe I'd found myself here. This drunken and grovelling man bringing me snacks while I bathed in his home.

"I'm not hungry," I said, putting my head under the water to stifle a smile.

"Okay, I'll just put this here." He put the items down on the closed toilet, not before spilling some of the tea into the bath. "I'll sleep downstairs."

TWO "I DO"S

I lay in his bed stirring. The power dynamic up until this point had been off balance. Tonight it shifted. He was a slurring mess of a man who stank of all-day drinking, who hadn't packed for the weekend and who had five hours to sober up before driving 600 miles.

———————

The next morning, I descended the stairs in Jonathan's flat. My suitcase had been pulled in front of the spiral staircase and was blocking the way with "I'm sorry" written on an unopened bill envelope balanced on top. I don't think I'd ever seen his handwriting before. It was nice to learn something new about him. He was asleep on the sofa.

"Jonathan," I whispered, brushing my lips against his. "We need to leave in twenty minutes."

He murmured, stirred and opened one eye. I smiled a forgiving smile at him. It was as if last night hadn't happened.

"Are you blushing?" he said.

I wasn't blushing. But I can see why he said this. Because our meet-ups were spread out, by two or more weeks at a time, things felt new each time we were together. It was like a one-night stand every time.

"I'll make us tea," I said.

———————

The journey was exhilarating. He drove fast. Out of London and onto the motorway while downing a two-pint bottle of milk he'd taken from the fridge. He assured me he was sober enough to drive (I doubt this retrospectively). The night before felt like a distant memory and as the sun came up, it was clear it was going to be a glorious weekend. I glanced sideways at him as he put his hand on my leg and smiled, his other hand tapping on the steering wheel to his new Ghostpoet album.

ALL BOATS ARE SINKING

Looking back, that car journey may have been our happiest moment together. The antics of the day before had forced him down from the pedestal I had put him on, and for a short time, I felt in control of my feelings and on a par with him.

It was a gorgeous ceremony. I introduced Jonathan to everyone I knew, and we told the story of the night before over and over. We circled the party together, and sometimes separately as we shared knowing smiles to each other across the room. I would watch as Jonathan charmed those he spoke to. It would sometimes verge into flirtation, but there seemed to be no prejudice as to who received this treatment, so I didn't particularly care. He would skulk at the back of the group photos, finding people to hide behind. Half of the party guests were from London, and he knew these photos would be on social media. Word could get out.

It was fine being there with my ex and his new wife, his friends and family. I had a wonderful plus one by my side who was charming and sociable. We sat with my friend Eric and his partner Amy at dinner. They hadn't been together long but were engaged to be married a few months later. Eric and I had worked together a few times over the years in my previous career as a theatre maker. I was a fan of his directing work, and we formed a friendship over late-night chats at the Edinburgh Fringe festival.

"What's going on here?" said Amy, whom I adored already, while Eric and Jonathan were deep in conversation.

I rolled my eyes. "God, don't ask," I said.

"Hm. He's lovely, but you don't think you can trust him or his intentions with you."

I looked Amy in the eyes and said nothing. She smiled and I smiled back. She had nailed it.

"You should both come to our wedding in September," Eric was saying to Jonathan.

"Of course, we'll be there," Jonathan said, shaking Eric's hand as Amy and I gave each other a wry smile.

We got in the car the next morning for wedding number two in Stratford-Upon-Avon. Ghostpoet playing, another beautiful day. We were speeding down the motorway when I saw a sign for Manchester.

"We could go and see my brother," I joked, pointing at the sign. My brother Matthias had just moved to Manchester from Liverpool with his wife, Ellie. My closest sibling to me in age, Matthias has certainly warmed to me over the years. When we were children, Mum says she couldn't leave us in a room together without him wanting to attack me. Thankfully things have evolved, and though we can be a little sarcastic towards each other from time to time, there's at least love there now. He is the intellectual one of the family, having spent several years undertaking his PhD as a medical researcher. His wife Ellie is a gallery curator. They'd been living a student life for many years but were reaping the rewards now, both excelling in their fields. They'd just had a baby boy; little John. I'd only met him once.

"Would you like to?" Jonathan asked.

"I was joking," I replied.

"Go on, we have time." And with that, he'd taken the next turn and we were headed for Manchester. What was going on? Why was I introducing him to my family? Were we now partners? We turned into the car park of their block of flats, a converted factory right by Manchester Piccadilly Station. I rang the doorbell a few times, but there was no reply. Eventually I got hold of my brother on the phone while outside the apartment block.

"We're in London, you dork," Matthias said down the phone. Jonathan heard this and laughed before rolling his eyes. I sheepishly hung up the phone.

"Come on," said Jonathan, "let's watch the football instead."

Jonathan's ability to turn anything into a positive was refreshing. We parked up and found a pub to watch a World Cup game. As we were unable to show any public affection in London, this was exciting. We snogged in the pub and walked the streets of the Northern Quarter holding hands. Just like a normal couple. An odd couple, sure, but a couple, nonetheless.

Jonathan drove us down to Stratford-Upon-Avon. This one was a reverse wedding: the party element was on the Sunday night and the ceremony on the Monday after.[45] There was nothing conventional about our weekend. We checked into the hotel and headed to the evening do, which was in a stately home on the edge of the town, with topiary in the grounds and lights illuminating the building's façade.

Fatigue had clearly set in for Jonathan, who was now on day four of a bender. Thankfully this wedding was more low key. I knew two other women there and we stayed together, the four of us chatting away over dinner. Jonathan popped back to the bar to get more fizz.

"What's going on, then?" asked Katie, a primary school teacher and a Crouch End restaurant pal, and another I'd managed to arm wrestle into joining the cruise ship life.

"I've no idea," I said, picking on a label from a beer bottle.

As the sun set, Jonathan and I found ourselves sitting on a bench by a pond, watching the party from afar. He was in a striped suit and yellow floral tie, his hair poking over sunglasses propped on his head. He had a champagne flute in one hand, the other was lightly touching my hair. I was in the more risqué of the three red carpet dresses from Michelle – a short wrap around, with orange and turquoise flowers. With the low sunshine casting our shadows across the grass, I looked at the two silhouettes before me. My silhouette looked like someone else's. This moment felt like someone else's. He wasn't my boyfriend. How could he possibly be? I knew he didn't have it in him, and I don't even think that's what I wanted. But these two silhouettes looked happy, and so deeply connected to one another. We sat in silence.

The next morning, we went to the ceremony in the same church William Shakespeare was buried in. We held hands. We were holding on to something. It being a wedding, the vicar gave a sermon on love.

---

45 Actors' weddings tend to fall on "dark days" for theatres, most commonly on Sundays or Mondays, but the "party *then* ceremony" thing was a first for me.

TWO "I DO"S

"A warm summer's weekend with sparks flying can evoke feelings of love. But it is not the same," he said.

Bloody hell, has this vicar been reading my diary?! Jonathan squeezed my leg. After the ceremony, we said our goodbyes and enjoyed an M&S picnic together by the river. With the end of the weekend approaching, I was feeling sombre.

"Talk to me, Hannah," he said.

I didn't want to talk. I didn't want to say or do anything. I just wanted to be in this moment, having this picnic, with this man, forever. I lay in his arms on the grass and admitted to myself what I already knew. I was painfully in love.

The drive back to London was different to the other legs. It was sad and quiet as I began to understand the depths of my feelings for a man I knew wasn't good for me. We arrived back to the familiar sight of rush hour in the city. While we were stuck in traffic near Battersea, Jonathan held my face.

"Would you like to stay over tonight?" He stroked my cheek.

"Really?"

I missed *Argie*, but I knew that as soon as this weekend was over, question marks would emerge over what we were doing. I was keeping this secret from people I loved. I trusted this man not one jot, and he had a fantastic ability to compartmentalise his life. I knew that the next day I would slide back down the ladder and to the bottom of his long list of priorities.

"Of course I'll stay," I said.

We ate dinner and fell asleep in front of a film.

Two days later I sat on *Argie* and hand wrote a letter to Jonathan. In it I described my longing for a committed partnership. That I wanted a teammate. That what we had was meaningful and loving, but that I couldn't just ride out the joyful part anymore. That I had dived into this and done a very scary thing for my heart, and if this wasn't something he could do, then fine. But I needed to know.

Chapter 22
My Time

It was my one-year boat anniversary. I sat out on deck on my blue metal chair and ate dinner alone with a glass of fizz. I'm not sure homeowner anniversaries are a thing, but it felt significant to mark the occasion. Learning how to navigate my boat and operate locks had been a new skill and a year in I was getting more and more confident at it. Despite the six-month hiatus in movements, I felt like a proper London boater now. I looked like one too. My clothes were a little tatty and my hands had become hardened from carrying out manual work. I'd spent a lot of time in my engine bay over the spring and early summer. There was always something to do. On days off work, I would lift up the deck boards that had been fitted into the new engine bay by Paul the welder and climb down into the steel compartment that sat below the water level. Inside, I would crane my neck at the sound of a swan. They would draw in close and eyeball me at their level.

My engine bay contains an engine (of course), a diesel tank, batteries (three leisure and one starter), an exhaust, propeller shaft, weed hatch, stern gland, bilge pump and several electrical and fuel cables. A year in and I could now point out parts of the engine and make minor adjustments where needed. I would straddle the engine wearing my dad's overalls and some old boots and tighten up belts or replace parts, as needed. The engine bay would need to be cleaned every now and again, and I would scoop gunk from the drainage trenches and remove any unwanted fluid from the sump, pumping it into bottles before disposing of it at waste removal points.

Replacing my engine stop cables was a job that took me a whole day. I marked the various components I needed to remove with different coloured nail varnish, to distinguish which ones went where. I'm definitely not afraid of manual work, but I'm a little slapdash from time to time, and so I was proud as punch to have changed over my cables all alone. Completing the task, I left the nail polish in place, to remind future Hannah of my achievement. It made me smile whenever I saw it. Anything larger or more complex, I'd call out an engineer and watch them closely working away in my engine bay. Anything to help me become more accustomed to the workings of the boat.

As I sat on deck with my glass of fizz, I looked at the boat. At the roof I'd repainted and the plants that were thriving on it. When I first moved on to the boat, I said to myself I'll give this lifestyle a year, and here I was about to give it a second. I'd turned this boat into a home, and it was already packed full of my personality and achievements. Boat life had been testing at times, and I'd made plenty of mistakes. But I was still here and loving it. It was right to raise a glass.

Chapter 23
This Charming Man

Just because Prosecco Sarah said she didn't want a hen do, it didn't mean we weren't going to throw her one. And the fact that Sarah and her partner Jamie had married in secret only spurred us on even more. Melissa, Angie, Sarah and I had become a tight-knit group over the past few years, holidaying together and enjoying many a night out in our little crew. Melissa and Sarah had been introduced by a mutual friend of theirs in the "I know another Canadian living in London" kind of way, and they had bonded with Angie from New Zealand, who they met in the Piano Bar in Waterloo one night. Angie became the third wheel, and when Sarah told me how great her new friends were, I joined as the fourth.

"Sarah, what the fuck is that?" I said, looking at Sarah's ring finger on a night out with the group.

"Oh, that? Yeah, we got married in Florida." She said it like she was telling me about a car boot sale she had visited that morning.

"What? We haven't even thrown you a hen night," I said. Melissa and Angie jumped up with their congratulatory hugs.

"We're having the proper wedding party in Canada," she said. "This was just the official bit."

"You're not getting away with it," I said to Sarah.

"Fine, we can have a hen do. Just us four, though. And none of those fucking sashes."

Planning the hen do was completely stress free. As long as it involved booze and dancing, I knew Sarah would be happy.[46]

It was late summer, and the canal was sealed in with the Kermit-green duckweed I had grown accustomed to, thick like carpet atop the water below. Sarah, Angie and Melissa arrived at the boat, which basked in sunshine in Mile End. Our outfits were also vivid in colour. Flowers and candy stripes that pinged against the green of the canal and the blue of my boat.

"This is so cool," said Angie. It was her first time on *Argie*.

"Maybe stay outside. It's a mess in there," I said, pouring out prosecco into coupe glasses on my outdoor table.

I'd spent the morning preparing a brunch that consisted of:

* Salmon, roe and creme fraiche on homemade blinis
* Homemade guacamole[47]
* Homemade tzatziki
* Olives
* Homemade breadsticks
* Homemade chocolate and pecan brownies
* Watermelon spritz and lemon meringue sour cocktails

The cabin of *Argie Bargie* was carnage. The walls and floor were splattered with flour and avocado goop. Mixing bowls and bake trays were piled up on the kitchen counters and sofa, cubes of discarded ice melting on the floor.

"I can't believe you made all that in there," Sarah said more than once.

---

46 Sarah is so low maintenance that when her faux wedding came around, she threw on a £40 dress from some wholesale outlet in Westfield with a pair of matching flip-flops, sauntered into the bridal room five minutes before the wedding and asked if someone could do her make-up. I'm not one for a long beauty care regime myself, but Sarah getting her toenails painted in the seconds before walking down the aisle takes it to the next level.

47 My secret ingredient is cumin. You're welcome.

"I'm surprised too, if I'm honest," I said. "I had to change the gas bottle halfway through so the breadsticks are a little underdone."

Sam used to say it looked like a bomb had hit whenever I cooked in our flat and he could never understand why I used so many pans. I don't make things from scratch often, but when I do, I get in the zone and can become quite the Pollock of the amateur small-plates world.

After brunch on *Argie*, I locked away the mess and we took a taxi into town – a black cab because we were feeling fancy. We had a manicure in a nail bar in Soho followed by cocktails in China Town. After a sushi dinner we danced long and hard at our favourite spot, The Arts Theatre Club on Frith Street, a tiny underground nightclub that plays disco and indie bangers and serves cocktails out of teacups.

"I've had the best day," Sarah said over "This Charming Man" by The Smiths.

"Good!" I said. "You deserve it."

"Who do you think will marry next?" said Melissa, leaning in to be heard over the music.

"Urgh, don't ask that," I said.

"Anyone in here take your fancy, Hannah?" Sarah held my hand and spun me around to take in the sweaty crowd.

"No. I'm not interested in anyone at the moment," I said.

"That's not entirely true though, is it Hannah?" said Sarah, who was one of the friends I'd told about Jonathan. She guided me under her arm and back into the circle.

It would have made perfect sense to flirt with someone that night. Jonathan hadn't replied to my letter and while I was still seeing him every few weeks, on the day after each of our meet-ups he would go quiet, and I would have to wait to be invited around again. We didn't see much of one another at work. My job was roaming, and I found little reason to go to the head office where he was based to meet with him. It was best that way. I didn't like seeing him at work. Sometimes when we were together, I would challenge him. Ask him why he disappeared like this. Say that the silence between our meet-ups was cold and hurtful. He would say, "I'm sorry you feel that way."

Sometimes in the gaps, he would respond but not as I wanted him to. He would say, "I'm afraid this has got to stop," or "I don't think we should do this anymore" and I would be angry and confused. Then I would remember that he hadn't promised me anything anyway. But then a week would go by and he would invite me around again. What was he doing? And more importantly, what was I doing? He hadn't promised me anything. He wasn't misleading me.

It was within one of these gaps between meet-ups that I found myself looking across the room on the dancefloor in Soho. There were plenty of men. Attractive men. Flirtatious men. But I just couldn't bring myself to think about anyone else.

"Tonight's about you anyway, Sarah," I said.

We danced. I shook off the feeling of longing and a growing temptation to text Jonathan. When the club shut, we jumped in taxis to take us home.

I stood by the entrance of Victoria Park looking for my boat. I couldn't see it. I walked up and down the towpath for what must have been half an hour. Then I remembered.

"I don't live here," I said to a swan.

My boat was in Mile End. I had forgotten I had moved it. I howled with laughter and walked the towpath drunk and giddy to find my floating home.

Chapter 24
Hanging

Being poorly on a boat is more challenging than on land. I would like to demonstrate why through the specifics of a well-known illness: the hangover.

Boat jobs will still need to be completed – the fire will need to be tended to, there will be maintenance jobs and God forbid the hangover falls on day 14 (or 15) of a two-week stay, requiring a boat move... in the rain.

There's no "change of scenery" option inside a boat. You're in a small space and so will be staring at the same four walls until recovery. And forget lounging under a blanket on a massive comfy sofa in front of the TV.

Temperature and humidity levels are variable, which is a subtle way of saying, you'll be sweating your bits off or you'll be shivering like a small dog until you recover.

Popping out for supplies in an unknown community can be unfruitful if you don't know where you're going. Takeaway services to boats are getting better... but are not perfect.

The general day-to-day boat anxieties around water in places it shouldn't be, and the fear of sinking, will be heightened during a hangover.

I like to be in company when I'm nursing a hangover, and my boat is just about big enough for my sorry hungover ass, but definitely not for two (or more) of us.

Compost toilets leave little to the imagination.

Boats are rocky.

Chapter 25
The Truth About
Winter

"Is it cold in winter?" closely follows "Where does your poo go?" as the most asked question from landers. And given the simplistic yes/no options available to me, and the feeling that the person asking the question has often already decided what answer they would like to hear, I tend to play around with my response. Anywhere between, "No, my fire makes it nice and cosy," and "Yes, it's winter".

The boat is made of steel and it sits in water that is sometimes (though rarely) covered in ice. Rain lashes down, and there's less sunlight on the boat in the winter. So yes, if the fire has gone out, or I return after a spell away, it is as cold as ice inside my steel boat and will take some time to warm up. I might also have a leak, so if it's raining the space can feel damp. Windy weather can circulate around the boat, entering through draughty spots; in the bathroom and by the main entrance.

My fuel-burning stove is enough to warm the boat if the fire is built properly. When sitting by the fire, I can feel the temperature drop, at which point I will stick in some more briquettes (slow release, lower heat), seasoned wood (faster/hotter burn) or heat logs (mmmm... real toasty) and maintain a fine temperature inside. Cooking and boiling a kettle will add additional heat. The problem lies in being out too often, in long days at work and not having enough hours on board to let the fire really "bed in" before I retire for the night.

I would come to understand that boat jobs are higher stakes in winter. Running out of fuel can be dangerous and with less daylight, more care and planning is needed over boat movements. But the winter nights are quieter, more romantic. With a lack of birdsong or outdoor socialising, and the sound of runners infrequent, it is a peaceful time of year to be on the water.

With my first winter full of mistakes – blocked chimneys, rushed fires – I was braced for my second and looking forward to making the boat cosy again with candles and blankets. Fire lighting is a competitive sport within the boating community, with Facebook posts every year from boaters saying, "I caved!" underneath a picture of a roaring fire. I wasn't going to risk holding out, not after the previous year, so had mine going solidly from October. On my second winter I still didn't really have guests like in the summer, but a few were successfully bullied into coming around. We'd sit and play Scrabble on the sofa by candlelight. Spring and summer really are our showcase seasons, but winter is special too.

But yes, it is cold in winter. It's winter, after all.

Chapter 26
Boat Jobs

DAILY
- Check bilge water and run pump as necessary
- Run engine to charge batteries
- Empty wee

WEEKLY
- Empty and clean compost toilet

EVERY TWO WEEKS
- Move the boat

EVERY ONE – THREE MONTHS
- Remove any water and other fluids from engine bay and sump
- Deal with a leak or two
- Clean chimney
- A surprise issue, including though not limited to: broken alternator belt, failed electrics, hole in water tank, damaged chimney, water in cabin, disintegrating pipework, broken stop cable, flat batteries, rotten wooden door, broken lock, attempted wasp settlement

ANNUALLY

- Engine service
- Stove service
- External rust treatment and paint touch-ups
- Deal with any known but long ignored (and expensive) issues

BI-ANNUALLY OR MORE

- Take the boat out of water and have the hull surveyed and/ or painted black
- Clean moss off cratch cover [48]
- Take out and reseal windows

---

48 A cratch cover is a stretchy tent-like material fitted onto the front of the boat. I had one fitted at Stanstead Abbotts. It serves as a tool shed.

Chapter 27
Cat on a Hot Steel Roof

I was developing a close friendship with Rox, executive chef and colleague from work. Her love of cooking was not limited to her job, and she regularly hosted dinner parties on Sundays at her home in Tooting. By winter 2018/2019 I had managed to infiltrate the group of professional foodies and become a regular at their gatherings. The crowd were a mix of chefs, food writers and movers and shakers from across the restaurant industry. They would arrive with unusual wines and present them with a speech before each course, saying who the maker was and how the wine was made. The meal, cooked by Rox, was always elaborate and delicious.

Before long, I'd given Megan a glowing reference, and she was invited to join the crew. We'd laugh as we scoured the supermarket shelves for a wine that would impress but not break the bank.

"Rosé's quite in at the moment, I think," Megan would say.

"Sure," I'd agree, putting a mid-range rosé in our basket.

As the months went by, we became more confident in our position within the group. We were all at similar stages in our lives, working in fast-paced jobs in industries that we loved and we had a shared appreciation for good company and conversation.

I'd turn up an hour before the start time and have a bath. Rox would open the door mid-prep and I'd scoot past and up the stairs before the rest of the guests arrived. Peggy and Rox are as trendy a London couple as they come, with a whippet called Zeus and a home of well-designed accessories and fancy toiletries. When the other guests had arrived, Peggy would hold court with tales of happenings since we last met, and Rox would call through from the kitchen with perfect comic timing, interjecting her side of the story, as Peggy continued topping up our glasses and circling the room. Peggy is ten years our junior, but you wouldn't know it.

After one of these fabulously long soirees, I travelled back to my boat in Broadway Market, a typical and trendy East London mooring spot with artisan bakeries, cocktail bars and a thriving weekend market all year round. I was pretty tipsy, but it was only 7 p.m. so I was in for a long night's sleep before the working week. I slumped into bed and was out like a light. I awoke at 5 a.m. to my doors flapping open in the February air. I jumped out of bed, assuming I'd not locked them properly, bolted the doors from the inside and climbed back under the sheets.

I woke to my alarm at 8 a.m., stuck a coffee on and went to retrieve my laptop. Looking at the space on the floor where my rucksack (containing my laptop) usually lived, and seeing it was not there, I realised my error. I'd left my keys in the door and I'd been robbed.

Nausea came over me as I thought of a stranger inside my boat. My home.

"Fuck. Fuck. Fuck. Fuck. Fuck," I said, searching for signs of anything else missing. A hairspray bottle was on the floor by the bed. It's likely that the opportunist came close to where I was sleeping, knocking the spray onto the floor right by me.

My phone had been in bed with me, so luckily it hadn't been taken. I went on my banking apps to cancel my cards and saw that my Monzo was showing the activity in real-time. I could see payments being made down Commercial Road, one convenience store after another. £19.00. £20.00. £17.99. I called the police.

There wasn't a lot I could do after that, except feel stupid and sad for my loss. The police sent someone to take fingerprints. I was pretty shaken up and spent the next night at Caz and Natalie's, both of whom I'm sure spent the evening biting tongues against a deep desire to tell me how careless I had been. The following day, I returned home, burnt some sage, had a tidy up and went to bed.

CAT ON A HOT STEEL ROOF

I awoke again at 5 a.m. on the boat, bolt upright, to the sound of shuffling and scratching on the roof above me. It had to be the burglar again. My heart was in my mouth.

"Get the fuck off my boat," I shouted as loud as I could. My pulse was thumping in my ears. I was terrified. My hands shaking, I reached for my phone in the dark and called the police. Two coppers turned up and assured me that there was no one on the towpath and I should go back to sleep. I explained that I'd been broken into two nights before and was admittedly on edge, but that it was unmistakably the culprit returning. Same time, same place.

They left, and I lay in my bed, terrified.

The next day, sleep deprived, I walked along my gunwales to my neighbour's front door to warn them of what had happened. I looked along my roof and saw the outline of fresh footprints. Or, more accurately, paw prints. I thought back to the noise at 5 a.m. The scratching. The shuffling. I put my head in my hands and laughed. Of course, this time the commotion had been caused by a cat pulling up my tulip bulbs. I'd called out the London Metropolitan police in the middle of the night because a cat was on my roof.

———

Jonathan had been back in contact.

"Would you like to come round tonight?"

When this happened, my reaction was always the same. I would think about it, deduce that it probably wasn't a wise decision, think about it for a bit longer, agonise, deliberate, question and, finally, say yes. Sometimes he would persuade me, sometimes I would talk myself into it then out of it, then into it again. But always, I would go. I would arrive to a hot bath with candles and a glass of wine while he rustled up dinner. We would eat together and retire to the sofa, where he'd put on his latest favourite album and we'd talk for hours and hours. He'd make jokes about some of my life choices but generally encourage any creative projects I had bubbling away. We'd touch on politics, though I'd steer this slightly, not wanting to admit our polar leanings. Each time I turned up, I'd feel nervous for the first 30 minutes or so. We'd never discuss work, which was odd given the part it played in both our lives. But if our relationship was already dodgy, using these intimate moments to gain further company insight felt very wrong. It didn't matter if it was a Friday, Sunday or a Tuesday, our routine was the same. We would sink some posh wine or champagne and retire in the small hours. Our working hours were different and the next day he'd leave me in bed to head off for a meeting he was already late for.

"Stay as long as you'd like," he'd say, kissing my forehead.

Being alone in his flat was wonderful. I would crank up the radio and mooch about like a pet that had been welcomed into a new family home. Sauntering between rooms, I'd enjoy his toaster, a hot shower and the ability to charge up my devices in every available socket. I might stay and work from his sofa for a few hours, enjoying his central heating and a tap that provided instant boiling water for tea. It would be a few weeks until I'd be there again, and so I'd be sure to make the most out of my visit.

Once or twice, I found a red hair in his sink, two wine glasses on the draining board, or an extra toothbrush, and I wondered if there were other women in his life, if he had the same rituals and the same moves with them as he did with me.

"Are you okay?" he said one afternoon in bed.

The sun was shining down through the window in his bedroom and warming our bodies. Over the course of the year, we had developed a physical shorthand to ensure we stayed connected for as long as possible in bed. We would lie together for hours, in and out of sleep, so it was important we got it right. On this occasion, I was lying on the mattress, legs slightly apart with his body in the gap. His head rested on my abdomen and his right hand gently stroked up and down the length of my ribcage. I'm not sure where our other limbs were, but it worked.

Except, my mind was racing as thoughts vied for attention in my head. I knew I was in trouble with this man. I knew it the second I saw him walking up those stairs in that pub on Tottenham Court

Road, and since then I'd grown addicted to his smell, his touch, his taste. I would feel this intensely when we were together, but even more so when we were apart. Was it really love? I don't know. At times I had felt sure it was, but at other times, it felt too sporadic, too compulsive to be love. But it was something as powerful as love. The fix I received every few weeks or months was more intense than anything I'd experienced before, and I'd be in agony until my next hit. I would begin to think about a life without him, and he would message, **"Can I cook for you tonight?"** And I would be confused and angry but relieved that he still wanted me. And I would go to him.

With Jonathan I was able to express a side of myself that I felt had rarely been encouraged in my previous relationships. My opinions were important to him and he'd listen intently, remembering details from our conversations, picking up from where we'd left off each time we met. When I was with him, I felt that the arrangement was mutually beneficial, that we both received a rush of chemicals that would surely be good for the soul. But when we were apart, I would wonder if this was just a game to him, an abuse of power he'd meticulously mastered over the years with other women who had fallen just like me.

Fundamentally, I knew this didn't have a future, but I couldn't work out what I really wanted from it. Was I empowered by the sexual awakening I was having? We'd been doing this for so long, though, that it couldn't just be sex, and he would say as much.

But here I was. A year later and still getting my fix.

As we lay together that afternoon, I had questions and yet little desire for the answers. Either I didn't want the truth to push us apart, or I didn't want him to lie to me. I think it was both.

"Talk to me, Hannah." He was still stroking my rib cage.

"I'm worried about my heart," I said, a tear falling onto the pillow.

"Don't be." He squeezed me tighter. "Life is short, and this is lovely, no?"

"Yes, it is—"

"I care about you deeply," he said.

"I know."

He lifted himself up and brought his face and eyes to mine.

"It's not simple," he said. "I'm much older than you... my life is very complicated." These well-rehearsed lines had come out before.

"You've not replied to my letter," I said, turning my face away.

"I know. I'm sorry." He kissed my cheek and then my neck as he lifted himself once more on top of me. "I do love you, you know," he said.

Hearing this sentence after all this time gave me no joy. In fact, as I lay there perfectly still in the afternoon sunshine, I felt numb and experienced nothing but a deep knowing sadness. He didn't love me. This was a game, and I knew it clearer than anything. I was only surprised that he'd lowered himself to this. He must have known it was something I could now use against him.

I sighed as one more tear fell.

And again, I left. The numbness stayed with me on the Tube home, and as I walked through the doors to my boat, I slumped on the sofa and lay staring at the ceiling, exhausted by the relationship and how lonely it made me feel.

Chapter 28
Things I Can't Do on My Boat

- Have a bath
- Host a dinner party
- Sit up in bed
- Have more than two people inside before it feels crowded
- Stretch
- Sit in another room for a change of scenery
- Have electrical appliances like a smoothie maker or espresso machine
- Have a long shower at a consistent temperature
- Receive post
- Have a day off
- Relax in a storm
- Predict what the next issue will be
- Keep ice

Chapter 29
Seville

Year one on the boat, I had booked myself into an Airbnb in Porto for a long weekend. A treat to myself to mark the end of winter in the boatyard. After the success of my solo adventure, I decided I would now make it an annual thing. My intention for these trips would be to get some sunlight, turn off from work (and more recently, Jonathan), and become lost in a new city on my own. In Feb 2019, I enjoyed the tapas and architecture of Seville in southern Spain.

My accommodation was styled like a Moroccan riad, with an indoor water feature inside an atrium that was surrounded by separate accommodations. My room had towels shaped like swans and breakfast crockery laid out for two. (Jeez, thanks guys.) I sent a picture of the room to Jonathan – "Wish you were here" – instantly breaking my "don't text Jonathan" rule. I deleted his number, writing it on the inside page of my holiday book in case of an emergency.

I spent the first few days walking through the city, stopping off for tapas at little bars here and there. I had received a comprehensive list of (mostly foodie) recommendations from Darren, one of the attendees of the Tooting Sunday Soirees. I was following the list to a T.

On day three I took a bus excursion out of the city to visit a Roman archaeological site (it was in *Game of Thrones*, apparently). This was the only time I was around other Brits, and there was the inevitable small talk you'd expect on a day trip with people you have a language in common with. They all seemed concerned about me holidaying alone and pressed me to join their couplings at any opportunity. "I'm fine, really," I'd say. It was a little exhausting by the end of the day, and I couldn't wait to get back to the bustle of the city and the remaining tapas bars on Darren's list.

I was at a locals' bar in the city centre later that night, perched at a high table with a napkin's worth of space to myself. The barman was making suggestions to me in Spanish. I was clearly struggling.

"You're about to order three different types of dried potato."

I turned and saw a woman of a similar age to me, with Princess Diana-style hair and a roll-neck top. She was smiling.

"Oh, okay… That's not good," I said.

"Do you eat *anything*?" she said.

"Pretty much."

She took my menu and spoke to the barman in Spanish, handing the faux leather book back to him before turning again towards me.

"Thank you," I said, relieved and pleased to be using my native tongue with someone my own age.

"I'm a Spanish teacher," she said.

"Oh, you're not Spanish?" I said.

"Austrian."

"Are you alone?" I asked.

"You bet."

"Me too. I'm Hannah."

"Theresa."

"Your timing is impeccable, Theresa. I was with a load of Brits today and couldn't get away quick enough. But I think I've underestimated the language barrier in these locals' bars."

We shared a bottle of wine and some tapas. Theresa would ask me what I enjoyed, and order for the two of us. She, like me, was getting away for a few days. From work, family, life.

"And a man," she said.

"Ah," I said, knowingly.

"A colleague."

"Me too!" I said.

"No way." We both laughed at our similarities: 32 and holidaying alone, both in messy work relationships.

ALL BOATS ARE SINKING

We ordered another bottle. And another. We talked about Austria, London and my boat. Food, our jobs, travel, men. It felt like she was a best friend I'd known for years. Bellies full, we headed to a cheesy bar for gin; played some pool, smoked cigarettes and exchanged numbers, agreeing to do the same again the next day.

I had a text from Theresa at 9 a.m.

"I'm just going for a run. Meet you at 6 p.m. tonight?"

"You're joking, right? I'm sooooo hungover!" I said.

We met at 6 p.m., me having achieved nothing with my day, and had a more civilised evening together.

"Will you end it?" she asked.

"There isn't really anything to end," I said, picking at the last remaining olive with a toothpick.

Jonathan had told me he loved me, but there was no sign of a relationship developing. Our meet-ups were as sporadic as ever, and if I questioned his commitment to me, he would respond by telling me how sorry he was that I felt that way.

"How about you?" I said to Theresa.

"Yeah. Same." I'm not sure how much I believed her, or how much she believed me.

My flight was leaving the following morning, so we said our goodbyes and agreed to meet in another European city in the future.

When my flight touched down, I had a message from Jonathan on my phone.

"Good trip? Let me cook for you tonight."

Chapter 30
Surprise Brunch

Little Venice to Ponders End

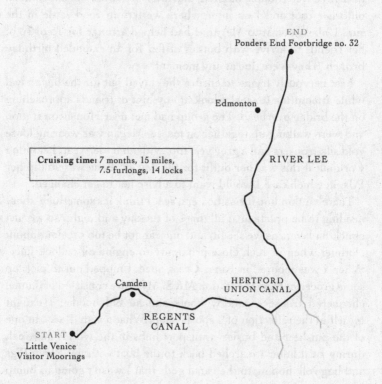

END
Ponders End Footbridge no. 32

Edmonton

RIVER LEE

Cruising time: 7 months, 15 miles,
7.5 furlongs, 14 locks

Camden

HERTFORD
UNION CANAL

REGENTS
CANAL

START
Little Venice
Visitor Moorings

ALL BOATS ARE SINKING

It was Megan's birthday, and we were moored side by side in Homerton, East London – a stretch of the River Lee that feels like it could be somewhere remote, deep in the English countryside, if it weren't for the sheer density of boats. The algae, weeds and lily-pads add to the already green vista of tall trees on the edge of Hackney Marshes. It's like being moored in a forest within the city. It's gorgeous.

It was a sunny day and I had prepared a breakfast of eggs benedict and Bloody Marys, which we ate outside on my back deck. We were double moored, and after breakfast Megan climbed onto her roof and I on mine where we let our food settle in the sun. Unbeknownst to Megan, I had helped arrange for 15 or so of her friends to arrive with bottles of fizz for an extended birthday brunch. They were due at any moment.

I sat nervously trying to ensure she stayed put for the big arrival while attempting to steal a look at any hint of friends approaching on the bridge overhead. The group had met near Homerton station and were walking up together en masse. Megan was wearing loose gold silk trousers and a grey vest top, with no underwear. I couldn't work out if this was her outfit for the day, or if she was still in her PJs, in which case I would want to advise her to get changed.

There's a thin line for us boaters, see. I think it's something about needing to be practical at all times of the day and night, so we just chuck on layers as we see fit, and one cannot be too precious about clothing when in such close proximity to engine oil or lock juice. When I was moored in Kings Cross once, I nipped out to pick up some groceries from the station M&S. My attire consisted of flannel chequered trousers, muddy boots and an old hoodie. I caught myself in the reflection of a sports shop. What a state I was, in one of the plushest and busiest transport hubs in the world; midweek during rush hour. I marched back to the boat with my Percy Pigs and bog roll, hoping to the canal gods that I wasn't going to bump into anyone I knew.

With the friends en route, and likely photographs and videos capturing the whole affair, I was increasingly nervous about her reaction to being shocked by 15 friends surprising her in her PJs. Then at the sound of "Happy Birthday" sung full blast from the bridge, Megan looked up.

"Why are all my friends here!" she said.

I waited for her to stand up and hurry inside, mortified as she changed into a new outfit. She didn't. And from the joy on her face and the following four or so hours in company with her friends, all the while wearing her gold silk trousers and grey top, it was clear that this was in fact her outfit choice for the day… phew.

Party in full swing, my boat provided the kitchen and prep area for Rox's canapes. Both mine and Megan's back decks played host to the group of friends, who sat, stood and perched against our respective railings. It was a glorious May bank holiday as we popped and enjoyed several bottles of cava together. Boaters that passed all yelled "Happy birthday!" across to Megan and towpath users looked on with envy at our Saturday boat soiree. As the friends departed, and I tidied away after a wonderful afternoon, I felt so unbelievably content. *This is the life*, I thought.

Chapter 31
10k

I was visiting Caz and Natalie's new flat in Walthamstow. A newbuild as part of the area's ongoing regeneration, it had cream carpets like the ones in Crouch End, two newly fitted bathrooms, a shiny inbuilt kitchen, two sizable bedrooms and a balcony.

"What do you think?" said Caz.

"It's lovely. Very smart," I said, removing a layer in her consistently temperate living room.

"I'm so pleased you like it," she said, taking my jumper from the sofa and hanging it up. Something in Caz had shifted. The new flat. Her clothes. Her smooth skin. An Apple sports watch on her arm.

"How's the boat?" she asked.

This was the go-to now. People always ask me how the boat is before they ask how I am.

"Still afloat," I said.

Lucy, our old school friend, arrived, and we stood in the kitchen with a glass of wine listening to the new homeowners and their plans for artwork; a feature wall of slogans and London landmarks.

"How's the boat, Hannah?" Lucy said.

I smiled at Caz.

"Afloat," said Caz. "Right, grubs up."

We sat down for roast chicken.

"You look good, Lucy," I said to our old friend, desperate to keep the chat away from me. The last time I saw Caz and Natalie, my home had been broken into because I left my keys in the door when I was drunk. My friends were growing up, and in their company I was feeling exposed, left behind.

"I've been running," said Lucy. "I love it. I have more energy. I feel stronger."

"Good for you," I said.

"You should try it, Hannah."

I stared at Lucy with mock approval.

"Seriously." She continued, "You have such a gift with the towpath outside of your door."

"True. There are a lot of runners out there. They're a bloody nightmare."

Natalie laughed.

"And your location is constantly changing, you're so lucky. What I'd give to run somewhere new each day."

"I've never thought of that before," I said. I'd embraced so much change of late. Maybe Lucy was onto something. *I could add this to my new lifestyle*, I thought, and I was definitely more open to trying new things nowadays. But running... really?

"In fact, I'm doing a 10k race soon. You should all join me. It'll be fun," said Lucy.

I look around the table. Caz is into her fitness but hates running. Natalie is into the gym.[49] And I am into neither running nor fitness.

I thought for a second about all the benefits that Lucy was describing. And then thought again about how unlikely it would be that I would fit running into my new lifestyle.

"Sorry, Lucy, I don't do running," I said, leaning over and grabbing the wine.

"Yeah, no way, Lucy," said Natalie. "Running's not for me." There's no beating around the bush with Natalie. She'd recently had a promotion at work and was rapidly climbing her career ladder. She hadn't got there by being indirect. She's younger than us, outspoken and determined.

"Oh, go on. You'll love it, I promise," Lucy persisted. "Hannah, think of all those smug towpath runners. You could be one too."

---

49 Or something called CrossFit?!

ALL BOATS ARE SINKING

I've never really done any sport. I walk a lot and I'm active at work. I suppose I was feeling a little less toned with age, and my lifestyle since moving onto the boat had become heavily based around socialising. And that meant rich food, meals on the go and booze. Lots of booze.

"I'm not about to take up a new sport at thirty-two. Sorry, Lucy, sounds great, but you're on your own."

A few bottles of wine later and Caz was on her iPad.

"What are you doing, Caz?" I said.

She was entering her bank details.

"Caz?"

"Booked," she said.

"What have you booked?" I said, peering over at her fancy screen.

"Four places for the Regent's Park 10k. Eight weeks away."

"No chance, guys," I said. "It's my birthday soon and I've got two festivals coming up. Sorry."

The next morning I awoke to a message on our WhatsApp group from Natalie:

"Lol, do you remember us signing up to do a 10k race?"

Followed by some gentle piss-takes.

"Can you imagine Hannah doing it?"

I looked out of my window. Toned legs and neon trainers were pounding past the boat. I'd got used to the sound, but now I could see just how many there were. Perhaps there was something in it, after all, and I supposed it wasn't a terrible idea to start taking a bit more care over my health and fitness. Plus, this perception that I was unfit and unlikely to succeed did not land well.

"Oh, I'll run it alright," I replied.

I had eight weeks to train.

I downloaded a running app and typed in my goal and timeframe (omitting the two festivals and my birthday), dug out an old pair of trainers from the bottom of my granny's shelled-out radio on the boat and started training.

I stepped outside and looked up and down the sandy towpath. I was nervous. The voice on the app said walk for five minutes.

10K

Easy enough. After five minutes, the running part started. Alternate 60-second runs and 90-second walks, for 20 minutes.

Sixty seconds of running was long. My chest was dry. My breath rasping. As my heartbeat sped up, my legs began to ache. Laboured steps, but I was running. As other runners sprinted past, it turned out I was very slow. But I pushed through and with each 60-second run my legs became looser and I fell into a rhythm. I looked ahead at the curved towpath. Like a racing track. Twenty minutes passed. I had done it.

"One run down," I messaged the group.

The way the runs were designed, the increase in distance and endurance happened without me thinking. By week six, I was running 35 minutes straight. It was quite fun, as it goes, weaving in and out of dog walkers and buggies on the towpath, and Lucy was right – every few weeks my location was different. It made progress more fun and varied. I listened to 1990s dance music through my headphones as I ran. The beginning of every run was tough, but by the end I was flying. The last five minutes I would even crack a smile. And the last 30 seconds I would sprint back to the boat and collapse at my front door, the boat shaking with the weight of my fatigued body. Thanks for the recognition, *Argie*. I felt fitter and more energised. (Who knew?)

I bought new trainers and headphones. I was 32 years old, and I had become a runner.

Chapter 32
Toilet Chronicles
(Part II)

Through Megan's contacts, I landed a job distributing wristbands to artists at Glastonbury Festival. I would arrive on the Monday before the festival started, work until Thursday, then enjoy the bands and festivities until the following Monday. I'd never gone to Glastonbury before, and I couldn't have been more excited. Friends and colleagues were also going – Megan, Rox (who was also wristbanding) and Peggy (with her younger friends), and my colleague and increasingly close friend Kelly was also going separately with her crew. Kelly is a powerhouse of a woman: strong, focused and passionate, with an insatiable appetite for letting her hair down.

A week at Glastonbury also meant a week off work, something I needed, and I couldn't wait to set my out of office for a whole nine days. Jonathan was continuing with his hot/cold semi-commitment towards me. We'd been out to the theatre, ballet, restaurants, pubs. He'd met several of my non-work friends – some of whom were charmed, all of whom were wary. He'd got to know the boat and had helped out on a few moves, which was risky, given we were cruising through London. This thing, whatever we were doing, was still a secret amongst colleagues. The situation had become increasingly problematic, and I needed to get away. Again.

Leaving the boat for a week wasn't something I enjoyed doing, but it had to be done if I was to have a break. The morning of, I had a few jobs at work before my train was scheduled to leave and I was rushing somewhat. I'd packed, was clearing down the boat, chucking away food that was on the turn and emptying my compost toilet into a big bag.[50] I wasn't going to let waste sit on my boat for a week in the summer sun. I booked a taxi to take me to work for my final meeting and to leave my laptop there. I stood out on deck sweating in the sunshine, with my camping rucksack, tent and the bag of waste in my hands, and looked out at the Tottenham landscape. Bins. Where are the nearest bins, I thought.

Bins are a bloody nightmare in the boating world. They're probably my least favourite thing about being a boater. I can name all boater bins in London on one hand. I'm not sure why there aren't more, and it causes many issues, with park bins overflowing and fly tipping rife along the towpath. Recycling points are even more rare.

With time against me, and in a panic about the bin, I had no choice but to take the waste to work. So, I triple bagged the contents of my compost toilet.

"Let me help you," said the taxi driver as he loaded my bags into the boot.

"Oh, it's okay. This one can go in the back with me." I couldn't give a bag of my toilet waste to this poor taxi driver. It was bad enough that it was going in his car at all.

"Such a hot day," he said.

It was a hot day. Sweltering, in fact. I sat on the back seat holding my bag of poo in my sweaty palm, desperately willing the traffic to clear.

"Have a great time at Glastonbury," said the driver as we arrived at work.

He helped me unload the boot. "You'll give me five stars?" he asked.

"Oh, definitely," I said, still holding on to the bag.

He drove off. I walked around the side of the building and dumped the contents of my compost toilet in the giant bins outside, and I never told a soul to this day.

---

50 This was pre-actually-composting-my-waste days.

ALL BOATS ARE SINKING

After completing a few last-minute tasks, I stuck on my out of office and headed for the train station. On the train, relieved to have made it, I texted the Glastonbury 2019 WhatsApp group:

"Have left work. WOOOOOOHOOOOOOO! ⛺"

Kelly replied.

"Ah you lucky thing! I'm still working. Will be with you on Thursday. 🍺⛺🎵"

And then with a follow-up message, "Just seen Jonathan's latest promotion. Mid-twenties, beautiful. Classic Jonathan."

A rush of nausea came over me. Everything I already knew and suspected was confirmed in that message. The hair in the sink. The jewellery and hair grips in the flat. He had done it again. I had replaced his previous plaything. And now this one would replace me. She had been promoted in the same way I had. Plucked from junior roles within the company to join him at head office. It was a horrible cliché, and I was disappointed in myself, and in her. I'd grown up watching these dynamics play out in film. The charismatic older man in a position of power. The younger woman, reduced to an object. I wasn't that... and nor was she.

I replied, "Right, no more work chat in this group pleaaasssssssseeee 🧘"

I stared out of the window on the train as tears fell down my cheeks. Tears of sadness but of relief too, in knowing that I had been right. I'd become addicted to this man and he was never going to be my teammate.

I knew I needed to move on. As I journeyed towards Glastonbury, I vowed to tell Rox, Kelly et al about Jonathan. I'd grown too close to them all to be keeping it secret. I wouldn't do it at Glastonbury, though. He wasn't ruining this trip.

I hoped he would fall into that large bin at work.

Glastonbury Festival was everything I dreamt of, and more. With Kelly, Peggy, Rox, Megan and a whole host of new festival pals, we danced day and night. We walked for miles and miles, sang in unison, connected with strangers, asked why the world couldn't always be like this. The festival was in technicolour, a fairground of wonder, as we played like children in a magical forest. It was a scorcher that week, peaking at 31 degrees. We were grubby, we were hot, we were barely clothed and we were happy.

Jonathan popped into my head from time to time. I would feel a pang of longing. Of missing him. Of being scared of my ability to say no if (when) he reached out again. Though these thoughts did arise, they were short lived, and as I sat on a hill by the stone circle at 5 a.m. on our last night and looked over the festival site, I realised: *I know who my people are, and he is not one of them.*

"What are you thinking about, Hannah?" Peggy stretched her legs out on top of mine.

I thought about it. About telling her and telling all of them. But it was such a beautiful moment and had been such a beautiful week.

"How on earth have you managed to break in a pair of new Dr. Martens this week?" I said instead.

Peggy giggled and jumped up.

"Come on," she said. "Let's go for one last mooch."

In truth, I wasn't ready to tell them. I was too ashamed. I'm sure they wouldn't have expected this of me. I am too strong, too individually minded, too much a feminist. I was embarrassed to say that I didn't know why it had happened, but that it had.

We took one final walk through the magical playground, arms slumped around one another. Fatigued bodies and *mostly* content minds.

Chapter 33.1
What I Thought Living on a Boat Would Be Like

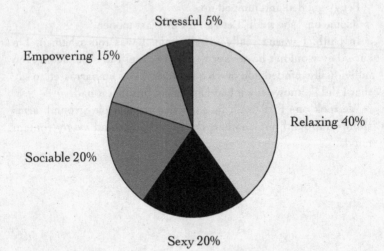

Stressful 5%

Empowering 15%

Relaxing 40%

Sociable 20%

Sexy 20%

Chapter 33.2
What It's Actually
Like

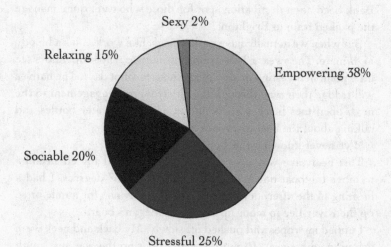

Sexy 2%

Relaxing 15%

Empowering 38%

Sociable 20%

Stressful 25%

Chapter 34
Phalange

Mid-July 2019 and London was having one of its heat waves. When the temperature reaches mid/late 30s, it never fails to catch us Londoners off guard. If the heatwave falls on a weekend, we'll flood the parks and lidos, and the city will be awash with drinkers perched at tables dragged outside by typically underprepared pubs and restaurants. Tourists are as shocked as we are, and the South Bank becomes a destination spot for those who can't quite manage the packed train to Brighton.

But when we actually have to do things, like work… it's a bloody nightmare. The sweaty Tube trains, businesses whose operators see little point in investing in air con for those few hot days. The natives will trudge their way through the city from one engagement to the next, open toes black with pollution, clutching water bottles and talking about the heat to anyone and everyone.

"I've never known it this hot," we'll all say.

This heatwave was no exception, and I found myself needing to move the boat one Wednesday morning in 37 degrees. I had a meeting in the afternoon, so I planned a short one for a mile or so up the River Lee to moor up alongside Megan's boat.

I untied my ropes and pushed off slowly. My back and neck were dripping with sweat. I found Megan's boat up the way just south of Ponders End and pulled in alongside, stepping lazily onto her back deck as I'd done many times before. She wasn't home. As I climbed onto Megan's boat I looked across at mine. *Argie* was still moving forward. I clearly hadn't reversed enough when I pulled in alongside, and the boat continued to move away from me. I held on tightly to my centre line to steady the boat while I stood on

PHALANGE

Megan's. The rope that was previously limp suddenly tightened like a seat belt. *Argie* slowed but continued forward. It all happened in a heartbeat. The rope I was holding in my left hand wrapped around my fingers and jerked me forwards. SNAP. The rope had become tangled around my hand, and it twisted and pulled my finger. I knew instantly that I had broken it.

I pulled the throttle back with my other hand, and my boat steadied in position. I looked down. There was a bend in my finger on my left hand that wasn't there before. An extraordinary wobble in my legs confirmed that adrenaline was coursing through my body. I told myself to stay calm, though my heart was beating like a train. I knew I needed to take myself to the hospital immediately. I looked around. There was no one nearby. I couldn't leave my boat untethered. I held my left hand to my chest and walked along the gunwales of my boat, legs still shaking like jelly. I leant down at the bow and tied up my front rope. It was impossible with one hand. I realised there was no pain coming from my broken finger yet, so I used that hand to tie up the ropes as I steadied myself with my good hand.

I knew I had a finite amount of time before the pain kicked in. I climbed inside the boat and grabbed a tea towel to mop up the rope burn graze that was bleeding on the good hand and ordered a taxi to take me to the hospital. Thankfully the taxi was quick, and the pain still hadn't started. In the back seat of the car, I looked down at my finger. *You idiot, Hannah*, I thought. Such a stupid mistake. How was I going to carry out boat tasks now?

I arrived at A and E and sat opposite a man who had mangled several fingers in a motorbike accident. I used the tea towel to conceal my comparatively pathetic break. The adrenaline was wearing off and my own finger had begun to throb. Pain deep enough to be felt in my whole arm. I could almost trace the journey from finger to brain and back again. I was called into triage and greeted by a friendly nurse. She looked tired and fed up. A doctor entered and asked her a question about another patient. She closed her eyes and responded wearily. As the doctor left the room, she said, "Sorry. Difficult day."

"I know," I said. I knew exactly what she was talking about. It was all over the news. Boris Johnson had just been made prime minister.

"I can't work for the NHS under him," she said. "I'm handing in my notice today."

"What a shitshow," I said under my breath. The nurse chuckled.

I left the hospital with a cast from my fingertip to my elbow. I was emotional and tired when Megan came home an hour later.

"Oh, Hannah," she said, giving me a hug. "... You've also broken my mushroom."[51]

"Oh, I haven't, have I? Oh, I'm so sorry, Megan."

"It's okay. It needed fixing anyway." She laughed. "Bloody boats, hey? Now, seeing as you look so pathetic, shall I cook you some dinner?"

~~~~~~~

I was referred to the plastics department of another London hospital. The break was a complex one and they needed to operate. A surgeon was assigned: a tall man in a linen suit with even stubble on a chiselled jaw. Possibly one of the most beautiful men I have ever met. He walked into the room followed by a team of three others.

"Hello," he said, pulling across the curtain. "I'm Dr Raj."

"Hello, doctor."

"How did you do this?" he asked.

My hand was gently balanced on top of his.

"My boat was still in gear," I said. "I was mooring up and the rope wrapped around—"

Dr Raj took a sharp inhale through his teeth. *Surely he's seen much worse*, I thought. Perhaps this was just his bedside manner. Dr Raj

---

51 Mushrooms are the vents on a narrowboat roof. Often made of chrome, brass or stainless steel, they allow air in and out of the boat cabin.

PHALANGE

asked me what I did for a living, to assess the speed and type of treatment he'd be giving.

"And because it's your ring finger," he said, "we'll want to get this straightened perfectly for you."

That was a rather strange thing to say, I thought, and he wasn't the last person to say it. A few of the healthcare professionals seemed to place particular significance on this being my "ring finger". Surely there's a medical term for that finger, apart from the antiquated name that suggests it's only valid if it has a ring on it? A quick Google search brought up the real names for each part of the hand. I was delighted to see that these parts of your fingers are called phalanges. The medical world must be sick of every hospital appointment about broken phalanges causing a whole generation of *Friends* fans (hi there) to giggle their way through their consultations.

I left the hospital after the appointment, wobbly at the knees from my beautiful surgeon and the high drug dose. I called Caz.

"Caz… I cannot tell you how beautiful my surgeon is," I said. "How appropriate is it for me to give him my number?"

"Not appropriate at all," she said. "Though let me do some digging anyway, find out what his status is."

I had faith in Caz's ability to find out if Dr Raj had made use of his ring finger before. Within half an hour, she'd sent me a string of messages containing information about my surgeon. He was married and had a business registered with his wife. Caz had found the pictures from their wedding, as well as an online copy of their wedding invitation. She'd also found his full address.

I wish Dr Raj a long and prosperous marriage, and if he's reading this, suggest he perhaps takes a closer look at his internet security settings.

~~~~~~~~

With a cast around my left hand and arm, doing certain things became difficult, particularly boat things. Megan took the lead on lock duties for a month or so and helped me change gas bottles, tie ropes and do all manner of things I didn't realise would be so much harder with one hand.

Dr Raj told me I couldn't run while my finger healed. That was the biggest blow. I'd built momentum with my training, and I was getting all the things out of it that Lucy said I would. It was a huge setback. I moved onto an exercise bike at the gym, determined to not let the injury stop me running the 10k race.

A week later and the cast was replaced by a plastic mould. One that let air get to the wound. I could see the finger, all blue and dry underneath. And the pin that stuck out of it. The plastic mould was kind of ridiculous-looking – a black and shiny claw, like Danny Devito's Penguin in *Batman Returns*.

~~~~~~~~

A month after the finger break, Caz, Natalie and I were in Regent's Park limbering up and queuing for the toilets in the rain. Technically I still wasn't supposed to run, but I felt I'd had my feet up for long enough now, and the finger seemed to be healing nicely. I just needed to make sure it was kept dry.

Our old school friend Lucy had missed her train back from Ipswich and would not be joining us for the race.

"So, how far have you run in training, Caz?" I said, circling my hips.

"About six, I reckon," she said. "How about you? How far had you run before you got the penguin claw?"

I continued stretching. "Oh, I dunno, about eight, maybe?" I said.

"Eight?!" Caz was visibly riled. "I thought you said you hadn't been training?"

"Well, you know… it wasn't fast or anything."

I felt a little guilty. But not that guilty.

We ran the race. Natalie ducked out after 5 kilometres. Caz and I continued on. Rain poured down, and with the stitches in my finger exposed, I held my hand under my vest for the duration of the run.

PHALANGE

At 7 kilometres, I turned around to see where Caz was. I couldn't see her. It seemed her tactic was to run just behind and overtake me in the last few kilometres. *Clever Caz*, I thought, staying out of view so I wouldn't notice her coming up behind.

At 8 kilometres, I turned around.

No Caz.

At 9 kilometres, I turned around.

Where the hell was she?

Aaand… 10 kilometres. I made it!

Caz crossed the line four minutes later as I stood huddled under a tree with Natalie. Well, I never. Caz is considerably fitter than me, with years of boxing and gym classes under her belt.

"Think you've found your sport, Hannah," Caz said, as she lay on the floor panting.

I couldn't believe I'd run it at all, let alone faster than Caz.

"I could have carried on," I said, trying not to sound too cocky.

"Oh, fuck off," said Caz, pulling me to the ground.

"Come on," said Natalie, "let's go find a pub."

A week later, I'd been accepted as a runner for the London Marathon the following spring.

Chapter 35
Things I've Smashed

- The kitchen window
- All the glassware
- All the crockery
- My rib
- A mirror
- Framed pictures
- My phalange (and Megan's mushroom)
- The side of my boat
- A 10k run

Chapter 36
Toilet Chronicles
(Part III)

Ponders End to Little Venice

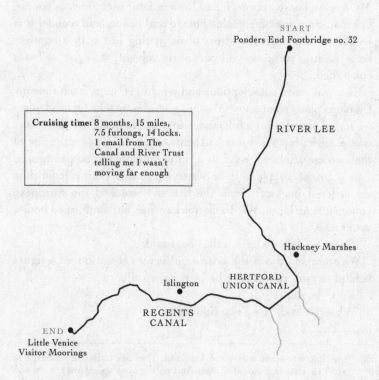

START
Ponders End Footbridge no. 32

Cruising time: 8 months, 15 miles,
7.5 furlongs, 14 locks.
1 email from The
Canal and River Trust
telling me I wasn't
moving far enough

RIVER LEE

Hackney Marshes

Islington

HERTFORD
UNION CANAL

REGENTS
CANAL

END
Little Venice
Visitor Moorings

ALL BOATS ARE SINKING

Before Sam and I broke up, we decided to give our relationship one last chance. We arrived in Thailand as a nervous couple trying to re-stabilise our relationship. But over the course of two weeks exploring the southern island hot spots, a handful of holiday mishaps stretched us to our already flimsy limit.

A week in, we swam in a deserted bay and Sam received a series of jellyfish stings across his waist, foot and leg that left him bedbound for the rest of the day. The next day we journeyed on a tuk tuk during a thunderstorm to a restaurant I'd been told about in the middle of nowhere which was average at best. And I booked us a few dodgy hotels for good measure. The way in which we responded to these adversities said a lot about our relationship. My free and easy approach had been at fault each time, of course, but that same attribute enabled me to find beauty and wonder that would far outweigh the stress of us getting lost with a stranger on a tuk tuk; and it was all part of the adventure, as far as I was concerned.

Sam was more conscientious and would get angry each time my frivolous plans went awry. Mounting tension reached a head when we found ourselves at a full moon party in Phuket. The atmosphere was electric, but we'd just had massages and at twice the age of the average attendee, were in a different state to the partygoers. Like a British couple in their 30s trying to save their relationship, we ordered buckets[52] from the bar and watched the European youngsters let loose. We drank quicker than our sunburned bodies could take.

"Come on, let's go for a walk," Sam said.

We stumbled down the beach and before long noticed a figure behind us who appeared to be carrying a knife.

"Run," he said.

"What?" I said. "Don't be ridiculous."

---

52 These buckets are notorious in Thailand. They are lethal: ice, a bottle of M-150 (a Thai equivalent of Red Bull with added ephedrine), soda and some very strong local liquor.

TOILET CHRONICLES (PART III)

"RUN!"

And so we ran back to our hotel, yelling at each other down the moonlit streets.

"You're being paranoid," I said.

"There was a man following us with a knife, Hannah."

For the remainder of our relationship, we would argue privately, and in public, about the validity of that incident. I would maintain that there was a man with a knife collecting his catch from fishing nets. Sam would insist we were being chased by a man with a machete. We will never know. I have a hunch, on the basis of our inebriation, that the man never had a knife in his hand at all. Indeed, there may not even have been a man.

The extravagant finale to our holiday was meant to be a weekend of shopping, Thai boxing and cocktails in Bangkok, where we would enjoy a more age-appropriate experience. There was a general air of politeness in our interactions, as we were still recovering from the full moon machete incident. We checked into a hotel with a rooftop pool in the centre of Bangkok. Sam had a sweat on. I guessed it was the humidity of the city.

"I'll catch you up," he said when we were about to leave the hotel for the day. "I'm just going to use the bathroom."

We went to the shopping district, and a pattern emerged. We would enter a mall and Sam would usher us in the direction of the public toilets. After the third time, I suggested maybe we needed to go back to the hotel. The next 12 hours were extreme. The bathroom visits intensified, and by 4 a.m. he had set up camp around the toilet. My reaction of eye rolling at his usual paranoia was replaced with fear as I saw the man I loved shrink into a damp ball on the bathroom floor in agony. Not wanting to fuel his terror, I began to do some googling. Lying on the bed at 4 a.m. I typed into Google Maps "Hospital Bangkok".

The Wi-Fi was freakishly good, and the pin, with speedy precision, dropped directly next to our hotel. What are the chances?

I let out a yelp of laughter.

"Babe. I'm so sorry, you will laugh about this one day," I said.

He remained in situ.

"I've just googled 'hospital Bangkok' and the pin has dropped right next door. It's called Bum Run Grad."

He didn't laugh.

Bumrungrad is ranked as the number one hospital in Thailand. We headed over and spent the remainder of our time in Thailand there. I was grateful for Sam's conscientious nature in booking a sturdy holiday insurance policy. He was put on a drip, and we just about managed to make it to the airport for our flight a few days later.

I had saved one final fuck-up.

"Babe," I said, "I'm gonna get us an upgrade on the flight because you're ill."

"Leave it, Hannah," he said.

I ignored him and walked to the desk to speak to the kind-looking airport assistant.

"Hi there," I said. "My partner has been in hospital with food poisoning. He's really unwell. Is there anything we can do to make this flight more comfortable for him?" I put an emphasis on the word comfortable, one wink short of spelling it out.

The man at the desk looked at Sam then back at me.

"Ma'am, he can't fly," he said.

"Excuse me?" I said.

Sam, who heard this, stood up and with the final bit of energy he had left, walked over.

"If he's sick," the airport assistant continued, "we can't accept him on the flight. And you just told me he is sick."

"Well, he's not—" I said.

Sam cut me off.

"I'm fine. I was discharged from the hospital," he said through gritted teeth. "Hannah, get the discharge documents out." My hands shook as I retrieved the paperwork from his rucksack.

"Excuse me for a moment." The man walked away from the desk to talk to someone more senior.

I stared ahead. Sam stared ahead.

TOILET CHRONICLES (PART III)

"I was just trying—"

"Don't, Hannah." Sam shot a look over at me. The hatred for his "happy-go-lucky girlfriend" was poorly concealed by a forced smile.

The flight assistant returned and handed back the documents.

"Okay, you can fly," he said. "But there are no seats in first class for you."

We returned to our seats in the airport and waited for our flight to be called, in silence.

Sitting in economy, tears of exhaustion and sadness fell down both our cheeks. The holiday had had its moments of joy. Floating together in hotel swimming pools. Boat trips between islands. Slow strolls in beautiful surroundings. But the holiday was over, and coming home on that flight, we were in our own worlds, and desperately sad. The gap in our relationship had widened during the trip and our differences were more apparent than ever. I think it was at that point that we knew the relationship was over.

Chapter 37
Autumn 2019

In the book *Can't Even – How Millennials Became the Burnout Generation* by Anne Helen Petersen, burnout is described as "reaching [the point of exhaustion] and pushing yourself to keep going, whether for days or weeks or years". Burnout is not the same as exhaustion. With burnout, you continue through the exhaustion and keep on going, and in the autumn of 2019, I kept on going. My working week was erratic and long, as I travelled across London every day, spinning plates like they were on fire. I was frantic and exhausted. My career in the events and hospitality industry had always been like this, but looking back, by this point I was out of control and the word "boundaries" had not yet entered the public lexicon as a way of managing the feelings I was having.

I felt like I had to perpetually prove my capabilities at work. Whether this was exacerbated by my embroilment with Jonathan, I don't know, but I was exhausted by it all, and at work the pressure was mounting.

I felt like I was living a double life and living it badly. Despite my Glastonbury awakening, he had once again reached out to me, and once again I had relented. I knew I was no longer his number one. But I was still a number, and for whatever reason, I felt I couldn't walk away from that. I had told some more friends about the affair by now, including Megan. She was too kind to say outright, but I could tell she was unimpressed.

"I know I shouldn't be doing it," I said to her one evening. "I just can't seem to shake him."

"I can see it's playing on your mind," she said. "Why don't you think about seeing a therapist?"

She was right, and I'd been toying with the idea anyway. I needed help. I was so confused. I needed to understand why I had found myself saying yes to him, when I wanted so much to say no. I needed to know why he was at the forefront of my thoughts at every waking moment.

And so, I started to see a therapist.

Anyone who has been fortunate enough to discover the wonders of paying for a professional to shed light on your character will know that soon into the journey, talk will move away from the immediate problems at hand and delve deeper into past experiences: the society in which you have existed, the feelings you have about yourself. It was an exercise in discovery of how I came to be and who I was at my core.

Being moored in a different location every few weeks, which in itself had become another erratic mode of existence, I would type the therapist's location into my city mapper app and take the Tube, train or bus to the small room up three flights of stairs, in a converted townhouse in North-east London. We would sit for an hour together. Each session, different. I would go in with one thing, and invariably, come out with another. I would cry more often than not, sit in silence, become impatient, accept things, deny things, listen, speak, pose questions, wonder, accept.

I was still running. I can't recall how or when I squeezed it in, but I did. It was another type of therapy. Another mode of self-discovery. Incrementally, I was gaining strength and learning to understand myself. My situation was the same, but my outlook was shifting.

I didn't know it then, but it was the best preparation I could imagine, for a world that was about to change.

Chapter 38
A Winter of Luxuries

By my third winter on the canals and rivers of London, I had mastered the art of "luxuries". The way I found I could operate working a 50+ hour week, with a boat (which can feel like a part-time job), while maintaining a social life and an ongoing, though less frequent, sexual relationship with my senior colleague, was by forking out every penny I earned (as well as a hefty overdraft) on things that made me feel (seemingly) better. Desperate to create some semblance of equality in my relationship with Jonathan, I had mostly insisted we went halves on our activities together. The theatre trips and restaurant visits had stopped, but in the early days with Jonathan, we would regularly go out on fancy dates, and I always paid my way. With my erratic work schedule, I was rarely home for mealtimes, so I would eat out several times a week. If I did go grocery shopping, it would be to small organic shops and farmers markets in East London.

"It's the yin to my yang," I would say to friends. And I believed this. If I was to excrete into a potty (as Jonathan called it) then I'd need a membership at a spa to balance things out. Megan and I would sit in a sauna once a week to warm our bones and I'd have long hot showers in the changing rooms, because, why the hell not. When life on the boat could sometimes feel quite merciless, these luxuries had become important to me. The whole "London is expensive" argument that I had spouted to my family was valid; however, my new-found taste for kombucha was not.

Every Friday I would say, "I'll sort out my money on Monday." Monday would come round, and I wouldn't have any food in, and there would be a new Thai restaurant opening in Chatsworth Road to check out, and it would be a little too far to walk, and I would just grab an Uber, and, and, and.

I was in some debt as a result. Not a huge amount, but enough to occasionally keep me awake at night. I would start to talk to friends about my small problem and saying it out loud made it real, of course. I was in my mid-thirties with an okay salary and few ties, but no savings. It wasn't good enough.

Anyway, I'd deal with it on Monday.

～～～～

One such luxury had become an extension of the Sunday dinner parties at Rox's, which now included meals out at fancy restaurants. Peggy was working in PR for high-end chefs and would let us know of any new openings and the hottest spots in town. The group had expanded out to include my old friend Lauryn and her new partner Janet. Peggy messaged the WhatsApp group, **"Who fancies a trip to Manchester? A new restaurant is expecting a Michelin star. I think we should go before the prices hike."**

I looked at the menu online... £105 for a taster menu, £80 for wine pairing. I'd say that was pretty hiked anyway, wouldn't you, Peggy?

"I'm game!" I replied.

Megan, Peggy, Rox, Janet, Lauryn and I sat around a large glass table in Mana, Manchester's newest restaurant, and ate a 15-course taster menu with wine pairing. It was the most remarkable meal I'd ever eaten. Dishes that appeared through clouds of dry ice and glowed with colourful jus dotted across stone plates. Vegetables and flowers of all colours and flavour pairings I would not have put together in a million years (probably because I'm not a Michelin-starred chef). I looked over to Lauryn and Janet at the other end of the table. Janet carefully pushed the dishes in the centre in order to get the best possible photo before she dived in. Lauryn had a bemused expression on her face. Like me, I think she was questioning how and why she'd ended up in this restaurant, and in her Mancunian accent she would ask Janet quietly, "What's this, then?" before every dish that was brought over. It was adorable, and hilarious.

We left the restaurant, shaking hands with the staff, who I think were glad to see the back of us as we had been noticeably the loudest table, and headed to Canal Street, where we danced for as many hours as our 15-course-stuffed bodies could manage. On the way home we picked up kebabs and chips, to ensure that the taste left on our lips the following morning was salty and fried, and not the exquisite £7/bite soon-to-be-awarded-a-Michelin-star flavours from our meal earlier in the evening. We stayed at Lauryn's flat and enjoyed a roast together the following day. We'd had an extravagant but wonderful weekend away.

I sat on the train home googling.

"What are you looking at, Hannah?" said Peggy.

"What living on the canals in Manchester is like," I said.

"Really?" Peggy looked shocked.

"Oh, don't worry, I'd never actually leave London," I said, putting my phone away. "I was just curious."

Chapter 39
London Boatwoman

The canals and rivers in London showcase an incredible array of colours and textures. The bridges that cross the waterways are caked in graffiti, with angry slogans, tags and revengeful comments about politicians or ex-girlfriends. This destruction and reaction to blandness shines a light on an underworld of anger, class politics, frustration and frivolity. They serve as reminders that we should hug each other, vote, take drugs, call Stacy on 07********** and fight capitalism. The slogans are loud; the artwork (often) beautiful. Luxury apartments and converted warehouse office blocks along the canal with their muted colours and streamlined edges almost appear to encourage bursts of canal-side artwork. The architecture, along with the artists, the boats, the birds, the bikes and the pondweed, create a lively patchwork of colour and style that really does epitomise my London.

Embracing the city's vibrancy and variety, I revelled in exploring. On my runs, I was forever surprised by what I stumbled across living on the waterways. Community gardens, luscious parks, marshes and abandoned waterways are plentiful on the network, and I delighted in getting lost in the new communities I came across. Learning more about my city from the waterways was a dream and I had no desire to live anywhere else; I wanted to continue exploring. Every boater I spoke to seemed to feel the same; that this was the best way to do London and that this special place within the city was somewhere we could be ourselves.

I would find myself mooring up alongside townhouses, trendy warehouse projects and high-rise apartment blocks, though I was never too far from a pocket of green. I'd often be moored up on tree-lined stretches of canal thinking that if it weren't for the sound of traffic, I could be anywhere. My friends would introduce me to new people as "a boater". They would comment on the lingering smell of wood burner that would accompany me as I walked into a room. They would chuckle as I squirrelled my electrical devices and plugged them in at the corners of pubs.

I had become familiar with the London network from Brentford in West London to Tottenham in North-east London, and the Limehouse Cut that breaks away at Mile End and heads southwards towards the Thames before looping back and emerging in Hackney. I knew I had earned it now, and I was happy to adopt the official title of London Boatwoman.

My favourite routine on the boat was my mornings, when I would hop out of bed and put on a coffee for one. The gentle rocking of the boat, the way the reflections of the water danced on the ceiling, it was my happy place. I'd stick on the radio, open up the blinds and stare out at the colours before me. I would smile at my boating neighbours. We would loan each other tools, discuss our toilet set-up and the changing seasons. I'd see the same people again and again. This was my community and I felt I had become one of them to my core.

Chapter 40
Last Flight

My annual solo weekend away was poorly timed with its proximity to the London Marathon and coming not long after my extravagant Manchester jolly, but it was tradition, and as usual I was craving some time away from work (and so on) and looked forward to walking the streets of Lisbon for three days in the spring of March 2020, and of course, sampling the finest Portuguese cuisine. I would need to be sensible, though, as it was only six weeks until race day. Training over winter had helped me rein it in during "silly season", and I'd found myself building a healthier schedule; sleeping better, planning and cooking meals, and starting every other day with a run or a workout. Sundays were saved for the big ones. I would go gentle throughout the week, Saturday night I would eat a bowl of pasta and head out on Sunday morning, each week increasing the distance – 6 miles, 7.5 miles, 10 miles, 13.1 miles, 15 miles, 16 miles.

Mornings were crisp on the boat, so I'd climb out of bed, quickly light a fire and jump straight into my running trainers. I came off the towpath and regularly ran around Victoria Park, with plenty of other runners and an even surface to run on. I'd head out in the dark wearing a headtorch (I had all the gear now) and as my body warmed up, my speed would increase and I'd arrive back at the boat just as the fire had reached its peak.

So as to not break form while away, I'd booked a run with a tour guide in Lisbon. Naturally, I'd also reserved a few spaces in fancy restaurants. Work had been increasingly stressful, and Jonathan in particular had been brutal in the week leading up to the trip. The day of my trip he suggested he put me forward for a new role; one which he framed as an "exciting opportunity" but which was, in its title, a demotion. I called him from the airport and stepped across my "no work chat" boundary to tell him off for being so hard on me.

"Are you trying to get rid of me?" I asked.

"No, Hannah, I'm not," he insisted.

"You knew I was going away."

"Yes, Hannah," he said, "but…"

"It could have waited," I said. "And you've been singling me out."

"Look, go away and enjoy your trip. We'll talk next week."

In Lisbon, my emails were turned off, and I walked the streets with the spring sunshine warming my shoulders. But I couldn't relax. It was March 2020, and the streets of Lisbon were eerily quiet. The restaurants had just a few patrons scattered across reduced table spaces. Staff were wearing masks and gloves.

On day two I ate at Minibar, a two Michelin star restaurant with an avant garde menu in a low-lit theatrical setting. I sat at the bar, alone. It was a delightful and unique menu, to rival that of Mana's in Manchester. The meal was exquisite, but the atmosphere was odd.

My phone was relentless with messages. One from Jonathan:

"Will you make it home okay?"

And one from Mum: "Hannah, change your flight. They are getting cancelled all over Europe. Come back now."

By the third course, I put my phone away – well, after one quick check on the BBC app first. The 2020 London Marathon had been cancelled.

I turned to the barman. "Could I order the wine pairing, please?"

I relaxed for the rest of my meal by chatting away to the staff behind the bar and comparing tales from the UK and Portugal. I told them about the toilet roll stockpiling that was happening. They couldn't believe it. Lisbon locals seemed to be taking it all in their stride, like they'd done this a hundred times before. Schools had already shut and I dined at Minibar on their final day of trading, watching staff take off their aprons not knowing when or if they'd return to work.

I spent my last morning in Lisbon feeling rather apprehensive. I hadn't changed my flight, and the city was emptying. There were no restaurants or cafés left to eat in, so I picked up pastries and ate them at the water's edge. The trip had been marred with uncertainty. Would I get home? What would be there when I got back?

I arrived at the airport six hours before my flight. I felt I needed to be prepared for any extra waiting time, or any chaos that might be playing out in the departure lounge. I approached a crowd of hundreds of people outside.

"What's going on?" I asked a British couple.

"They're not letting people in until their flights are called. So we have to wait out here," said the man. "What time is your flight?"

I already needed a wee and my phone (which had my boarding pass on it) was dying.

"In six hours," I said.

They looked at me with a concerned expression. I walked to the front of the gathered group of travellers and found a security person.

"Excuse me." She looked around, clearly fed up of me already. "My phone battery is about to die and my boarding card is on it. My flight's not for another six hours."

"I'm sorry, you can't come in," she said.

"I also need the bathroom," I said.

Her face softened slightly, "I'm sorry."

I walked away, with no idea how this would play out.

"No luck?" asked the man.

I shook my head.

"Here, have my charging pack," he said. "That solves one issue."

"That's so kind," I said. "Thank you."

Before he handed it over, the security guard approached and signalled me to follow her.

"Come on." I followed her as she led me through the main entrance. "Toilets there and charging point there."

I smiled and mouthed "thank you", knowing she was attempting to be subtle in front of other needy passengers. I charged up, went to the toilet and passed through security and into the waiting area for flights. The board had a dozen or so flights listed on it when

ALL BOATS ARE SINKING

I arrived. Every half-hour that passed, another flight came off the list. I saw a flight's worth of Budapest-bound passengers break down into tears and disbelief as their last remaining flight home was cancelled.

There were five more flights on the board, with mine the last of the day.

Until my arrival at the airport, I had fantasised about an enforced stay in Lisbon. I'd bunk up with a local family offering support. They'd put me up in their annex and feed me wonderful meals made from recipes passed down the family as I worked away on an old-fashioned typewriter. Their adult son would come home from his job working on vineyards in the Douro region, duty-bound to be near his aged mother. He'd be tall and strong, and we'd get acquainted on long walks around the deserted city together. We would fall in love that summer and be married in the autumn. I would bring him back to the UK to meet my parents for a British Christmas. He'd cry the first time he ever saw snow.

In Lisbon's airport, abandoning my McDonald's meal, too nervous to eat, the fear that I wouldn't make it home turned my stomach. In reality, I had no idea what I would do if I was stuck there. Eventually, my flight was called. It was the last flight to leave Lisbon before my world turned upside down.

Chapter 41
Boat Names I Have Seen

- Kids' Inheritance
- Knot so Fast
- Ship Happens
- Fishizzle
- Fishy McFishface (Boaty McBoatface is still the funniest thing the British have ever done [53])
- Unsinkable II
- Nauti-boy
- Aboat Time
- P45
- Rosé and Gin

---

53 In 2016, there was an online vote to name a £200-million polar research ship. A presenter from BBC Jersey came up with the suggestion *Boaty McBoatface*. Despite the fact that this name received 124,109 votes against the second choice (34,371 *Poppy-Mai*), the voting was overlooked, and the vessel was named the *Sir David Attenborough*. Thankfully, the campaign wasn't entirely wasted, with a tender on board receiving the title *Boaty McBoatface*.

Part 3

Locked Down

"When all of this is over, the world won't be the same."

Francesca Melandri, *The Guardian* 27 March 2020

Chapter 42
A Small Knitted Carrot

It was almost unheard of that I would say no to Jonathan but last night, I had done it. He invited me around after I touched down at Luton airport, and I said no. Maybe it was Lisbon's warm spring air that gave me the strength to do so. I went to sleep on the boat feeling powerful and resolved. Grateful to be home and alone.

After a long night's sleep, I awoke and straight away looked at the rejection message I had sent the night before. A rush of anxiety came over me. He would surely be angry that I turned him down. Had I blown it forever?

I sent him a message.

"Good morning. Sorry I didn't come round last night. I was pretty tired after the journey."

He read the message, but didn't reply.

"I could come over tonight?" I said.

No reply.

I checked my work email. There was one from Jonathan.

"Morning Hannah, I trust you had a good holiday. Could you come to head office for 11 a.m. today please?"

I replied to the email in the usual way, as a dutiful employee of the company we both worked for.

"Certainly, Jonathan. Would you like me to prepare anything?"

"No need."

As I unpacked my suitcase, I thought about how ridiculous this relationship had become. I was playing a character at work, but at least I knew where I stood. In our personal interactions, I couldn't have been more uncertain.

As I travelled in on the train, I started to feel nervous. I was always anxious about seeing him at work. Any excitement about our secret had long disappeared and been replaced by feelings of shame and paranoia whenever I saw him across a room, particularly with the sinking feeling in my gut that I wasn't the only one looking at him this way. But today something else had provoked my fear. What was I being called in for? I'd turned down the offer of a new job before I went to Lisbon. Would they try again to convince me to take the job? Did I have an option? I could tell things were strained at the company. They were before this pandemic thing had reared its head, but all the additional uncertainty must now be adding to their worries.

I was right to be nervous.

The air at head office was bleak. The staff who were based there – a melting pot of talent from across the globe – usually spoke energetically across desks with passion and dedication that was palpable. But this morning, their numbers were down, and those that were present sat in silence, heads bowed, sombre.

Jonathan stood as I approached the shared desk that he was working at and clapped his hands together loudly. He asked the younger woman he had promoted to make him a cup of tea and bring it into the meeting room.

She stopped what she was doing and stood up.

"Would you like one, Hannah?" he said.

"I'm okay thank you."

He smiled at the woman and she walked to the kitchen area in her thick black heels to make his tea.

"Right, shall we?" He signalled me into a small office.

We sat down in two high-backed conference chairs. His hands were clasped together on top of the table that separated us. His posture was as straight as ever.

Even when he was relaxing, he would sit up straight. At home, in the pub; at the theatre I'd lean forward in my chair and feel his presence behind me. I'd fidget throughout the performance, and had wondered if it bothered him. If it did, he never showed it. He never really showed any frustration towards me in private – very occasionally, if I swore too much, and the rare late-night argument when we'd differ in our opinions about the latest political movement and one of us would spark a debate. But other than that, he was calm and seemingly happy in my presence.

On the boat, his stature was at odds with the environment. I'd clamber and squeeze through the small space while he sat still and upright on my sofa or out on deck. I remember one morning in the summer, I was tidying up from the previous night in my kitchen. Jonathan had pulled a chair off the roof and was sitting outside in a shirt and boxer shorts, wearing a pair of my sunglasses. I'd loaned him a play text the day before, *Oleanna* by David Mamet, and he'd brought it out with him to read as I stayed inside and prepared breakfast. The boat was moored in Victoria Park, with towpath users metres from us. He would greet them with a smile as they walked past, saying "hello" and "lovely day".

I'm sure they were as surprised as me to see this elegant man sitting on a small blue boat in East London. He read the play from cover to cover, enjoying the cups of tea I brought out to him. I glanced through the open door and marvelled at the sight. A backdrop of different coloured boats lined the water's edge, and a green summer willow hung down over the canal. A man I adored was sitting in the sunshine on my boat reading a play I'd recommended, for the whole world to see. Was there anything more beautiful?

Back in the meeting room, he began. "I'm afraid I've been asked to inform you that you no longer have a job with the company," he said as if speaking to a child about their poor grades at school.

I couldn't stop my mouth from opening. What had he just said? Did my recent lover just say I didn't have a job any more?

Before I had a chance to respond –

"It's not just you, Hannah. This has been a difficult few days for the company, I know. And the hardest of my career to date."

ALL BOATS ARE SINKING

My heartbeat quickened. I had worked tirelessly for this company for seven years. I looked through the glass panel into the room next door to see another one of my colleagues being let go by another senior colleague. Why couldn't I have had that colleague, I thought? This man in front of me had invited me to his flat last night, and now he's telling me I don't have a job any more?

He continued, "With this virus, we don't know what the future of the company looks like, but we do know it will not be sustainable as is."

He had said this speech today already, I thought.

The younger woman Jonathan had promoted knocked on the door and entered. She placed his tea in front of him.

"Thank you," he said, following her out of the room with his gaze.

He carried on talking. Something about handing back my laptop and formal letters, as I stared into his bright blue eyes, looking for a glimmer of emotion. He gave nothing away.

"I understand," I said, robotically.

I didn't. I didn't understand why he had to carry out this meeting, or why he couldn't have waited five minutes for his cup of tea.

"You've done what you had to do," I said.

Jonathan ran his hand across his ringletted hair. Hair that I had played with many times.

I felt confused, sickened by him, by his formality.

Remaining in character, we both stood up to leave the room. I habitually went to sit down at one of the shared desks. The younger woman looked across to me and smiled a sympathetic smile. I smiled back. It wasn't her fault.

I stayed for the rest of the morning sending out emails to partners and cc'ing in my personal address, trying to remember all the individuals I had worked with who may be of use to me in the future, whatever that looked like. I was numb. I had never been let go from a job before. I had no idea what I would do next. Finally, when there was nothing more to do, I logged out of my laptop and stood up to go. I looked around at the remaining team members: a third or so were left. There were people I had got to know really well over the years, and some I knew I hadn't given the time that I should have. I regret that.

He was sitting at his desk, looking calm. Focused. I said my goodbyes. I hugged the younger woman he had promoted. I left.

Jonathan caught up with me on the staircase and laid a hand on my shoulder. I wasn't sure what it meant. I smiled through the sadness, and carried on walking.

That evening I texted him, "I'm scared I'll never see you again."

In all the confusion around the redundancy, the pandemic on the news, the virus that was our relationship, I don't know what I was thinking by messaging him this. I was sickened with myself. That I had spent the last two and a half years of my life at this man's behest. That whenever he messaged, after anything between a week or a few months of silence, I would go to him. No matter how much I knew it would hurt me in the long and medium term. That I just couldn't seem to say no. Even now, as I believed our relationship to be firmly over, all I wanted was to see him and to make sure he knew that I was still there.

He replied with a photo of a Christmas decoration that I'd bought him, a knitted carrot, left hanging from a sculpture in his flat when the tree had come down. He'd only bought the tree for a Christmas soiree he'd hosted. He wouldn't have got one otherwise.

Below the picture of the hanging vegetable was his message: "Of course you will, Hannah."

~~~~~~~

Two days later, I received an email from the Managing Director. After all that, in light of the government furlough scheme, our redundancies had been revoked. I would stay employed... for now. The letter came as a relief, but there was a bitter taste in my mouth. I understood from a logical perspective why I had been in that room. My role in live events would be useless in the new

ALL BOATS ARE SINKING

world if the headlines were to be believed. I therefore accepted my
redundancy above most of my colleagues. But I did not accept that
he had done this. And with that unnecessary cup of tea.

Chapter 43
Lockdown

Two months moored in Little Venice and Kensal Rise

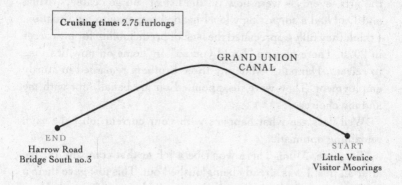

Cruising time: 2.75 furlongs

GRAND UNION
CANAL

END
Harrow Road
Bridge South no.3

START
Little Venice
Visitor Moorings

"You know where I wouldn't want to be during
lockdown? On a boat."

Overheard on the towpath

Megan and I were moored in West London when the UK went
into lockdown on 26 March 2020. The weekend before, I had
looked out of my cabin window and watched the mass exodus of
boats head further west and out of London for greener climes.
While most of the population had little choice where they would
spend their lockdown, save those with multiple homes, the moving
communities did, and many took advantage of this. If we wanted

to spend the time in central London, now deserted, we could. If we wanted to go somewhere greener, we could. As each boat passed, I felt more and more anxious. Why wasn't I doing the same? I had nothing to stop me from leaving.

I had phoned Mum.

"I've no idea what my career prospects are now, Mum."

I found it implausible, laughable even, that my attempt to expand my repertoire of "fallback" jobs over the years had left me stumped in the pandemic. Every single one of them – cruise ships, hospitality, the arts, events – were now on the list of "no go" careers. Mum and Dad had a surprisingly level-headed response to my situation. I think they fully appreciated the lack of predictability for my career in 2020. There was no "I told you so" or "come on now, it's time to retrain, Hannah," while my three brothers remained in sturdy employment. They were disappointed on my behalf, not with me and my choices.

"Well, let's see what happens with your current job," she said, remaining optimistic.

"Trust me, Mum. There won't be a job at that company for me after all this. I was already being pushed out. This just gave them a brilliant excuse. And it's for the best, to be honest." Though Mum knew about Jonathan and me, she didn't know the extent of it. Nor how untenable the situation had become.

"Anyway, it's not like I haven't got time to think about what to do," I said, as my eyes followed another boat heading out of the city.

"Why don't you go and visit your brother on the boat?" she said, catching me off guard.

"Which brother?"

"The only one on a canal?" she said, with more than a hint of sarcasm.

"Matthias?" I said, incredulously. "That's crazy, Mum. It would take me forever." After their stint living in Manchester, Matthias and his family now resided in Todmorden, West Yorkshire – a beautiful town on the edge of the Pennines.

"Well, I just thought it might be nice," she said.

LOCKDOWN

My mother never fails to surprise me with her ideas. Wilfully rejecting her nervous tendencies, she's an adventurer, and despite a long marriage to my father, has kept an independent mindset. She's got fire in her. I'm not saying all her ideas are good. But this one was interesting.

"I'm not sure I could go all the way to Yorkshire on my own," I said, "but maybe somewhere outside of London might be nice."

When I moved on to the boat, I never imagined I would cruise away from the London waterways. It hadn't really been the point. But the option to breathe in the fresh countryside air with abundant wildlife and overgrown towpaths during this time was a tempting prospect. I felt like there was nothing keeping me in London anymore. I mooted the idea of heading west out of London to Megan as we queued outside Sainsbury's in Kensal Rise.

"How would you feel if I took the boat out west for lockdown? You could come too?" I said.

"Not great," Megan said with a look of sadness in her eyes.

Megan wanted to stay put and be near the action when things kicked back into gear and didn't want to be stuck out in the middle of nowhere in case she needed to travel again for work.

She continued, "I feel like we really need to look out for each other during this time. I hoped you would feel the same?"

I stayed silent, confused as to what my reaction should be. I guess there was some sense in being near a friend, but I didn't want to make this decision for anyone else. I wanted to do what was right for me. Was I being selfish? My heart and instinct was telling me to run away. I was desperate to gain some semblance of control in a situation that I felt was beyond mine. I hadn't been happy in my job or in the mess I'd found myself in with Jonathan, and so there was some relief there. But it was a fragile relief, and my ability to see clearly was on a knife's edge. I felt I needed to take matters into my own hands to ensure a positive outcome after having everything taken away so suddenly. Unlike Megan, I had no idea what my career prospects looked like and knew little would change in the coming weeks and months.

ALL BOATS ARE SINKING

"I feel like this is an opportunity to press the reset button on my life," I said. "Take the boat out of London and spend some time in the countryside."

"That makes sense." She paused as we took two socially distanced steps forward in the supermarket queue. "But perhaps you could wait and assess it again when we know a bit more from the government?" Megan seemed upset and I didn't want to add any more stress to the situation by putting strain on our relationship. I thought about the summer before. How she'd helped me with the boat when I'd broken my finger. I supposed I could hang out in London for a few weeks, then head off.

"Yeah, of course I can wait," I said.

I agreed to stay until the prime minister's next announcement, and we created a support bubble between our two boats. I'm not sure this was entirely compliant with the rules at this point, but we made the allowance based on being like flatmates and agreed that if one of us became symptomatic we would both isolate. I was moored near the water point in Little Venice and Megan was half a mile away to the west in Kensal Rise. The distance between our boats was appreciated by us both, I think. It gave me a chance to experience and process a range of emotions in the comfort of my own home, and while Megan continued working from home, she was able to get her head down and maintain more structure to her weeks. The walk between our boats would provide an opportunity for us to stretch our legs and change our environment, even just for a bit.

Once the lockdown officially started, instructions were emailed to all liveaboard boaters from the Canal and River Trust. We were told to stay put, only moving for essentials like water or toilet facilities. The usual rule of cruising every two weeks was suspended. For those whose boats were a second home, they were asked not to visit them. The decision to move the boat out of London was taken away from me, and I was gutted.

LOCKDOWN

"It's better being here. Trust me," said Megan. "We can do yoga together in the park and you've got all the facilities you need right nearby."

Megan may have been right, but I was still gutted. All those boats that had left in a hurry would now be out of the city and enjoying life in the countryside. And I was stuck in West London. In normal times, I wouldn't ever stay very long in West London, and generally preferred the bustle and excitement found in East London, as well as its convenient location for work.

Little Venice, it turned out, wasn't a bad place to be holed up for lockdown. With so many boaters having left London, the area was considerably quieter than usual. Moorings in Little Venice can be hard to come by, but during lockdown, while boats were still double moored, there was considerably more space between the moorings.

In London the waterways are packed, bow to stern all the way along the network. In central London spots, it's expected that boats double moor. It's a game of Tetris as different shaped vessels find gaps to slot into. With *Argie* being 45 foot I don't struggle to find places to moor, but if I do get a towpath space, it's never long before a boat joins mine. In my first year, I would tentatively pull in alongside a boat, and if the owner wasn't on board, I would leave a note:

"Hope you don't mind! here's my number. My name is Hannah, I'm your new neighbour. X ☺"

But after a while, I realised that as long as you were polite, no one seemed to mind. Boaters outside of London find this concept bizarre. "Why would you want to double moor? You might as well share a flat," they'd say. But for Londoners, it's part of the deal.

I'd arrived at my lockdown location before I went to Lisbon. I remember thinking it was a shame I'd got such a premium spot but would be spending some of my precious two weeks there away from the boat. How little I knew. I would end up spending two months there, moored a short walk from Hyde Park, with plenty of options for grocery shops, a laundrette and a bin facility just a few minutes' walk away.

ALL BOATS ARE SINKING

The stretch of water from Regent's Park and around Paddington and Little Venice is a postcard perfect image of the London canal network. Pubs and restaurants flank the water's edge with bridges that boast ornate cobalt blue railings curving elegantly across the canal. The white Regency houses in neat rows throughout Maida Vale and Warwick Avenue dressed in purple wisteria, from whose front doors Mary Poppins might burst at any moment. Boats sit along both sides of the water; cruisers like me on the Royal Oak side and some impressive permanent floating homes on the Warwick Avenue side. Of course, in lockdown, with everything shut, the pubs and restaurants were merely relics, with a particularly torturous reminder stamped on the awning of the closed down restaurant just opposite:

Summer and Seafood all year round

On the first few days of lockdown, the boats around me shuffled as folk snuggled into their preferred spots. Knowing I wasn't going anywhere, I resolved to make the best of my location. I shifted the boat slightly forward so my solar panels and back deck received more direct sunlight, and away from the impending blossom coverage from trees hanging over the canal. Once I was happy with my new location, I retied my ropes.

A fellow boater slowly pulled in alongside as I was crouched down over my new mooring ring.

"Hope you don't mind…?" he said.

Wearing a sleeveless T-shirt that showed off his biceps, the man, with black sunglasses and thick strawberry blond hair, hopped off his boat and onto my gunwales.

"No, not at all. I'm Hannah," I said.

"Andrew," he said. "I wasn't keen on my neighbours." They were two boats down, so he was whispering. "I thought I'd shuffle along and join you."

LOCKDOWN

"Welcome, neighbour," I said with a casual nod. I went inside my boat and locked the doors behind. I opened my mouth aghast while holding myself up against a kitchen surface. My new neighbour was beautiful. I sent a WhatsApp voice note to Syd, **"This could be an interesting lockdown."**

For the next few days, I would find every excuse to potter about on deck. I polished my brass mushrooms, planted herbs and painted my barge pole the two-tone blue of *Argie*. Andrew was working from home and would pop out with a cup of tea every now and again, but not as often as I'd hoped. When he did come outside, we'd talk about lockdown, the weather and the various boat jobs we both hoped to tick off our lists during this time. He had a gentle manner and seemed as happy to talk to me as I was to him. There was no mention of a partner, so I assumed he must be single, and perhaps that was one of the reasons he brought his boat over to join mine. Then, a few days later, while he was admiring his lavender plant on deck, he said, "So Hannah, are you seeing anyone?"

Here we go, I thought. I was out of practice but had just about remembered how to keep it cool.

"No, not really," I said, climbing onto my roof. "You?"

"Yeah, but he's studying in Brighton," he said.

"Oh, that's sad," I said, too quickly in a way that might have come across as curt. I tried to recover from the bombshell with a sympathetic smile, as Andrew continued.

"We had to make a decision for lockdown, but he'll join me once things are back to normal and come and live with me on the boat."

"Oh, that'll be nice," I responded quickly again, but this time I meant it. Andrew *was* lovely. He wouldn't be my future husband, I think that was clear by this point, but I hoped he might become a friend. Flirtation well and truly over, I told Andrew about Jonathan... the first new person I had told in a long time. It felt shameful to say it out loud, but it was good progress, I thought. Something I could say was a part of my past now. My relationship with Jonathan as a colleague as well as my lover had become particularly hard to stomach since that day at head office, and I knew this was my best chance to move on.

"Wait… he was the one who made you redundant?" Andrew said.

"Yep."

"Oh wow. That's rough," he said. "Shame they didn't wait a few days for the furlough scheme announcement. Would have saved you some heartbreak."

"I think it needed to happen that way," I said. "And they did put me on furlough in the end. But the redundancy certainly shook me out of myself."

"Will you go back after furlough?" said Andrew.

"I don't think I'll have a job to go back to," I said, resigned to this reality.

"But if you do?" he said.

"I'll cross that bridge when I come to it."

I also told Andrew of my desire to move the boat out of London, head out on a voyage.

"Maybe as far as the North of England. My brother lives up in Yorkshire." I pulled out a map across our two back decks and showed him the route. He looked at the map. "Whatever happens with this lockdown and with my work, I can always turn back or work from a field or something."

"If you head out of London, I'll come with you," he said after a pause.

"That's brilliant." I gave another lightning speed answer without really thinking it through. I liked Andrew, what I knew of him anyway. But I did want to do this alone. There was something about the quiet ease of not being answerable to anyone that I was clearly craving.

"I mean, not all the way, but I could join you for a bit… say to Rickmansworth?" he suggested, following the line from London with his finger.

Rickmansworth in Hertfordshire is spoken about as a kind of pilgrimage by the London boating community. The first rural spot outside of the capital on the Grand Union Canal, it's where horses roam along the towpath and boaters wild swim in the reservoirs. During that first lockdown, many headed there. I had images of these city expats out in the wild, with suntans, bottling up homemade elderflower and smoking rollies in their turned-up corduroy dungarees. Going to Rickmansworth with Andrew instantly became a deep desire. He would turn back at some point, but I might carry on.

"That would be perfect," I said.

But we had missed the window of opportunity for leaving London and were bound by government guidelines to stay where we were. That didn't stop Andrew and I talking about it daily, though. "Shall we go tomorrow?" became a regular conversation starter. We joked that neighbours would overhear and shout out of their windows, "Jeez, just go already!"

It felt mischievous to be planning the trip with Andrew. After my initial conversation with Megan, I think she had thought the idea had passed. But it hadn't, I just didn't want to upset her by mentioning it again. Andrew and I were egging each other on, and the prospect became an obsession for us both.

Chapter 44
Brasso Bandit

Like many others, in March 2020 my calendar was wiped clean overnight. Every engagement from friends' birthday parties and work meetings, to theatre trips and report deadlines; all the colour-coded calendars on my phone had gone. It was liberating, if I'm honest, not being tied to promises and commitments across my social life and work. The weight of pressure had lifted and it was freeing. Sure, it was sad that I wouldn't be attending that friend's wedding or seeing through any of the projects I'd worked so tirelessly on at my job. But I didn't need to worry about them anymore and the best thing about it was that the decision was out of my hands.

A week in and I was getting into my lockdown stride, catching up on what felt like a lifetime's worth of sleep and spending my days cleaning, sorting, baking and watching episodes of *New Girl* on my iPad. If I wasn't doing any of that, I was catching up with friends over FaceTime or scrolling through endless articles about the pandemic. Of course, concern and uncertainty around the whole affair was very present, but I was enjoying being on my boat like never before and embracing the simplicity of my new life. I found I had space to sit and breathe. I was going to bed early and I was waking up early and when I sat out on deck in the mornings, with barely anyone around, I would watch the water and the wildlife, see carp swimming in the canal and birds building their nests for the arrival of their young. These are things that had been going on around me all this time, but I'd never seen them before.

The pace of everything I did was slower. Making breakfast, cleaning my windows, baking bread. I took my time with it all. Everything in my previous life had been so rushed. I was constantly running late for appointments, squeezing in meals and taking shortcuts with everything I did. I had got ill because I wasn't taking my time to build my fire properly. I had broken my finger because I was lacklustre and tired on a boat move. I had been burgled because I was drunk and hadn't taken the time to take my keys out of the front door. If this lockdown was teaching me anything, it was that I had been living my life brilliantly and fully, but it was madly chaotic and making me ill. As I sat out on deck and let my coffee go cold watching my new coot neighbours, I could see that as clearly as anything.

~~~~~~~

I was filling my time with boat jobs. I'd painted my bathroom – a job I'd wanted to do since buying the boat three years earlier. I fitted a new shelf in the bathroom and discovered the total ineffectiveness of a spirit level on a moving boat. I cleaned all my internal walls; I hadn't noticed how grubby they'd become. I played about with the layout inside, creating space by putting things in places that actually made sense. I sorted through my books and put the ones I'd read out on the towpath with a sign saying "Take me" next to a bottle of hand sanitiser. I cleaned out my engine bay, bottling up and disposing of the oily water in the sump and clearing out leaves and muck from the drainage system.

By the second week of lockdown, I'd run out of boat jobs I could do without enlisting help or spending a load of money, and I was on the lookout for a new project. I signed up to volunteer for the NHS telephone service, but it was oversubscribed and I never heard back. I googled more volunteer projects locally, finding that they were all oversubscribed. I wanted to help, to be part of the effort, but at the end of week two, I made peace with the best I could offer – to stay home.

I was still running. Not as much as during training, but several times a week I would head out and loop the grand concourse around Hyde Park. It was a novelty living so close to the famous landmark. I'd barely been before, the odd sightseeing day out when I first moved to London, and a gig the summer before, Florence and the Machine. I found the same bit of grass that had hosted the concert, now cordoned off with red and white tape. It was strange to imagine the area filled with thousands of revellers enjoying live music.

I stood and looked out at the dried grass that would have been prepared for another set of shows and I smiled at the memory. Lauryn had invited me to the gig, and Silly Season Will had bought a ticket too. The three of us stood shoulder to shoulder facing Florence on stage, a tiny speck in the distance made visible by two large screens either side of her. Her ethereal voice filled the sky.

I remember Will putting me on his shoulders. He was surprisingly strong, and my body floated up and above the crowd. He carried on dancing as we swayed in time with the music. I remember looking around the vast expanse of live music junkies. It was London at its finest. I looked to Lauryn, who was dancing in a world of her own and held out my hands to hers.

"You okay, Will?" I said to my packhorse.

"Never felt better," he said. I remember stroking his face. This was where we belonged.

I carried on with my run.

~~~~~~~

One morning I ran past a café by the Serpentine lake in Hyde Park. It was shut, obviously, and looked forlorn on a sunny afternoon when it would otherwise have been a hive of activity. The café had a chain and padlock across the brass handles – they were in need of a good polish. They wouldn't be shined for some time. In fact, no brass fixtures on any hospitality business would be polished while they were shut. I vowed to come back the next day with my Brasso and polish the handles.

So I did.

BRASSO BANDIT

And so began my next lockdown project, with anonymous Instagram account and published manifesto:

@thebrassobandit
5 April 2020
I am the Brasso Bandit.
Like many in the hospitality industry, my work has been stopped because of Covid-19. On my daily exercise trips I have been saddened that once shiny brass fixtures are shiny no more. Therefore, as your premises lay dark, I gift you my now unused skill of Brasso'ing. I will rub each day that I am furloughed.
May the world shine on.

I would go for a run each day, stuff a pot of Brasso, a rag and some gloves in my pocket and polish the outside brass of businesses that were shut because of Covid-19. I would post the before and after pictures on Instagram, tagging the location and any neighbouring businesses that may want to benefit from the same service. Finding businesses with brass fixtures was easy in West London and I would get up and do my Brasso'ing in the early hours to avoid the possibility of human contact. It was giving me some focus and the Instagram account seemed to be making people smile. I polished pub kick plates, shop handles, library door-knobs, a tanning salon letter box, a pizza restaurant push plate and a sign on the great tourist attraction of Madame Tussauds. I carried on polishing brass fixtures on closed businesses daily around Paddington, Maida Vale, Bayswater, Marylebone and Notting Hill. I would come back to the boat and tell Andrew about my latest Brasso antics as he ate his cereal out on deck and laughed along with his neighbour's strange new project.

I was stopped by the police in Hyde Park one day as I sat on the floor polishing a Princess Diana Memorial Plaque in the rose garden. It was a toughie; larger than any of the others with an intricate inlaid design. Two officers who had been moving people on approached on horses.

"Do you work here?" one said.

I stood up quickly, as if I was midway through a run and had only stopped to do up a shoelace.

"No, I just had some leftover polish and thought this could do with a shine." I could feel my face reddening, realising the absurdity of what this must have looked like.

The officer was confused. "Rrrrrright." His expression turned to pity as I think he concluded I must be a royal super fan; an admirer of the late princess paying my respects.

"It's okay," I said, "I'm done now." My heart was racing as I stuffed my rag and gloves into my pocket.

"That smell takes me back to my childhood," he said to the second officer, who looked less convinced. I walked to a nearby bin to chuck away my empty can of polish, took a deep breath and ran off.

Chapter 45
Listless

As the weather warmed up and encouraged us all outside, Andrew and I would spend time together on our respective back decks. Like the daffodils and tulips all around, our friendship was flourishing. Talking to Andrew had become an important daily check-in. As new friends, it felt there was no expectation and we were able to support each other as we came to terms with the ongoing pandemic and shared stories and jokes together across our decks.

"Have you seen Megan recently?" he said. Andrew and Megan had met on the towpath a few times now.

"A little, but not as much as before. I guess she's been working a lot," I said.

Megan and I had started our lockdown by doing yoga together in a green space nearby, but it hadn't lasted. In normal times we communicated through laughter and sharing, but with less to share or laugh about and very little variety in our lives, we were struggling to keep our relationship and conversations light and positive. I couldn't work out what was going on in her head, and I'm sure this was reciprocated. It seemed that the disruption going on in the world was not only felt in our own lives, but in the way we related to each other. I was finding it difficult to express myself with an old friend, but with Andrew I felt I could start again.

"That fucking sign on that restaurant," Andrew said one morning, pointing to the awning opposite.

"I know. It's cruel, isn't it?" I said.

"When this is over, let's go and eat there," he said.

"Great idea."

ALL BOATS ARE SINKING

We'd talk about what we wanted to do when we got back into the real world. What food we'd order and from where on our first night out, who we'd be with. It was lovely to imagine, and we indulged each other's suggestions by asking questions that really got to the crux of the fantasy. I was beginning to get an idea of Andrew's life pre-lockdown. He had a solid group of friends and clearly used to enjoy a busy social life. His partner was at university, but they'd make an effort to see each other on weekends. They'd been together for a few years and it sounded like a great relationship.

"I'm looking forward to meeting him," I said.

"God, I miss him," Andrew replied, looking out at the canal.

~~~~~~

A month in and colleagues were calling at all waking hours for friendly catch-ups and check-ins. They would process their own situation over the phone with me, trying to guess what the outcome would be for them following their time on furlough. Some were calm and confident that the company and their careers would return to normal soon enough. Others were nervous and starting to look for other jobs. I would remain consistent in my reaction, that I suspected I didn't have a job to return to, while hiding from them all the additional emotions that were bubbling away under the surface. In truth, my mind was racing with questions. Would I ever look that man in the eyes again? Was he thinking of me? Would he and the company survive this pandemic? There was little escape from these thoughts in the days and weeks that followed.

With the majority of my friends working in the arts, events and hospitality industries, the sudden change of circumstance had been much the same across the board. Theatre shows cancelled during rehearsals. Friends left homeless when tour contracts were postponed indefinitely. Some held onto positions by the skin of their teeth, knowing full well that the situation was volatile. Some hoped their roles would be taken too, joining the furlough contingent and bringing forward what they suspected to be inevitable.

LISTLESS

The speculative talk amongst my peers about the length and severity of what we were beginning to go through was all we had to talk about. And boy did we. My phone rang relentlessly. All the usual crew – Lauryn, Will, Sarah, Kelly and Caz, the Sunday soiree lot, Syd, and some friends who had been in my life less frequently – were now calling too. I was reconnecting with old friends – what a bizarre situation to have brought us closer together.

～～～～

I was structuring my days now with lists.

- Morning Pages [54]
- Meditate
- Short run / Brasso
- Read
- Lunch
- Write
- Job hunt
- Dinner
- Netflix
- Bed

---

54 If you've not already come across them, Morning Pages, a concept coined by author Julia Cameron in the book *The Artist's Way*, are like a dump of inner monologue first thing in the morning. Strictly three pages' worth. I've been doing them on and off for years.

ALL BOATS ARE SINKING

I had lists for boat jobs, creative projects, meals I wanted to cook, films, podcasts, books. Businesses I wanted to "pay it forward" to as soon as I was in employment again. Restaurants to support once this was all over. I seemed to spend all day every day rewriting my lists, desperate to combat the feeling of anxiety that had started to sit in the pit of my stomach. I wanted to be productive, but I was spending a lot of time agonising about my lack of productivity, and less time being productive.

There was ample to feel lucky about. I had the comparative fortune of being a homeowner, with no ties, and no danger of going hungry or being at risk of illness or injury like others. I had less income than usual through the furlough scheme but less outgoings too. I knew money would become an issue eventually, but for now there wasn't much I could do except spend as little as possible.[55] I took joy in living in every small corner of my floating home. Having spent years on a perpetual loop of career and social burnout, I knew this was a precious time to recharge. But I would flit between this peace and comfort and a heavy hopelessness. Feelings of loss, confusion and anger weighed on me and, like so many, if not all of us, my emotions were pushed to their extremes. Things I thought were beautiful before were even more beautiful now. The canal, my friendships, the stars that could be seen in the London sky as the pollution levels reduced. And things I despaired over were even more despairing; our government's slow response to the crisis, my future career prospects, the effect this would be having on my aged parents, my brothers grappling with work and home schooling and the strain on them and their partners. It was a complicated set of emotions.

The clap for carers brought all us boaters out on deck every Thursday at 8 p.m. Residents hung out of their windows from the tall blocks of flats and the houses around us. We rang our bells,

---

55 I understand buying things on the internet became popular during lockdown. With no address for home deliveries, I didn't fall into this trap, thankfully.

honked our horns, banged our saucepans and stood for a minute or two together, clapping for our key workers. The claps changed a little each week. They went from being humble and grateful to determined claps and thankful claps, and then sad, angry and lost claps. I would come outside just before it started, poised. Andrew would invariably rush to join once it started saying, "Gosh, is it Thursday already?"

Time had both stood still and passed us by.

~~~~~~~~~

Though the tourists were nowhere to be seen, and there were fewer boats, the towpath in Little Venice was busy. It had become an escape for residents and those walking from further afield during their allocated exercise time slot. Some of the London parks had been shut due to overcrowding, which added to the numbers walking up and down the narrow path. I didn't take umbrage at this myself. I felt folk were doing the best they could. For a lot of people, walking along the canal would be going somewhere to improve their mental health during this time. Some boaters did struggle, however, for their own equally valid reasons I'm sure, and would put up red tape around their boats, with signs telling dog walkers and runners to find somewhere else to go.

The towpath had become a place of increased tension, and arguments regularly broke out. I saw a woman scream and fall to the floor one day as she was being shouted at by a fellow towpath user. People were on edge. When I did take myself out for a run, I would run to Hyde Park and St James's Park. If my route included a bit of towpath, I would ensure my unmistakably boaty cork keyring was hanging out of my pocket so I didn't get yelled at by my fellow boaters. My London and my canal were starting to feel a little oppressive, and my frustration upon staying in the city was building.

ALL BOATS ARE SINKING

I was closing down from Megan. Our responses to the circumstances were very different and this was taking its toll on our relationship. I was struggling to adapt and desperate to do something. Megan appeared to me to be unaffected, and if she was struggling, she was doing better than me at internalising it. We were both trying to support each other but grappling with the need to put ourselves first in a complicated arrangement that had us thrown together. I resented staying in London and I could tell she was becoming increasingly impatient with me. It wasn't working, and we both knew it. Though I should have been grateful for human contact, I just wanted to be alone.

Chapter 46
Things That Never Got Crossed off During Lockdown

- Pass driving theory test
- Expand cocktail repertoire
- Tile kitchen
- Learn British Sign Language
- Paint boat exterior
- Knit scarf
- Learn boat knots
- Make cheese
- Keep plants alive
- Get a job

Chapter 47
On the Turn

Andrew came out of his boat in lockdown jogging bottoms and a hoodie I had seen quite a lot of since we had met. I seemed to rise earlier than most of my neighbours and spent an hour or so writing my morning pages on my roof to the soundtrack of birdsong and refuse collections. Occasionally I would write a date at the top of the page and it would trigger a distant memory. Something big was supposed to have happened on this date, I would think. Was it tickets to a show, or someone's birthday party? It was an odd feeling of missing out on something, but a thing that was now not happening anyway.

"Today's the day," Andrew said through a yawn. "Are you excited?"

"Most exciting thing that's happened in weeks," I said, closing my notebook and hopping down from my roof.

I was taking the boat to the waterpoint.[56] A short trip, but a chance for us to shift our boats around and something else to fill the time. When the water tank on *Argie* is nearly empty, the pump starts to overwork, and water splashes out of the tap in bursts. In normal times, I'll start to ration my dwindling water supply at this point, and I'll carry extra bottles on board for emergencies. I can go without showering for a few days, and regularly do, but inevitably after day three or four there will be a point when my skin and hair starts to feel a bit sticky. Megan calls this being "on

---

56 Getting water was an exception to the no-movement rule. For obvious reasons.

the turn", and though us boaters are used to it, I do worry that land dwellers are less tolerant of my grubby tendencies. Water points are located all along the network, so in theory it shouldn't be too long before the tank is full up again, it just takes a bit of planning. During lockdown, though, with a tap so close, we had no excuse.

Andrew planned to do the same manoeuvre a few weeks later. *His tank must be bigger than mine*, I thought, or else he showered less. (I doubt that.)

Andrew's boat is a few feet longer than *Argie*, navy blue, with decking and plants and storage boxes on the roof. I hadn't been inside so couldn't say what the interior looked like. His boat was canal-side and mine was towpath side, so Andrew would need to untie his ropes to let me out.

We were giddy with excitement as we started the manoeuvre. My ropes were damp with spring dew as I untied them and placed them on my roof. Andrew loosened a grip on his rope and let his boat drift out into the centre of the canal. I started my engine and reversed out carefully. Andrew reached his arms high and cracked his rope along the roof of my boat, ready to pull his in once I'd cleared the area.

"See you in a bit," he said, bringing his boat towards the towpath where mine had once sat.

"Make sure no one else takes my space," I said over the sound of the engine.

"Oh, of course," said Andrew.

The voyage would see me cruise west for 20 minutes or so, turn around at Sainsbury's at Kensal Rise and travel back on myself to the Little Venice waterpoint. Filling up my tank would take 30 minutes, watering my plants another two and journeying back to join Andrew's boat ten.

Taking the boat to the waterpoint was the most exciting thing to happen during lockdown.

Water tank full, I returned to the mooring spot where Andrew's boat now occupied the towpath side. I pulled my boat in to join his. The light was different, the view was different. It was the change neither of us knew we were craving.

Chapter 48
2.6

St Mary Magdalene Church in Maida Vale had a statue outside of Jesus nailed to the cross. I'd been eyeing it up as a potential Brasso job. I was still doing my polishing. It was the only structure I had to my days, and while I found I was unable to concentrate on any bigger projects, this low-level engagement was perfectly manageable. It was Easter Sunday, an appropriate day for this one. I ran up to the church and stopped at the base of JC, though I soon realised it was a golden statue and wouldn't take well to being Brasso'd.

I stayed put for a moment, looking up at the son of God. We were going into the fourth week of lockdown, and his helpless expression felt perfectly relatable. Now, I'm an atheist, there's not an ounce of religion in my being, but I grew up with it. My grandfathers were both vicars, my dad a church warden and my mum wouldn't be the steadfast human she is without the strength she finds from the God that she follows. My respect for (and sometimes outright defence of) the Church in which I was brought up is a powerful force, and while I feel guilt and shame at times when I'm in the presence of anything remotely religious, I also feel a strength and a sense of place within the context of Christianity. (I know, confusing huh.)

I mark these festival days as if I was Christian. Caz and I usually observe Lent each year by giving something up (she is my only other friend brought up in a faith household). This year, though, it felt like a stretch, having inadvertently given up so much already, so for the first time in my life, I hadn't. Despite the lack of festivities, Easter Sunday felt significant. The experience of loss and the prospect of starting over was more relevant than ever. I stood fixed to the spot looking up at the shiny naked beauty before me and my bottom lip began to wobble. I hadn't cried since the lockdown started. My shoulders felt like they had been tense for a month. As I cried, the tension within my body released. I stood there in the morning sunshine outside the closed-up church and sobbed.

I missed my family. Easter would have been an occasion for us all to be together, and I had no idea when that would happen again. We would often all travel back to Ipswich for Easter Sunday. My brothers and their partners with an extra niece or nephew in tow, the faction expanding year on year. The family home would be loud with Mum and Dad performing their well-rehearsed partnership in the kitchen. The smell of roast lamb and simnel cake filled the house. Jazz or folk music would blare from the record player in the lounge as we dusted off Dad's record collection. It was a memory that warmed my heart and made me desperately sad.

As I looked up at Jesus's statue, I realised I was grieving all that I had lost. I longed to see my friends sitting together on a picnic table in a beer garden, watching the day unfold together. I wanted mine and Megan's friendship to return to how it had been before lockdown. I wanted to be held in a man's arms again. Any man, any arms. Hell, I was that close to hugging the statue. I stood for several minutes wiping tears from my cheeks, sighed a deep sigh and walked the last bit of the journey back to my boat to be greeted by Andrew, who was out on deck eating his usual bowl of cornflakes.

"I'd like to cook lamb for Megan later," I said. "Do you want a plate?"

"Sounds lovely," he said.

Later that day, Megan sat on my deck chatting to Andrew, who was sitting out on his, while I prepared dinner inside. Roast lamb, followed by hot cross buns and the requisite amount of sickly chocolate treats. It was comforting hearing them bond while I cooked. There was less formality between Megan and me. Maybe it was Andrew's presence. Maybe it was the gesture of a cooked meal. Maybe we just needed some space to reconfigure. Either way, things seemed to be improving.

ALL BOATS ARE SINKING

I called out to Megan, "Oh Megan. I've messaged Ben."

We'd met Ben at a Tooting soiree a year or so before. He and Megan had got on well, but he had a girlfriend at the time. I had recently found out that Ben and his girlfriend were no more, and he'd taken a job working in a fish shop down the road in Notting Hill while the restaurant he worked at as a chef was shut. I took the opportunity to message him and invite him to say a quick hello on Easter Sunday.

"Innnnntterresttttiinnnggg," Megan said. "What did you say to him?"

"I told him to pop by for a towpath chat." I was being purposefully blase, but I knew this would be big news for Megan.

He came by, just as he said he would, gifted us some lobster butter, spoke mostly with Megan and left. I looked at Andrew, who gave me a wink and mouthed "well done".

~~~~~~~~

Two weeks after Easter Sunday was the day I was supposed to have been running the London Marathon. I wanted to continue raising funds for the charity I was signed up with, Children with Cancer UK, knowing their fundraising shortfall would be enormous with the event not taking place. But after spending weeks living off a diet of chocolate and bread, I was far from match fit. I had the "one hour a day of exercise" to use, but I wasn't using it religiously and I didn't have long distance running in me.

I asked my friends to come up with a load of challenges involving the numbers two six two – 26.2 miles being the length of the London Marathon. I would complete some of these challenges on the big day, film it and ask Caz (who was also currently not working) to edit the footage together.

The suggestions I received were:

* Eat 262 Maltesers
* Drink 262 shots

* Think it's unfair to use Covid-19 to get out of this tbh. Just run the 26 miles?
* Do a headstand for 26.2 seconds
* Do 262 slut drops
* Fit 26.2 marshmallows in your mouth
* Have 2.62 orgasms
* Brasso 10 things (2+6+2)
* Eat 26.2 Snickers bars

And these are the ten I went for:

* Run 2.62 miles
* Eat 26.2 Mini Eggs
* Have a 2.62-hour nap
* Do 26.2 sit-ups
* Write a poem in 26.2 words[57]
* Eat an ice cream in 262 licks
* Eat 262 ingredients
* Wiggle my bottom 262 times
* List 26 things I love about my life
* Make cocktails with 26.2-millilitre measures

For the running part of the challenge, I ran to the Mall in St James's Park, which is where the marathon would have ended. I saw other runners wearing their charity vests like me. Some were crouched down in contemplation. Others were crying. Some were being hugged by their partners. It had been quite the journey training for the marathon, and the disappointment to not run it was amplified by being in St James's Park. The whole experience of lockdown

---

57 "Have no doubt"
   Boris will shout
   There's a flour drought
   Baking is the new Out Out
   Kids are doing their work-outs
   And I'm not doing the Ma... :(

just felt like one big disappointment. So much had been missed; by everyone.

I came back home and completed the rest of the challenges, filming as I went. In order to achieve the high count needed for the "eat 262 ingredients" challenge, I cooked elaborate dishes from my Ottolenghi cookbook, gifting baked treats to neighbouring boats. I drew some attention during my bum wiggles and felt sick and exhausted from everything else.

A new neighbour, George, had shuffled his boat away from flowering trees that were covering his solar panels and tied up next to mine and Andrew's, so his stern was facing ours. We quickly became friendly. A hairdresser and upholsterer by trade, and a mean cocktail barman, he had set up a makeshift bar on his bow for the final hour of the day's challenges. Megan, Andrew and I had a socially distanced cocktail hour, each of us leaning towards George's boat to have our glasses topped up by our very own mixologist. Ben (the fish chef) messaged to say he would pop by for another towpath hello.

Megan had put on make-up this time.

Chapter 49
Black Swan

Caz had done a great job on the video. She had taken the clips I had sent her and edited together a nifty little fundraising film. I'm not sure why I forwarded it to Jonathan... maybe just to let him know I was surviving fine without him. We'd been messaging a bit. I said I hoped he was okay. He said he hoped I was. He asked if I would like a visit. I said no, we're in a fucking pandemic.

I would text him in the evening after a glass of wine and regret it every single morning. All superficial rubbish really. I wanted to ask him about how he was feeling about me, but true to form, I didn't. I know he could have explained himself and his actions... he had no choice but to make me redundant, it was unprecedented... and so on. But I felt nauseated about the whole thing. He'd made me feel inadequate in the months[58] building up to this, that was clear now. It wasn't just a response to Covid-19. This had been brewing, and the pandemic had given him an out. I knew I needed to never see that man again.

———

I was in St James's Park sat on the grass across from Kelly. We were friends from work, but weirdly, since lockdown and our numerous phone call check-ins, we had grown even closer as friends away from work. Kelly had cycled up from South London, and we were drinking non-alcoholic beers and having our first in-person

---

58 Years

catch-up since lockdown started. The park was strewn with people doing the same. Despite the media coverage, the environment was mellow and in no way exhibiting the usual summer frivolities found in London parks. No music systems, no boozy picnics. Just pairs having precious and brief catch-ups in the sunshine.

"How are you getting on?" I said, though I could tell Kelly was owning her lockdown experience. It had been months since I'd last seen her and she was looking fantastic.

"I feel fucking amazing," she said.

"You *look* amazing," I said.

She'd given up alcohol and taken up fitness in a big way.

"I feel positive and energised and I'm sleeping really well."

She was living alone and using her free time to enjoy painting and exercising. This lockdown was having a great effect on my friend. She'd worked hard for years. The career break was deserved, and she was using it well.

"I've got you a present," she said.

Kelly took a brown envelope out of the basket on the front of her bike and gave it to me. I opened it and pulled out an A5 painting of a black swan against a backdrop of *Argie Bargie* blue-themed swirls.

"It's the black swan you told me about."

On my runs in Hyde Park, I had been enjoying watching a solo black swan swimming gracefully in the Round Pond. I'd sent a picture of the swan to Kelly and she had painted it for me.

"Wow, Kelly. It's beautiful," I said. "Thank you so much."

I was emotional and sad that I couldn't give her a hug. There was something sobering about being here with Kelly. Apart from Megan and Andrew, I'd not really seen anyone for months and felt like I had become consumed with a few small aspects of my life. Kelly and her gift had the effect of waking me up to that. As if intuitively, she stretched her legs out in the sun and asked, "Are you still thinking about going away?"

"I was," I said. "But I guess with things likely to open up soon, I'm not sure it's wise anymore."

"Hannah, do it."

Kelly doesn't mince her words, and I think she also knew I wouldn't have a job to go back to.

"You enjoy your own company, right?" she said.

"Oh yeah," I said. "More than ever."

"You won't get another chance. Do it," she said, pointing her finger at my face.

"Yeah, you're probably right."

"I *am* right."

I laughed. "It's good to see you, Kelly."

Our hour was up. I walked back to the boat thinking hard about what Kelly had said. She was right, this was my chance. I was so ready to leave London and to embark on something new. What excuse did I have? I decided I would tell Megan the next day that I was going away as soon as lockdown lifted. She had started to see more of Ben and didn't need me around anymore. As soon as I could, I was taking my boat out of London and on a voyage to the North of England.

I came back and told Andrew.

"I'm doing it," I said. "Are you coming?"

"Really?" he said.

"Really."

Chapter 50
Adios, Amigo

I had a plan. I would take the boat to Rickmansworth. Andrew would follow a few weeks later. We'd spend a week moored together in the countryside before separating. My goal was then to journey up to Todmorden in West Yorkshire where my brother Matthias and his family lived. Travelling all that way on my own, through 250 locks, did feel a bit ambitious, but it was something to aim for and I figured I could always turn back.

I typed the journey to my brother's into CanalPlanAC, an online resource for calculating journey times. It said it would take me 28 days if I cruised seven hours a day. I surmised that some additional time would be needed for any unforeseen boat issues. I would plan to stay in Todmorden for five days, then turn around and come back down to London in time for autumn, when I figured businesses would likely be recruiting again and I would get a new job as the UK workplace surely returned to some normality. Or, I might find a job on the way, and a new community to live in. I might find love and never come back to London. It was all up for grabs.

I was beyond excited about the plan and eager to get going. I had a few days left in London before boats were allowed to move again, one of which was Megan's birthday. She'd requested a Mexican-themed feast for her birthday, and she brought her boat to join mine, George's and Andrew's, so our four back decks played host as margaritas and an abundance of Mexican-style dishes provided by Ben were plated up for each of us. I was in good spirits, knowing I was leaving, and Megan was delighted with her day.

The following day, we said goodbye to each other. It was an understated farewell, and we didn't talk about where I was headed, or what my plans were. I was a little confused. Things had been getting better between us, but this felt formal again. Perhaps Megan thought it was all a little too far-fetched and I'd be back soon enough. It's also entirely plausible that we had just spent too much time together during an already very intense period. We'd been seeing each other three or four times a week in early lockdown for coffees on the towpath, yoga in the park, trips to the laundrette. It had been a lot and once things returned to normal, I imagined a healthier friendship dynamic would surely resume. I hoped so. She'd been my friend for years, and it seemed a shame to let a global pandemic come between us.

Chapter 51
A Popular Lockdown Cocktail

LOCKDOWN LEMON MERINGUE SOUR (MAKES 1)

To be served in a coupe glass

Ingredients:
25 ml gomme syrup (50/50 water sugar mix)
1 x egg white
50 ml limoncello
25 ml lemon juice
25 ml vanilla vodka
Ice
Crumbly meringue (supermarket is fine)
Lemon zest

Method:
Dry shake (no ice) the egg white with the gomme syrup
and lemon juice in a cocktail shaker.
Add the ice, limoncello and vanilla vodka.
Shake well.
Strain into glass.
Crumble the meringue over the top and sprinkle lemon zest
shavings on top.

Chapter 52
Cooties

On the morning of 27 May 2020 I sat on my blue garden chair watching the activity from the coots' nest opposite, which had been built two months prior. The female had since laid eggs and the couple were doing everything in their power to keep their young alive. I'd witnessed it all. I'd watched the female with her splayed toes accidentally knock two of her eggs into the water and try desperately to retrieve them while the male stood on the bank cleaning his wings, totally unaware. He joined her, still seemingly none the wiser, just as she tried one last time to scoop them out while they fell further down into gaps in the weeds like a marble run. A futile attempt. That marked the end of that short chapter in their young's life. She swam off from the nest, for what I imagined to be time alone to grieve. It was heartbreaking to watch. The other three eggs hatched. Two were strong and one frail. Andrew and I would message each other from inside our boats whenever we caught sight of the third cootie.[59]

"Number three spotted at 0900 hr. It's looking a bit stronger."

I'd watched them take their first swim a few weeks earlier, shouting to my neighbour inside his boat, "Andrew! They're off!"

I didn't consider that he might be working or on a call to colleagues. I knew he'd want to see this. He rushed out and stood on his back deck leaning across to get a closer look.

---

59 The actual name for a baby coot.

"Go on, little one. You got this," he said. We stood watching like a proud auntie and uncle as the cooties gained confidence in the water.

I sat and watched one final time and smiled. Though a recent turf war had broken out between the coots and a mallard, I had strong hopes for the family's survival. They'd come this far.

It hadn't been so bad staying put in West London for lockdown, as it goes. I'd met Andrew, a funny and kind soul. I would laugh to myself that I ever thought him a potential lover and was excited to see how our friendship would develop in the future, with his partner joining as we ate in that "fucking restaurant" opposite. I was going to miss him and suspected he might not actually follow me to Rickmansworth. Though we'd only known each other a short while, we'd been through a lot together.

I'd also discovered many corners of Hyde Park and the picturesque vicinity during lockdown. In my last week there, I'd managed to go on a few walks with friends to say goodbye. I didn't know it at the time, but these encounters would become confined to nostalgia far quicker than I imagined.

It was a gorgeous summer's morning as I prepared to leave my lockdown perch. I'd cancelled a Zoom quiz the night before, stating to the organiser Lauryn that I needed to get ready for my big voyage. A fair excuse, I thought. Except on this occasion, I had nothing to prepare. I didn't need to pack or make any arrangements for going away. Everything I owned was coming with me, and I had no loose ends to tie up.

I put my chairs and table on the roof, quietly so as to not awaken any neighbours that had slept through the morning's bird fights. I untied Megan's birthday bunting from my tiller and placed it under a plant pot on her deck. I lifted up my boards and climbed into the engine bay to do my checks and have a look in the weed hatch. I was shocked to see a beard of weeds attached to my propeller. It was alien green. I suppose that's what happens in stagnant water: things grow. I put my hands in and pulled on the beard, dragging clumps of the stuff out of the canal and chucking it on to the towpath. Small black leech type creatures were wiggling around inside it.

Andrew came out in his signature dressing gown and watched as I secured my weed hatch and put the boards back down.

"Big day. How are you feeling?" he asked.

"I'm a bit nervous, actually, but excited too," I said.

Aside from getting water, I hadn't moved my boat in over two months. I was unsure how my driving would be after all this time, what lay ahead of me in unknown waters and whether *Argie*, and more specifically *Argie*'s engine, was up to the voyage. I'd never journeyed more than a mile or two at any time, and being in London I had numbers for engineers to call if I encountered issues with my engine. In London I knew where to go for anything boat related. The right chandlers for gas, coal, diesel, ropes. Which taps had the best water pressure. I knew where moorings were easy to find and where it was trickier to get a spot along the towpath. I knew which areas were well lit and where taxis could drive close to the boat at night-time. I knew where the bins were and the location of the nearest B&Q. I was familiar and comfortable with this city. My home for the past 11 years, and my canal home for the past three.

"This might be the last day I ever live in London," I said, starting my engine.

"Ah, you'll be back," Andrew said.

I wasn't so sure, and the thought made me very sad indeed. My friendship groups and my career had been created in London, and I adored all that the city had to offer. It had been a strange place to be over the past few months. Without culture and a bustling nightlife and the underground trains and the pubs, it hadn't felt like London at all. But it was still home.

"I'll miss you," I said, untying my ropes.

"I'll be joining you in a few weeks," Andrew said, handing me my back line.

Our boats had started to separate. I looked back towards Andrew, gave him a smile and a cursory Covid-friendly wave, and was off. I had built up to this day for months and had surprised myself that

ALL BOATS ARE SINKING

I was actually doing it. I knew I would make it to Rickmansworth. But how far thereafter? I had no idea. I'd been nervous in the days leading up to this moment. But as I turned to face the canal and looked ahead at just the first small bend, it didn't look so scary.

"Are you ready for your next adventure?" I said in a low voice to the boat beneath me. "Because I am."

Chapter 53
Culinary Achievements On Board

- Hot spiced cider atop stove
- Baked potatoes (regular and sweet) in the stove
- Lockdown cocktails
- Posh canapes for a hen do
- Pastel de nata [60]
- Home grown veg and salads
- Roast dinners
- Mince pies
- Bakewell tarts
- Orangettes (caramelised orange peel dipped in chocolate)
- Hot cross buns

---

60 Doing this without a fridge, in the height of summer, deserves a big Portuguese snog.

Part 4

Down a Lock

Chapter 54
Contentedness

The Grand Union

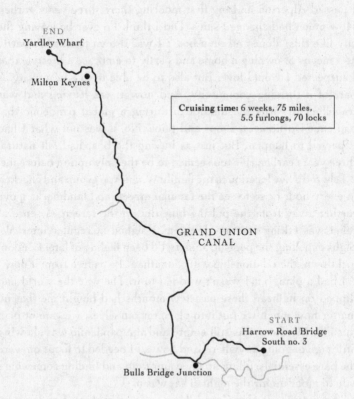

END
Yardley Wharf

Milton Keynes

Cruising time: 6 weeks, 75 miles,
5.5 furlongs, 70 locks

GRAND UNION
CANAL

START
Harrow Road Bridge
South no. 3

Bulls Bridge Junction

ALL BOATS ARE SINKING

Lack of activity had given way to crystal clear waters. I spotted all the usual suspects on the canal bed as I left West London – a bicycle, shopping trolley, a child's scooter, remnants of a busier world sat motionless at the bottom. I was pleased to see abundant plant life too: rope-like vegetation dancing under the surface, lily-pads with buds reaching towards the May sunshine, and birds' nests built on floating logs in the centre of the channel. Nature taking advantage of lockdown. I felt guilty moving through the water, so I journeyed slowly, keeping clear of birds and their young.

As I meandered west, the boats thinned and the waters widened. I passed Alperton and my first mooring there three years earlier. How much had changed since. Did I think I'd ever be leaving the city like this; alone and on a boat? I was drawn to this life partly as a means of owning a home and partly to embrace a lifestyle that I suspected I would love. But also to be able to live in my city as part of a thriving community. And now I was leaving and was travelling towards the unknown, during a global pandemic that had shut workplaces, shops and pubs. No, it was not what I had expected to happen. But just as buying the boat had felt natural three years earlier, this too seemed to be the only option before me.

I shared a live location to my family WhatsApp group and checked in every hour or so to see the familiar streets and landmarks move further away from the pulsing blue dot on the screen. A sense of relief was taking over my body, as I sighed at regular intervals. Sighs expelling the pent-up anxiety I'd been feeling of late. London, lockdown, the relationship with Jonathan. I was free from it now.

I had a plan, but I wasn't wedded to it. The way the world had flipped on its head these past few months had taught me that no matter how much we put into place for ourselves, we cannot plan this life. My diary was still empty and the pandemic was showing little sign of going anywhere, and now all I needed to focus on were the bare essentials; filling up my water tank and finding somewhere safe to moor up for the night. That was it.

The stretch of the Grand Union Canal out of London was flat and I journeyed through several miles of lock-less water.

CONTENTEDNESS

There were stretches through industrial estates, a golf course and over an aqueduct above the North Circular motorway. As I cruised to the edges of the city, there were far fewer boats, people and buildings. Several hours in, I arrived at Greenford, where I stopped for water. I pulled in on the bend I'd seen marked on my Nicholson canal map,[61] hopping onto the towpath and securing my boat to the rings. In central London I felt self-conscious manoeuvring the boat in front of fellow boaters and gongoozlers,[62] but here, away from watchful eyes, I felt capable. I could do this, I thought. I could travel solo up the length of the country. With my newfound confidence, I hooked up my hose to the tap, went inside and showered with the doors open. It was wild. As my tank filled, I made up a light lunch, and with clean skin and hair, headed off for the next leg of the first day on my voyage.

From Greenford I continued west and found a stretch of concrete in front of a row of houses in Southall, where another boat was tied up. It looked like a sensible place to moor for the night. I pulled in, confidently again, and tied my boat on to the rings. As I bent down to secure my backline, I noticed a cyclist had stopped a few metres from me. I recognised him from earlier on in my journey when he'd given me a wave and a warm hello. This time, however, his presence felt less comfortable. He pulled out a camera phone and held it up to me.

"Smile love," he said.

Really, I thought. A familiar fatigue for such an obvious sexist trope that was at worst slightly threatening, but mostly boring.

"No, thank you. Please don't take a photo of me." I was staring down the cyclist. He laughed and put his camera away and I went inside before he had a chance to say another word. I locked my door and stood for a moment, waiting until I could hear him leave

---

61 A canal map book. Apps exist, but they're not quite as good as the printed versions yet... plus, a book is a little easier to use in the rain.

62 A gongoozler is "a person who enjoys watching boats and activities on the canal" (*Cambridge Dictionary*).

before I moved again. I wasn't going to let this encounter affect my mood, but it was perhaps a necessary pointer. I was travelling solo now, in unknown parts with fewer neighbours. Showering with the door open, I decided, was a little silly. I would take more care going forward.

~~~~~~~

I set a routine of running to my next mooring spot before moving the boat for the day, which gave me a chance to scout out the journey and ensure there was space for my boat. Plus, I'd be achieving some good mileage on my runs. So, on my first morning waking up outside of central London I ran about 5 miles from Southall to Uxbridge. The towpath was dry in the summer sun and as I ran, I kicked up dust and dandelion seeds into the sky. Once I could see the stretch at Uxbridge with plenty of mooring spaces I turned around and ran back to Southall, ate breakfast and started my engine, ready to do the same journey again, this time by boat.

I left my spot and began cruising. The landscape I'd just run through looked different from the boat. The distance from the boat to the towpath is only a few yards, but the architecture of the canals tells another story from my back deck. The way the bridges frame the vista and the water paves a line through the lowest point. The relationship between the canal with its solid course and the tumbling surroundings isn't captured from the towpath. It's uneven and awkward. But from the centre of the canal, it's purposeful and spectacular. I would continue marvelling at this difference for the rest of my voyage.

The further I travelled west, the bigger the sky appeared. It was less built up, with more space between buildings. The canal widened and the towpath turned from concrete to gravel to dust. The air smelled different, with more vegetation and less fumes. I reached the turning that would take me either left to the Thames and where I'd first picked up the boat, or right, to the North. *How easy it would be to loop around at this point*, I thought. Head down the Thames and back up through Limehouse to join my bustling East London community; to meet up with a friend for a coffee on the towpath or while away the hours chatting to a friendly new neighbour out on our back decks. But I didn't. I turned right at Bull's Bridge Junction and headed north. Straight after the turning I pulled into a marina, filled up my diesel tank and purchased some mooring chains.

"You're the first boat we've had through in months," said the man who filled up my diesel tank. "Where are you headed?"

The quiet setting and the man's question evoked that common scene from films set in Midwest America. The rickety motel and petrol station, with a solo traveller stopping by to fill up their truck with gas.

"To West Yorkshire," I said.

"On your own?" he said.

"Yes."

He exhaled sharply through his lips. "You're brave."

Brave about what? I wondered as I left. Travelling along unknown waters? Doing a bunch of locks on my own? What did he mean? I didn't ask. I'm not sure I wanted to know.

Tank full, I cruised to Uxbridge, where I found a shaded spot to moor up. I went inside and stared at my map – a fold-out map of canals and rivers[63] that I had cut down to size and mounted onto my cabin wall with Blu-Tack – while the kettle boiled. Each canal grouping is a different colour in accordance with the corresponding guidebook. The Grand Union (book 1), green. The Kennet and Avon (book 7), purple, and so on. Arrowhead symbols on the map mark the locations of the locks. I took out a biro and circled the areas where the lock symbols were particularly dense. The circles grew bigger the further north I drew. The canals and rivers, like roots on a tree, scurried their way along the pages, hard joins between colours, gaps where tunnels took the boats through

---

63 The Collins *Inland Waterways Map of Great Britain*

land, lines perforated when the waters were unnavigable. I took out some stickers from a drawer. Little coloured dots. I stuck them along the London network, where I'd travelled to date. I would add a dot or two each time I moored up, creating my own tree root. I put the stationery away and thumbed the line between London and Todmorden. I finished making my cup of tea and stood back leaning against the kitchen counter and looked up at the map. *Could I go all the way to Todmorden?* I thought. It was 250 miles and roughly the same number of locks. It would be an epic voyage if I made it. But could I do it on my own?

My excitement had waned. But in its place was something I've always valued more. Contentment. My boat and I were headed for the countryside now. Uxbridge was giving me my first taste of freedom in months and the view out of my window was surprisingly green and as beautiful as I'd hoped it would be. Apart from the man at the marina, I'd not spoken to anyone all day. I'd need to get used to that. But maybe I already had.

Chapter 55
Rickmansworth

To my delight, Andrew did catch me up, just as he said he would, and we found ourselves once again side by side in Rickmansworth. His partner Danny had moved in, having just finished his degree in Brighton. After Rickie they planned to carry on cruising over the summer, up the Oxford Canal and back to London via the Thames. Andrew was working from home, but only half-days, so he'd work in the mornings and they'd head off in the afternoons. They had their own adventure ahead of them and I could tell they were excited.

At Rickmansworth there were elderflower trees along the towpath, and, just as we'd dreamed, we were woken by horses cantering past our boats every morning. Boaters that had left London and come here for lockdown had well and truly set up camp, with awnings and extensions spilling out onto the towpath and plant pots marking each boat's territory. Probably because of lockdown, it felt like we'd turned up to a festival on the last day. It was all a bit scruffy and unkempt, with no one around but shells of firepits and well-used barbecues.

I spent my time in Rickmansworth running, baking brownies for Andrew and Danny and making bottles and bottles of elderflower cordial for, well... me, I guess. Danny and Andrew were reconnecting after their time apart, so I was keen to respect their alone time. It was just like lockdown had been, though. Andrew and I had catch-ups out on deck in the mornings and on a few evenings the three of us lay on our roofs and watched the sun go down together. After our week was up, it was time for me to head off again. We'd already had the big goodbye, so this one felt easier.

Less significant. That said, I had a strong sense that I was now on my own. He was my last connection to London and this was the start of the next big leg. I was flying solo now.

"Would you like a hand with the locks?" Andrew said as he helped with my ropes.

"I'd love you to," I said, "but no."

Until this point in my time as a boater, remarkably I'd had friends and strangers help with every lock I'd ever been through. Either I'd timed my moves with others, or enlisted people to assist. Three years, and I had never operated a lock solo.

"It's time I did one alone," I said.

I left Rickmansworth on the morning of 9 June 2020 and approached Stockers Lock just north of the town. I pulled into the lock landing at the bottom of the lock and hopped onto the towpath with my rope in my hand. I looked up at the impressive lock ahead of me. It was big[64] and powerful, with water seeping from gaps in the gates. The chamber was full of water, and I needed to empty it before I could cruise in and travel up the lock. I tied my boat up to the black and white bollard marking the first stage of the lock operation, tightly, so that the boat wouldn't be pulled away by the current as I emptied the water from the lock chamber. I took each movement slowly, with a care I hadn't taken since I first moved onto the boat. It felt new again, the ropes heavy and awkward in my hands. My feet felt small and precise. With the boat tied up securely I walked up the hill to the first set of gates with my windlass in hand. I attached my windlass to the cog-toothed bar of the paddle gear – the mechanism that opens the paddles (like underwater mini gates) – and turned slowly, lifting the underwater paddles to release the water. I'd done this before, but I took my time, setting a precedent for the next 250 or so locks.

The water whooshed out and into the pound below, where my boat was tied up. *Argie* bounced against the bank with the wash,

---

64 Double-width to allow for more than one boat.

and I stared at the centre line, hoping I'd tied it up tightly enough. After ten minutes or so there was calm, the lock empty and my boat where I'd left it. I leant against the lock gate on the same side as *Argie* with my whole body and waited for the remaining water pressure in the chamber to ease. Once I felt a slight movement from the gate, I pushed my body hard against the gate and it slowly opened. I walked over the footbridge and opened the second gate.

I ran back to the boat, untied the rope and cruised the boat in. Once in, I took my centre line in my hand and climbed the ladder inside the lock, tucking my windlass into my denim short belt hook. The steps were slippery. I knew this was something I'd need to consider each time I climbed these ladders; any lapse of judgement could be very dangerous. I climbed up to the top of the lock chamber, still holding the rope, tied the boat onto the centre bollard on the edge of the concrete and laid the rope alongside, ready to run and grab it if needed. The boat was clear inside the chamber and secured in position. I returned to the gates and shut them one at a time.

Andrew had told me that the best way to operate a double-width lock is to open the paddle on the side where the boat is sitting first. This way, the water bounces against the opposite wall and on to the boat's edge, keeping it in position. This stops the boat from bouncing about inside a lock that is designed for two. Once this first paddle is opened and the lock is half full, the second paddle can be lifted, and the boat should stay still, hugging the same wall. I did just as he'd told me, opening the paddles on the side the boat was positioned in first, and sure enough the boat stayed still. As I waited for the chamber to fill, I sat on the lock gate and watched as *Argie* rose up to my level.

Someone approached from a group sitting at a picnic table nearby.

"Can I help?" he said with the voice of a heavy smoker.

"No thank you, I'm fine," I said cheerily.

"You get on the boat. I'll open the gates and you can cruise out." I could tell he knew what he was doing and was keen to help, but I explained the situation.

"It's okay, I'd like to do it alone."

"Oh right," he said, looking a little disappointed.

"I've been on the boat for three years and never done a lock on my own before," I said, explaining my reasoning.

"Oh goodness. Well, good luck, then," he said with a thumbs up, walking away.

The water levelled and I opened the gate on the side where *Argie* was tied up. With the lock so big, I decided that I didn't need to open both gates. I could just slip out of the one gate. I walked back to the boat and climbed on to the back deck. I slowly cruised out of the lock, tying the boat up once again on to the landing at the top of the lock and shutting the gate behind me. I hopped back on to the boat and cruised off. As I left, I heard rapturous applause. I turned to see the man who offered to help sitting with his friends. They were cheering and waving and clapping.

I burst out laughing.

"Thank you," I said, shouting over the engine. I turned back around and faced the direction of travel. I was beaming with pride.

One down.

Chapter 56
Grand Union

Over the next few weeks, as I cruised through Hertfordshire along the Grand Union Canal, I had helpers assist with locks, including an old friend, Johna, and his partner, Laura. Johna and I had worked together as theatre makers in our early twenties. He is a master of puns and extremely well turned out, with an extensive wardrobe of fine waistcoats and tailored suits.[65] They lived in Watford and popped along for the stretch through the shaded woodland of Cassiobury Park. Sadly, Johna wasn't sporting a waistcoat, but they were both excellent helpers and enjoyed getting out for the day with their cameras and a million questions about boat life.

While Laura ran up to a lock gate, Johna took the opportunity to tell me his big news.

"I'm going to ask Laura to marry me."

Knowing she was watching, I kept calm as I said under my breath, "Ahhhhhhhhh. So wonderful."

"I've had the ring for ages," he said, "but our dream holiday to Canada was cancelled, of course."

Johna and I had been friends for years. He was a beautiful human, and I was delighted with the man he had become. Laura was fantastic.

"Let's do this again on the way back," I said to them both as they left.

---

65 Interesting fact: Johna is a quadruplet. And he looks just like Ewan McGregor.

"When will that be?" Laura asked.

"I've no idea." *But you'll be engaged*, I thought.

Silly Season Will had chosen to spend lockdown with his mum in the East Midlands. In part this was due to his desire to be close to her, but also because of his love[66] of fishing and her proximity to canals and rivers. He drove to see me one afternoon, arriving with a fishing rod and wearing a facemask. Maintaining social distance, he stood along the gunwales of my boat as we cruised along, a fake rubber fish (bait, apparently) trailing through the water behind us.

Dressed in navy football shorts, long white socks and an Oxford University football team rain mac, he looked, as ever, young and boyish. It was a different Will to the London version I'd got to know so well, and the rod was a novel addition to on-board accessories. He was in good spirits and would shout across to fellow anglers on the towpath.

"Caught anything?"

"Yeah, couple," they would say. "You?"

"Nah." There was an acceptance in his voice, like he knew it was never going to happen.

"You know you can't really catch anything when the boat's moving?" one fisherman said to Will.

"Yeah," he said, in the same happy-go-lucky manner. Will was working for a big pub company when the pandemic hit and had been furloughed indefinitely. He had the air of someone who had been waited on with cooked meals and countryside living for the past four months.

"It's like retirement," he said, throwing the rod back out and narrowly missing my ear. "I'm well rested, breathing in clean air. It's great."

"Reckon you'll go back to burning that candle again?" I said.

"Oh, definitely," he said.

---

66 Obsession

I smiled and marvelled at his zeal. Lovely Will, who is capable of living entirely in the moment. Watching him hang off the boat, I pined to be closer to him. Will would be on board when I approached my first swing bridge. A swing bridge is a structure that enables traffic (foot or cars) to cross the canal but can be swung on a pivot out of the way, allowing for boat passage.

"Right, how does this work, then?" said Will, hopping off the boat and onto the towpath.

"I've no idea," I said, wrapping my centre line round a bollard but staying by the boat. "Is there any signage?"

Will stood by the bridge and looked around for a sign.

"Got it. Okay, we need a British Waterways key."[67]

"Oh great," I said. "I'll grab mine."

I found my BW key hanging near the doorway and grabbed Will's fishing rod. I hooked the key (with cork keyring) on to the end of the rod and carefully hovered the rod in Will's direction.

"What are you doing?" he said, laughing.

"Social distance, Will," I said, giggling so much that the key fell off and into the canal.

"Ah, I always wondered if those cork floats worked," I said.

"You muppet, you could have just chucked it," Will said, retrieving the key from the canal. He ran up to the swing bridge and inserted the key. The electric mechanism kicked in. The bridge dislodged from its position and slowly pivoted open, accompanied by a low electric rumble.

"This is so cool," said Will, hopping up and down as I passed. I smiled and rang my bell to really hammer home the experience for Will (and for me). He shut the bridge and ran back to the boat, returning to his position on the gunwales with his fishing rod. I would come across several swing and lift bridges[68] on my travels, each one unique. Working out the different mechanisms can be

---

67 This is a special key provided by the Canal and River Trust (for a fee) that enables you to access canal features and boater facilities.
68 Lift bridges are principally the same, except the mechanism is vertical.

a fun guessing game. Having Will on board for my first was a real treat.

I knew the visits would start to reduce after Will, and his company, even if he was hanging off the other end of my boat, was very welcome.

Chapter 57
Pub

Having bid goodbye to Will and with my first swing bridge experience under my belt, I ventured on through quaint Hertfordshire villages. Canal-side pubs are dotted along the network, and in the height of summer they should be bursting with trade. But in June 2020 their picnic tables were adorned with empty tinnies from wishful locals, and bored school children leant up against their walls taking selfies next to dead flowers in hanging baskets.

I was cruising along one afternoon when I passed a bridge with a sign on it:

PUB AND BEER GARDEN

I looked down the road to seek out the pub. Like a mirage, there it was in all its glory: an open pub. A string of festoon lights illuminated a beer garden packed with patrons sitting at a dozen or so picnic tables, and a queue of people were lined up outside the door. Pubs were still not meant to be open in the UK and the sight of it was startling. Was this a film set? Had I imagined it? I needed to know. I tied up the boat as soon as I found a suitable place to stop and wandered back down to find the revellers. As I approached, the people at tables looked across at me with "you're not from round here" eyes. I joined the queue to enter.

"I don't understand," I said under my breath.

A man on a nearby table looked at another man, and then at me. They said nothing so I stepped forward in the queue. One of the men stood up to approach me, as another stopped him.

"She can stay. It's fine." He took a sip from a delicious-looking stout.

I faced the queue again and saw a sign propped up against a table.

LOCALS ONLY

"Oh, I see," I said, turning once again to the men at the table.

"It's fine. He's the landlord," said one man about the other.

I approached the bar in a bit of a daze, unsure what I was doing. I ordered a local amber ale. I was served through a sheet of Perspex and followed the arrows on the floor, out the back and around to the front of the pub. The men signalled me over. "Come and join us." I approached and sat at the table next to them.

"Oh my God, I can't believe I'm having a pint in a beer garden." The landlord cut me off.

"Correction. This isn't a beer garden. That is." He pointed to the other side of the road, and a small patch of grassland 65 or so feet away.

"Oh," I said.

"This bit in front of the pub is parish land. So, you're drinking takeaway and allowed to sit here as a member of the public."

"Right," I said.

I looked around at what was unmistakably a beer garden. There were ashtrays on tables and bar-stools dotted about between picnic benches.

"Bit of a loophole, and the local bobby knows about it. So it's all fine," he said.

"Oh, okay. Great."

"Don't get me wrong, we still kick everyone off when it gets to ten p.m."

I laughed to myself. I'm sure this was legit, but it would never have been allowed in London. Even if it was parish land, the view was clear as anything. After a pint and a half, I started to feel uncomfortable. I had definitely got swept up in the moment. I said my goodbyes to the locals and walked back to the boat. A fun little excursion but laced with a strange unease.

One and a half pints, it would seem, was now my limit. I was hammered as I walked back to the boat, leaving a loud and long voice note to Will about my trip to the pub. I wished he'd been around to see it.

Chapter 58
Space-Saving Hacks

- Own less stuff
- Hooks everywhere

Chapter 59
Slip-Up

The infection numbers were coming down, and with businesses on course to reopen in a few weeks, my friends were making plans to see one another. Some thought this marked the beginning of the end, others were less optimistic. I would flit, and at times worry that I'd removed myself from a potential social life and kick-start of my career just as things were opening up again. My helpers had been and gone and I was too far from London now for any assistance or visits. It was nice to be alone, though, living life at my own pace. I could see the benefits of this inward-facing time, even if it meant missing out on an actual pub visit or two.

On the whole, I judged my moorings with care. Cross-referencing Google Maps with descriptions in my Nicholson's guide, assessing the nearest access to civilisation, bridges and gaps in hedgerows. Popular locations, mooring rings or a sturdy bank in which to hammer my pins. I'd look out for other boats too, particularly in towns or more populated areas where I may have felt vulnerable to others. I'd be wary of a lone boat, but if there were two or more, I'd join them.

From time to time, I'd bypass these safety measures, cruising around bends in abundant countryside and pulling into a spot with no one else around. In these remote locations, birdsong and skies full of stars were my only companions. I guess that's the attraction of wild camping, or parking a campervan on a cliff that overlooks the sea. You can be alone in the wild. We're a dense country, and with my life centred around towns and cities to date, I was enamoured with having nothing else man-made in my field of vision. I would be on high alert at night, locked inside...

but I liked the thrill of it. The sense of danger added to the wild abandonment.

I arrived at a new mooring spot just north of Leighton Buzzard. I'd found a secluded bit on a bend of the canal, with a rolling field of wheat cascading down from the towpath edge next to me. The air was thick with pollen and the nettle bushes that lined the side of my boat were giving off a sweet odour and creeping in through my kitchen window as the boat moved gently with the breeze. There were no shops for a couple of miles and only a few boats dotted about here and there. The horizon was now hilly as I passed by the Chilterns to the west.

I lay on my roof with my Nicholson guidebook and looked over my journey so far. Forty locks, more than I could ever have imagined when I lived in London. Passers-by and other boaters had helped with a fair few, but a significant number I had done single-handedly. *I must be physically stronger*, I thought. They were definitely getting easier. I turned to the next section of my route and planned how many locks I'd do tomorrow. Lock days excited me now.

"Drop me your location," came the message.

I ignored it for several hours and cleaned my boat. I baked a loaf and did everything I could to think away what was happening. I knew what today was: it was his birthday. I wondered what had happened for him to have made no plans, however restricted by the current climate, only to decide that he wanted to spend his big day with me instead. How did this make me feel? It made me feel sick. And mistrusting. And confused. And, unfortunately, a little bit special.

I'd made good progress moving on from the relationship. I'd identified it as an addiction, in that each time I saw him I received a chemical hit, whereafter I would sink into withdrawal. The only solution was to be found within. To have the self-control to abstain, one day at a time, and eventually I would find myself no longer desiring the connection. I thought about him every morning and every evening. But with each week that I didn't see him, I knew I was getting stronger.

SLIP-UP

Here I was, alone on my boat and facing the temptation again.

Would it be so bad to see him, I thought, *just for one day?* I knew in my heart that this would be a setback and that I would be left once again in a vacuum of loss and disappointment. But I was curious also to see if this would be the case. I'd gained confidence since leaving London, found more stillness and contentment within. Perhaps I'd made such good progress that I wouldn't be affected by one small visit.

Aspects of the country were beginning to return to normal, but we were still living with a pandemic, and since leaving London I'd been abiding stringently by the rules. Anyone who had helped with boat moves had maintained a 2-metre distance from me (at least) at all times. And no one had been inside the boat. This would be a rule break.

"I'm pretty sure this isn't allowed," I replied.

"I haven't seen anyone," he said. "Tell me where I can find you."

I left it another hour before replying.

"Happy birthday," was all I could muster.

"Pin?"

"Fucking hell, Jonathan," I said.

"Charming."

I dropped a pin to my location.

"Bring ice."

It was on. I would be scraping together a last-minute birthday celebration for my old lover and colleague and behaving irresponsibly during a global pandemic. Risking all, and for what?

Though I was ill prepared I had the necessary ingredients to make homemade pizza, and a bottle of cava left over from Megan's birthday. I laid out a blanket on my roof, with candles and cushions, and I wore a flowing maxi dress, baby blue with purple flower detail. We would watch the sunset together and eat pizza on the roof.

As I prepared for his arrival, I began to imagine a romantic afternoon together. A new dawn marking a profound escalation in our relationship. Why else would he be coming to me on this, his birthday, but to tell me that he loved me and wanted to spend every birthday with me forever more?

I was inside covered in flour when the familiar weight of his footsteps hit my back deck. My heart was full and empty at the same time. I pulled across the curtain with my unfloured fingers and stood back from the doorway. He descended my short staircase, put a bottle of Bollinger down on my granny's shelled out radio and wrapped me in his tanned arms. A hug from anyone was going to be nice at this stage; I'd not had physical contact for months. I craved human touch just as I had craved my independence. We stayed in the embrace for a minute, and I breathed in his smell before whispering, "God, you're old."

We snogged with the beauty of a first kiss but the knowledge of a lifetime. We loved kissing and we were good at it. I held back the tears that were forming and channelled the emotion into him and our embrace. I think it was the human contact that made me well up, or maybe it was guilt that I was feeling. Guilt that this precious moment, this precious hug, was with him.

~~~~~~

The next morning, we ate breakfast outside on the back deck; marmalade on homemade toast.

"You seem relaxed," he said, buttering his toast.

"It's been good for me, this," I said, gesturing out to the canal and the field beyond.

"Good. I'm pleased to hear that, Hannah. You deserve it." He continued buttering his toast.

"I needed to get away," I said.

"To get away from me." He looked up, smiled and went in for a bite of his toast.

There was glee in his eyes. Of course he was pleased with himself. I cleared away the breakfast bits and he walked back to his car.

What a monumental fuck-up, I thought as he left.

Chapter 60
What I Have Out on Deck When I'm Cruising[69]

- Phone
- Sunglasses
- Water bottle
- Snacks
- Nicholson guide
- Windlass
- Rain mac
- Keys
- Suncream/woolly hat, gloves, scarf
- Serrated knife [70]
- Lip balm
- Radio
- Hand sanitiser

---

69 Feel free to cross reference with items I've dropped in the water.
70 I keep this near me in case any ropes get caught in a lock. If they did, I might need to move fast, so having a knife nearby to cut the rope as necessary is useful.

Chapter 61
Arrived

I was so angry the week after his visit. More so than ever before. Within a day he had gone back to ignoring me and I rued the day that I let him back onto my boat and into my life. It was all there at our breakfast together. His comment, "to get away from me" with a boastful smile. It had turned a light on in my head. He was unchanged. But this time, I had changed.

Finally, after this time away, I was beginning to understand the compulsive and addictive nature of our interactions and why I had got myself involved with Jonathan. Why I stayed in the cycle for so long was still a mystery. He never forced me. He was always friendly when we were together. The issue wasn't him. It was my inability to say no, even when I wanted to.

A line had to be drawn. I was on a journey, emotionally and physically, and it was time I grew up. Seeing him was not only irresponsible and selfish, but it was pointless. Summer was in full swing now and I was so lucky to be doing what I was doing. I was some way from reaching my destination of Todmorden and the 28-day goal had long gone by the wayside. It had been a month since I left London, and I was only a fraction of the way there. But my goals had changed. This wasn't about speed. It was about enjoyment and clarity. I would continue on. Inspired by my plan, I would move on from the hiccough with Jonathan with renewed determination and strength.

After a week of silence, I sent one final message.

"I'm going to save myself the heartbreak of not hearing from you by deleting your number. I need to move on. To remove the constant sickness of wondering where you are, who you're with or why you've pulled away from me again in that gut-wrenching cyclical way that you do. I've no remorse in doing this as I'm sure you have none for spending your birthday with me, only to decide you've simply had enough of me being in your life, again."

I archived our chat and put my phone down. I looked out across the canal and the fields beyond. The view was more beautiful than ever. I had a sudden urge to move. I started my engine, lifted my mooring pins out of the ground and took position at the tiller. It was time to confidently move forward and up.

And so, I continued along the Grand Union Canal, alone – a stretch of water that is grand both in name and structure, with bridges and locks that tell a tale of Victorian industry, red brick and steel making up the colours and textures of its fixtures. Some parts were as straight as Roman roads and others had ornate kinks that revealed new and dramatic landscapes at every turn. What I didn't know at this point was that each canal would exhibit a different quality. They were designed and built in their own right, after all, by canal engineers who brought their styles and experience to their construction. It was like they all had different personalities. Sometimes it was clear through architecture and design. But sometimes it was just a feeling. The Grand Union Canal was dramatic and proud, and I adored it.

In part, I'm sure, the personality of each canal was brought out by the seasonal changes I was experiencing so acutely. My journey out of London had started with newly hatched ducklings and unopened lily-pads. By now I was surrounded by nettle bushes in full flourish and spectacular midsummer sunsets. Later in my voyage I would be cruising along the canal with the sweet smell of meadowsweet in full flower filling the air. These seasonal changes would bring a whole new character along on my adventure.

Enormous trees towered over the canal as I cruised and slowly travelled north. It was the height of summer now, and as I stood at the tiller of *Argie* I would put-put-put along for hours and days, basking in glorious sunshine. When rain was forecast, I might give myself a day off and stay inside – cleaning, cooking, baking, reading, writing. I was in the swing of it now, this new existence. I would check in with Mum and Dad. Mum had sorted through every room in the house twice over. Dad had picked up the piano again. They had bought an exercise bike and would swap in with each other for half an hour before dinner. They were looking after themselves and each other. Mum was particularly anxious about the state of the world, but on a personal level, I was so proud of how they were coping. When I spoke to my brothers, they didn't reflect so much on how they were doing. All three of them spent their lockdown with partners and children (two each) and had worked full-time throughout. They didn't have the time to reflect. I'd check in with friends, giving an ear to those who were struggling. And on some days, I struggled too. The weight of the pandemic was a constant presence, as well as a fear that my future had an uncertainty now that I hadn't prepared for. I searched for work, limited to jobs I could do from home. There was little out there. I contacted pub companies to see about becoming a post-Covid auditor along my journey. I had this idea that I would pay my way across the country by popping in as a secret shopper, being fed pub lunches and reporting back my findings to their bosses. They didn't bite.

Intoxicated by boat moving, I would set off early with a belly full of porridge, a strong coffee on my gas locker[71] and a day ahead of me, not knowing where I'd get to or what I might see on the way. Cruising had become my solace. On the days I cruised, I was euphoric. I would plug a podcast into my ears and perch myself against the railing at the back of my boat, or stand on my little blue footstool in my Dr. Marten boots. My body was at one with the boat now. I would let it drift in neutral to run inside and use the bathroom in five seconds flat, returning to the tiller to regain control with confidence and a giggle that I'd left the boat without its helmswoman. It was a risky game of chicken, but it was better

---

71 My gas lockers live out on deck. They are two steel containers; one for the gas canister in use, and one for back-up. Gas heats my water and runs the cooker.

than mooring up just to use the loo. I would text while I cruised, steer with my buttocks, slow down if I saw something I wanted to photograph. I was untouchable, untraceable. I would spend my days gasping audibly at the wildlife. Flashes of blue from skating dragonflies and the rare sighting of a kingfisher. Bees that would hover at my control panel as I moved through the still water. Herons peering into the canal, kites circling above. I was in awe of the beauty that surrounded me and awash with this new sense of place and belonging that I am struggling to find a comparison with from any other time in my life. When I was cruising, I wasn't lonely or worried or confused. I was centred. I had arrived.

~~~~~~~

The boaters I came across on my journey were split into two types. The liveaboards, like me, were distinguished by well-worn boats with scuff marks and rust patches, attempts at roof gardens and stains from chimneys giving away our year-round existence on board. The second community, typically older, were the holiday boaters. Those with a land life and a boat as their summer retreat. Their boats were shinier than the liveaboards', with boxes of rosé wine and art supplies on display in their windows a sign of their retired habits.

For several weeks I hardly spoke to anyone, and if I did catch a smile or a nod with another boater there was a real sense of "gosh, aren't we the lucky ones". Travel otherwise wasn't really happening for anyone in the UK, but with our moving homes, we were able to experience some level of freedom. During the lockdown, holiday boaters were told not to make overnight stays on their boats, but now with restrictions having been lifted, they were out in full force. Unlike London, where everyone was a liveaboard, I was now a minority amongst the rural boating community of retirees.

One afternoon I met a holiday boater in a lock, taking his boat on its final voyage. It had been a retirement present to himself, and he was selling it now in order to appease his family.

ALL BOATS ARE SINKING

"Here, would you like these?" There was a sadness in his voice as he held a cushion in one hand and an enormous mooring pin in the other.

"What are they?" I said.

"The cushion, it's to go on your railing." He passed it over. "And you might need this pin if you find yourself moored up somewhere boggy. It's rainy up north."

The pin was 3 foot long. I'd never seen anything like it.

"Oh gosh, thank you," I said.

"No problem. I'd rather they went to someone who I know will use them."

He was about 75, I'd say, his world very different to mine, yet we had this common ground. We operated the lock together, and then another afterwards before I stopped for the night. It got me thinking about the locks and the encounters that would have happened in them a century or two before, and since. The exchanging of gifts, money, words. Lock keepers. Working boats being pulled by horses. Nomadic families. Operating a lock with another boat requires time, working together in synchronicity. It's based on trust and communication. My encounter with this boater was brief but kind of beautiful. I used the cushion a lot thereafter. I never used the enormous pin.

~~~~~~~

The canal looped around the city of Milton Keynes in a stretch of turns, with immaculate towpaths and rows of trees designed with military precision. The canal, with the River Ouzel alongside, was a meandering water feature wrapped around the community within. Cruising through this stretch involved just one shallow lock, and there were herons everywhere. I'd never seen so many. Statuesque on the water's edge, ready to pounce on a fish, or launch into the sky, their heavy bodies dropping down as they fall into flight.

ARRIVED

I stopped overnight in Milton Keynes at a bridge that signposted a laundrette[72] and used the facilities, continuing on the next morning. Beyond the city, the landscape transformed into farmland, a sight I would get used to throughout the Midlands. The transition from woodland and my boat hidden under a promenade of trees into vast arable land was smooth and wonderfully pleasing.

As my journey continued on, I began to start my cruises later in the day so I could enjoy the sunsets from my back deck. I wasn't doing recces anymore. I was just pootling up without knowing what was ahead of me. The mystery was part of the fun. Moving the boat at dusk was calming. The water was silky with reflections of the warm sky and the air was still as wildlife settled in for the night. I would cruise until I found a new spot to call home for a day or two, sometimes knowing where I was headed based on a conversation with another boater. But I'd also now got used to winging it, cruising until I found somewhere that looked nice, with grass I could put my pins in, or mooring rings attached on to concrete.

I loved not knowing where I was going next or for how long I'd be travelling each day. I started when I started, and I stopped when I stopped. It was simple. I was only going one way: up.

---

72 Big regret of mine not doing a photo project around the various laundrettes I came across. I love a laundrette, me.

Chapter 62
Redundancy 2.0

Texts came through from colleagues.

"Have you had the call?"

The company's managing director was contacting all employees with the outcome of our redundancy consultations following a period of furlough. I dreaded the conversation. Not because I wanted to have my job back. I didn't. But because the phone call would be awkward and loaded and I just wanted it over with. My call came at the end of the day while I was moving the boat.

"I'm very sorry, Hannah. You understand, don't you?" said the managing director.

"Uh huh. Sure." I was navigating a tight turn with an arm on the tiller, another on the throttle and my phone pressed up to my face with my shoulder.

"It's been a very difficult decision," he continued.

"Yeah, no. I totally understand," I said.

"You will receive an email with details about your redundancy payment."

"Okay."

"We're going to miss having your smiley face around." God he really was scraping the barrel.

"Mmm yeah. Well, I hope everything works out for you and the company, and I'm sorry it's been such a difficult time," I managed to say over the engine revs. "I'm actually moving the boat…"

"Yes, of course. Well good luck—"

"Yep."

"—with everything."

"Yep. Okay, okay, bye now," I said.

REDUNDANCY 2.0

I hung up and threw my phone onto the sofa inside my doorway as my shoulders dropped several inches. This phone call had been hanging over me, and over the course of the day I had started to wonder if the outcome might be different from the one I had expected. Maybe I would still have my job. Maybe I would be asked to return straight to work. That would have left me in a very difficult position. I couldn't afford not to work, but I was very far from that job now. Practically and emotionally. I was relieved by the outcome of the call. I could move on now.

Chapter 63
The Midlands

The Midlands

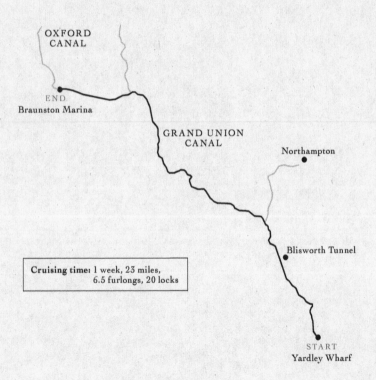

OXFORD
CANAL

END
Braunston Marina

GRAND UNION
CANAL

Northampton

Blisworth Tunnel

Cruising time: 1 week, 23 miles,
6.5 furlongs, 20 locks

START
Yardley Wharf

THE MIDLANDS

The canals widened as I entered the Midlands and curved through agricultural land like a playful doodle on a notebook. Trees no longer flanked the water's edge and the view of fields with grazing sheep would become the norm for several weeks. Canal and River Trust workers were not around so much to maintain the towpaths, so wherever I moored up I would use a pin to hack away at tall grass and nettle bushes to establish an entranceway to my back door. I would become accustomed to being the only boater around, and on long summer nights my mooring spots felt secure and private as the wild towpath had become my camouflage. Most days I barely saw another soul.

As I found myself further from civilisation, my diet became compromised. Supermarkets were often more than an hour's walk away, and local shops would be limited to a few shelves in a post office, or a Londis with little in the way of fresh produce. Occasionally I would stumble across a farm shop, and it was like hitting an oasis in the desert. I'd stock up on eggs, seasonal vegetables, cheese and flour and carry it all back in my rucksack.

One such drought in supplies and facilities coincided with a visit from Peggy, Rox and Zeus the dog. They joined me to keep me company through Blisworth Tunnel near where Peggy's parents lived. Peggy had brought some local treats with her, cakes and Irn-Bru[73] from Corby. I hadn't hosted a meal for friends since I was moored in Little Venice and I was mortified to present lunch to these two, my foodiest of friends. I'd only been able to find a small mini market before they had arrived, and it had slim pickings on the shelves. I had bought a cold tub of mixed beans marinated in an oily vinaigrette sauce with wilted mint leaves, thinking it could be added to some pasta. And that was it. Over the years, these friends had educated me with exquisite food, and this was my repayment for their hospitality at our Sunday afternoon lunches. Cold pasta with beans.

---

73 Apparently, Corby has the highest sales of Irn-Bru outside of Scotland.

ALL BOATS ARE SINKING

After the pitiful lunch washed down with Irn-Bru, we approached a lock. Another narrowboat came up behind.

I ran up to the other boat, which was hovering behind us.

"Shall we share the lock?" I asked the couple on board.

They looked at each other.

"That would be great," said the man. "It's our first boat move."

"Oh right! Well, between us we should zip right through," I said, thrilled to be speaking as an experienced boater now.

It transpired that Claire and Robert were a retired nurse and builder, and they had bought a holiday boat after they'd spent time with friends on theirs.

"Where are you headed?" I asked.

"We're going down the Oxford Canal after Braunston and taking the boat to a marina on the Thames."

"Sounds lovely," I said. "We're going up to Braunston, so we can travel together before you join the Oxford."

Between our location and Braunston there were several locks and Blisworth Tunnel to navigate through. I could sense their trepidation about the journey and decided to impart as much wisdom as I could in our short time together, taking advantage of my extra pairs of hands to demonstrate lock operation to the newbies.

We headed through the first lock. I shouted up instructions to Peggy, Rox and Claire from my back deck as they worked together to operate the locks, with Robert and I on the tillers of our respective vessels. The first lock went smoothly enough, so we continued on with the next few. Zeus spent his day on board curled up on the sofa inside, occasionally popping outside to have a run up and down the towpath when he could. We were getting into a rhythm with the locks and the couple were gaining confidence, but after several locks together I could tell they were getting tired. We made it through the sixth lock together as the sun started to dip.

Robert emerged from inside their boat with a bottle of New Zealand Sauvignon Blanc.

"Thank you so much for all your help today," he said, passing me the bottle.

"That's really kind," I said. "And it was a pleasure. Will you tackle the tunnel tomorrow?"

They looked at each other, then to me. "The tunnel?"

"Yes. Just round the corner." I pointed ahead of us. "We're doing it now, but do you want to stay here and tackle it tomorrow? I could come and help you in the morning."

"We'll just follow you in now," Robert said.

I wanted to tell them that they looked exhausted. That they had a long voyage ahead of them back to the Thames and should take their time.

"Are you sure?" I said.

"Robert, I think we should do it tomorrow," said Claire.

"We just stay in a straight line behind you, right?" said Rob, confidently.

"Well, yes."

Their boat had a bow thruster – a nifty little device that enables the boat to move from side to side. Mine doesn't have one, and I was impressed watching them moor up inside a lock straighter than I'd ever managed to. Perhaps they would be fine going through the tunnel now after all.

"Try to focus on one side of the boat. It'll help you stay in the middle," I said, trying to keep things as simple as possible.

Rox, Peggy, Zeus and I entered the nearly 2-mile tunnel, followed by Claire and Robert. As soon as we were inside, I regretted allowing them to navigate the tunnel on their first day moving a boat. I had taken for granted my three-plus years' experience of cruising and going through tunnels. Even with a bow thruster, this was a tall order.

Journeying through tunnels is a unique experience. All boats are required to have a working horn and a light at the front. Aside from the fire exit signage (a horrid reminder that something could well go wrong once inside, which doesn't bear thinking about), any modern amendments to the integrity of the 1800s structures are not obvious, and I cannot help but feel like I'm going back in time, as phones lose signal and the walls close in. In the eighteenth and early nineteenth centuries, owners would have "legged"[74] their boats up the tunnels by lying on the roof and shimmying them along with their legs so that they were only a few feet from the walls at any given time. The light at the end of the tunnel is exactly as you'd imagine it to be. Tiny, blurred, then incrementally bigger, as it remains the only focus during your time inside.

Blisworth Tunnel was narrow, damp, dark and long. As we cruised through, I saw the dot at the end get bigger and the dot of Claire and Robert get smaller behind us. They were making very slow progress. I didn't want to slow down too much, as it's harder to navigate at slow speed in a tunnel, and I couldn't take my eye off the journey for long enough to see what was going on behind. With no way of communicating with the couple, my fear for them was increasing.

After 45 minutes, Peggy, Rox, Zeus and I reached the other side of the tunnel. We moored up and waited. Twenty minutes later, the headlight on Claire and Robert's boat finally signalled their arrival, and two pale and shaken up new boaters moored up next to us.

"Are you okay?" I said to Claire.

"That was interesting," she said, visibly shaking.

"I'm sorry. I should have gone through with you," I said, feeling terrible.

"We were just zigzagging along and bumping into the sides." Claire had started laughing, thankfully.

"It gets easier, I promise," I said.

They retired for the night, and I sat with Rox, Peggy and Zeus as we polished off the Sauvignon Blanc before they left and headed back to their London home.

The next morning, I climbed outside the boat to check on Claire and Robert. Though it was early, their boat had gone. I felt awful after the antics in the tunnel the day before. I thought of my first cruise through a tunnel. It was the Islington Tunnel, a mile long

---

74 Where the phrase "legging it" comes from... apparently.

and wider than the Blisworth Tunnel. Megan had helped take me through. She had been so wise and patient, instructing me to concentrate on the light ahead, and to keep up a bit of speed to help with the control of the boat. I wished I had persuaded Claire and Robert to wait and helped them through myself, but it was too late. They would be well on their way now and off down the Oxford to head for the Thames. I guess they would know for next time. Keep up a bit of speed and focus on the light.

Chapter 64
Culinary Disasters

For guests
- Cold pasta with mixed beans
- Homemade pizza, affectionately named "soup pizza"
- Bread - many loaves
- Meringue for the Lockdown Lemon Meringue Sours (luckily, I foresaw this and bought pre-made also - crisis averted)

For me
- Gone-off ham
- Many salads (I didn't have a fridge pre-2020)
- Bread - most loaves

Chapter 65
Oxford and Coventry Canals

Braunston and the Oxford Canal

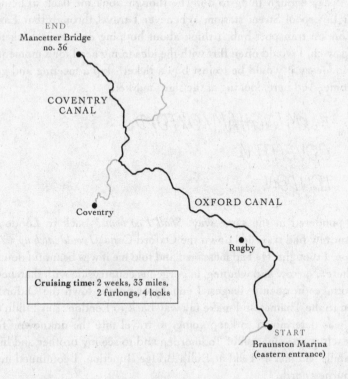

END
Mancetter Bridge
no. 36

COVENTRY
CANAL

OXFORD CANAL

Coventry

Rugby

Cruising time: 2 weeks, 33 miles,
2 furlongs, 4 locks

START
Braunston Marina
(eastern entrance)

ALL BOATS ARE SINKING

The village of Braunston is a hub of canal activity, with a toll office signalling where the Oxford Canal joins the Grand Union Canal, and a boatyard and marina that are well populated with holiday boats in various states of repair and usage. The white and black theme of the British canal network is at large in Braunston, with pedestrian bridges and signs painted in thick glossy coats of the stuff. It was busier than I'd been used to for the past six weeks but not half as busy as it would normally have been.

The turning from the Grand Union onto the Oxford Canal heading north or south presented itself as another moment for me. Just as I had at Bull's Bridge Junction in May, I took a look down the south arm of the Oxford and fantasised about turning back – an easy enough thing to do. The thought took me back to being at Liverpool Street station. Whenever I travel through that East London transport hub, I think about hopping on a train back to Ipswich. I would often flirt with the idea in my head for a moment. How easy it would be to just buy a ticket, skip a meeting and go home. And here, looking at the signs marked,

BIRMINGHAM/OXFORD

COVENTRY

LONDON

I pondered in the same way: *Shall I go home?* Back to London. Andrew had travelled down the Oxford Canal. *I could catch up with him*, I thought. He had messaged and told me it was beautiful down there. Narrow and winding, in gorgeous countryside with thatched cottages in quaint villages. I could just pootle down the Oxford, on to the Thames and make my way back to London. But I didn't. I was determined to keep going, to travel into the unknown. To reach my destination of Todmorden and to see my brother and his family. So just as I did at Bull's Bridge Junction, I continued my journey north.

Chapter 66
Coventry Canal

The Coventry Canal

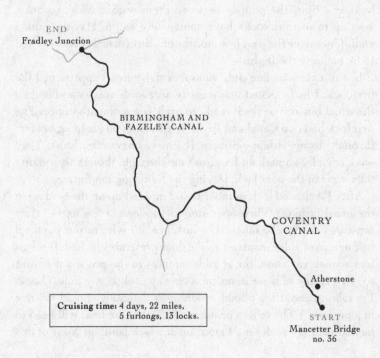

END
Fradley Junction

BIRMINGHAM AND
FAZELEY CANAL

COVENTRY
CANAL

Atherstone

Cruising time: 4 days, 22 miles,
5 furlongs, 13 locks.

START
Mancetter Bridge
no. 36

ALL BOATS ARE SINKING

Now, the first solo lock is one thing. But a first solo flight of locks – another. The 11 locks at Atherton on the Coventry Canal were my next challenge. When they're close together like this, upon leaving one lock, you'll head straight into the next, and then the next, and so on. The locks on the Coventry Canal are single width, wide enough for one narrowboat at a time. I had never seen a narrow lock before I hit the Midlands. The Grand Union locks were double width, allowing for two (or more) boats. Thereafter the narrow locks can be found on several canals in the UK, restricting these waterways to narrowboats only and not wider vessels. While the single locks are designed to accommodate one boat at a time, the pounds between them remain wide, so boats waiting to use the locks have somewhere to go. Having gained confidence over the past few months of solo cruising, I was excited to be tackling the flight.

It was a glorious late July summer's day when I approached the first lock. I had stocked up on easily accessible snacks and had all the usual bits out on deck ready to grab at a moment's notice. The first lock had two Canal and River Trust volunteers helping boaters through, to my disappointment (I know, ungrateful, huh). They were friendly enough and assisted me through, though they didn't follow me to the next lock, leaving the following ten for me.

After I'd cleared lock number two, I moored up on the landing in the usual fashion. When operating locks alone, a few extra safety measures need to be taken. For instance, it's wise to put personal belongings of value inside, with the door preferably locked. It seems like a small variation, but it adds minutes to the process if I want to retrieve any of these items for a cheeky peek at any time. (Look, I'm talking about my phone which most definitely should not live in a pocket.[75]) The other consideration is that the boat will need to be tied securely each time I moor up at a lock landing. None of this

---

75 Ref. Chapter 8: Things I've Lost to the Canal

trailing of ropes or holding on to them with my foot. The boat needs to be tied up and left, while I go and operate the lock.

I was in for a long day in the sweltering heat. The majority of the locks were sheltered by woodland and there weren't many people around to watch (or assist). Three hours and five locks down, my energy levels dipped. I was hungry. *I'll stop and have lunch after the sixth*, I thought.

As they were single-width locks, I was able to drive the boat into the chamber and step off the boat and onto land, holding on to the centre line and pulling the boat out of the lock rather than driving it. On the descent, I find this easier than climbing up and down ladders to drive the boat. Being single width, the boat isn't moving about inside the lock and I can just pull the boat out with the weight of my body and a bit of momentum.

Lock number six. I drove in, hopped off, lowered the boat and walked it out. Now at this stage, I usually tie the boat up to the lock landing in the pound, but on this occasion I decided that the water was nice and calm, and I'd got into a rhythm so it would be safe to trail the rope along the floor and quick as a flash go and shut the gate. I did exactly this, but sadly, I had misjudged the situation. Upon shutting the lock gate, the force from the movement of water gave my boat a little nudge, and I witnessed *Argie* and rope drift off into the centre of the pound of water. I stood still and stared at the sight before me. My boat – irretrievable in the middle of the canal. I'd never seen it from this angle, in the middle like that. It looked so pretty. I peered up and down the towpath. I'm not sure what the presence of another human being would really have added to the situation, but I was searching for them anyway.

"What am I going to do?" was coming out of my mouth on repeat. I knew exactly what I needed to do. I would have to jump in the canal and swim to my boat. At this point I was glad for the lack of human activity. I started untying my boot laces, replacing "What am I going to do?" with "for fuck's sake". I took off my socks and tucked them into my boots. I wasn't stripping any further... the humiliation of what was about to happen would be enough if anyone saw me. A bike approached, and I changed my position to stand as casually as I could looking down at the floor. As I stood and waited, I thought about the error. It was a classic Hannah mishap. Not dramatic or big, just bloody silly. It had been a while since I'd had one.

The bike continued. I was waiting a moment for the coast to be clear, when a small but mighty gust of wind hit my boat and *Argie* drifted gently in my direction.

"Come on, *Argie*," I said out loud, coaxing my inanimate boat over towards me. It seemed to listen and continued to drift. A minute or so passed and finally, my boat found its way to me. I leaned across and grabbed hold of a fender as soon as I could, retrieved my boots and hopped on to the back deck. I cruised clear of the lock landing and moored up for the night. *I'll save the next five locks for tomorrow*, I thought, enjoying a rather large glass of wine with my inanimate boat.

At Tamworth a few days later I reached Fradley Junction, where the canal would head either north-east towards Nottingham or continue north-west towards Stoke-on-Trent. At the junction stood another beautiful set of canal features. Two locks either side of an eye-catching canal-side pub, and a swing bridge. I stayed overnight at the junction, enjoying my first (official) pub visit since lockdown began. I sat alone on a pub bench and drank a cold crisp beer, as perfect a pint as I could have imagined, and true to form, I was drunk after one and a half.

The next day, I turned off the Coventry Canal and onto the Birmingham and Fazeley Canal towards Stoke-on-Trent, where I skirted around the north side of Birmingham, joining the Trent and Mersey Canal for the next stage of my adventure. I was sad to wave goodbye to the Midlands. I knew there was so much more to see, not least of all Birmingham City itself, which has more canals than Venice. The Midlands had been green and pleasant, which had come as a bit of a surprise, to be honest. I'd grown up in the 1990s, when the Midlands was in receipt of some bad rep. Across popular culture and in the playground, the accent, the drawl, was mocked, and sweeping remarks were made about that part of the UK. All totally uncalled for, and very dodgy, looking back. To experience the Midlands for the first time via the waterways had debunked all my childhood hangovers. It was winding and vast, hilly and flat. Varied and luscious.

But onwards and upwards. Quite literally. The green open landscape with smoothed stone bridges that joined fields together across the waterways gave way to the industrial landscape on the edge of Stoke. Eight weeks after leaving London, I had reached the Trent and Mersey Canal.

Chapter 67
Things I Sometimes Miss

- Reclining on a big sofa in front of a TV
- Baths
- An unlimited supply of water
- Wardrobe hanging space
- An ice compartment
- Space above my head in which to stretch
- Kitchen appliances — smoothie maker, coffee machine, food processor
- Central heating
- Clean nails
- Soot/oil/diesel-free living
- Underfloor heating [76]

---

76 I've never had this... but I still miss it.

Chapter 68
The Trent and Mersey

The Trent and Mersey Canal

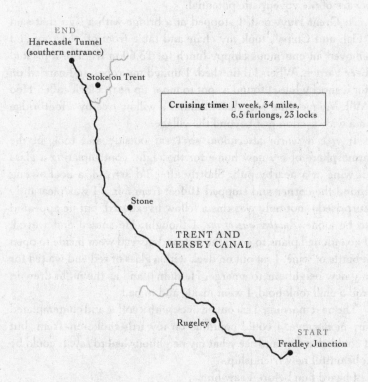

Cruising time: 1 week, 34 miles,
6.5 furlongs, 23 locks

END
Harecastle Tunnel
(southern entrance)

Stoke on Trent

Stone

TRENT AND
MERSEY CANAL

Rugeley

START
Fradley Junction

271

ALL BOATS ARE SINKING

The Trent and Mersey Canal snaked and looped through villages, towns and cities against a hilly backdrop that would become the edges of the Peak District. The canal presented an ever-changing aspect, with no two bridges the same. I travelled through rural and industrial settings in a fervent zigzag. It was late July, and the canal-side plant life was in full bloom, with fluffy and colourful flowers coaxing the bee and dragonfly populations out en masse.

Travelling through Rugeley meant cruising along water at the end of back gardens, where I saw flamboyant decking, extensive gnome collections and home projects, with makeshift lockdown bars made from wooden pallets. It was quintessentially British. I navigated this curious sight with a modest speed; eyes on the horizon, acutely aware of the voyeuristic potential.

At Great Haywood, I stopped at a bridge with a sign that said "Fish and Chips", took my chair and table from off the roof and enjoyed an enormous chippy lunch for £3.60 in front of a packed beer garden. When I'd finished, I untied my ropes and carried on for a short while. I found a spot to moor up near a lock called Hoo Mill. My mooring was shaded under a willow tree by a footbridge at a wide section just beyond the village.

It was a warm afternoon, so I sat outside and took in the atmosphere of my new home for the night, contemplating a glass of wine at a nearby pub. Shortly after I'd arrived, a boat swung round the corner and stopped 10 feet from mine. I was pleasantly surprised – not only was this a fellow liveaboard, but he appeared to be alone. *Another one of me*, I thought. He smiled and waved. I abandoned plans to go to the pub and instead went inside to open a bottle of wine. I sat out on deck with a glass of red and waited for my new neighbour to emerge. He didn't, and as the night drew in and a chill took hold, I went inside and to bed.

The next morning, I sat out on deck with a coffee and contemplated my next move. I could continue on towards Stoke-on-Trent, but I could also stay and see what my neighbour had to say. It could be a beautiful new friendship.

I heard him before I saw him.

"Alright, bird?" The southern accent and choice of greeting jolted me.

"Hi," I said, now hoping to keep our interaction short.

"How's it going?" The man was of a similar age to me, wearing low-fitted jeans and a faded red T-shirt.

"Yeah, all good, thank you. You?"

"Nice spot, innit." His voice had a rasping tone. "I've only been a boater for two weeks. I was with my mate up in Liverpool. We come down, but he had this bird with him, and she was a right bitch. So, I tolds him it's me or her. He chose her so now I'm on me own. He's a prick. She's even worse."

"Oh, right." I stood to pack away my table and chair.

"You leaving?" he said.

I didn't realise I was, but I was.

"Yeah, I'm heading off now," I said.

"Ah. Shame. Thought I'd found a new friend."

I think in normal circumstances I may have found this interaction fine, jolly even. But I'd spent a lot of time alone, and this was like going from 0 to 100. I was not prepared for his over-familiar energy. Having only moved the day before, I kept my pre-cruise checks brief and started the engine, giving it a 30-second watch and putting my deck boards back down. Before I knew it, my neighbour was standing inches from me.

"What's wrong?" he said over my engine.

"What?"

"Your engine," he said. "What's wrong? Need a hand?"

I paused, recalling his comment earlier about being a new boater.

"Nothing's wrong," I said.

"Oh," he said. "Why are you staring at it then, bird?"

Bird was increasingly becoming my least favourite word.

"I'm just giving it a little look before I head off," I said.

"Oh," he said.

I think he was a little embarrassed to have made the journey over only to be told that I was alright. But while he was here, he continued...

"Those locks are hard, hey."

"Yeah, they do take a bit of time to crack," I said.

"Do you tie your boat up?"

He wasn't leaving, clearly.

"In a lock?" I said.

"Yeah."

"Loosely on the ascent, yeah," I said.

"You shouldn't."

I bristled.

"How long did you say you'd been a boater for?" I said.

"Nah, I mean —" He paused. "I was told you shouldn't."

I put down my deck boards, getting ready to head off.

He was still there.

"My engine's smoking," he said.

"Yes, I noticed that when you were coming in yesterday."

I had two options here. I could drive off or I could offer a hand. Given his assumption that I needed help from him, I was quite keen on demonstrating my capabilities with the latter. Plus, my mother taught me to treat everyone with kindness.

"Would you like me to have a look at your engine?" I was already following him to his boat.

He lifted up his deck boards and I peered in, keeping a distance from him and the boat.

"Okay. Let's see where you check your oil?" I said.

"Oh, I dunno," he said.

"I think it's that." I pointed to a loop of metal. The man pulled on it, and a dipstick came out, with thick black oil dripping from it.

"Okay, I'm no expert," I said, "but it looks like you need to change that oil. That might be a good place to start."

"Oh right," he said.

"It would be a good idea to book in a service —"

"I've also got all this water in my engine —"

"Yeah, I'll come on to that in a second," I cut him off in return. "Get an engine service and watch the engineer. Ask them questions and you'll start to learn the particulars for your engine. Now, this water in your bay…"

I explained where the water was coming from, teaching this new boater all about his stern gland. The water was dripping in rapidly and his bilge pump hadn't been working to remove it. I was amazed he'd travelled so far without drowning the engine.

"Get that pump fixed," I said. I walked back to my boat and drove off. I relished every moment of the lesson and did pretty well, I think, for a bird.

~~~~~~~

I took a few days' break while in the beautiful Staffordshire town of Stone. With glorious weather due, I caught up on some boat maintenance and enjoyed a relaxing bit of time off from boat moving. I ticked off a list of outstanding jobs:

Fixed fibreglass patch on water tank
Painted roof
Touched-up paint on the sides of boat
Cleaned up and reconnected my leisure batteries
Swept chimney

Engaging in some boat DIY gave me a revived sense of satisfaction and a routine, as I made regular trips into the town to gather tools and materials. It had been a while since I'd experienced any familiarity in my surroundings. I wondered about staying longer in Stone. I had a perfect mooring, with countryside views, a town and train station nearby, and even an M&S next to the canal. I'd fallen for Stone and thought it might be a good place to stop before the second lockdown that we all knew was coming. I contacted pubs in the area to try to get a meeting for future work, but to no avail. It wasn't great timing. After a few days, I gave up on my job search and decided it was a sign to keep moving. I stocked up on ingredients for my new favourite breakfast snack. I had been told about Staffordshire oatcakes in a deli in Stone. It's a local delicacy and I ate it every day for a week.

Oatcake Breakfast (serves 1)

Ingredients:
1 (or 2 – probably 2) x Staffordshire oatcake(s)
2 x rashers of bacon and/or grilled mushrooms
Some local crumbly Staffordshire white cheese
Sticky relish – I went with jalapeno jam from Single Variety Co.

Method:
Grill the bacon or fry up the mushrooms then lightly heat the oatcake under the grill on both sides while your bacon/mushrooms are crisping up real nice. Dollop on some sticky relish to the warmed up outcake followed by the bacon/mushrooms. Crumble the cheese over the top. Wrap it up like a taco. Eat it out on deck with a coffee. Delicious.

Had this not been the year 2020, I think my trip up the British waterways (and this book) may have been about food. Canals and food… and maybe beer. But given the lack of human contact and the closed-up businesses, as well as the need to be discreet and responsible, it wasn't possible for me to go exploring or searching those things out. It was a joy to learn about a local dish and made me wonder what else there was out there in the British Isles aside from Corby's Irn-Bru and Staffordshire's oatcakes.

~~~~~~

Stoke-on-Trent from the canal was a sight to behold. The Trent and Mersey was first commissioned[77] for the ceramics industry, and the potteries are still visible along the route through the city, with doors right on the water's edge and bottle-shaped kilns standing proud. The cruise was fascinating and unexpected, with deep locks that worked their way around the country's pottery manufacturing hub in a kind of layered maze and cast-iron walkover bridges between one industrial lock and another. With so much to see, it was a stimulating and somewhat exhausting leg of the journey. The day-long cruise culminated in a journey through Harecastle Tunnel, which is 2,962 yards long. I didn't stop in Stoke-on-Trent, but I vowed to return in non-Covid times to experience the city from another angle. At the end of a long day, I moored up in a quiet stretch on the outskirts of the city and turned in for the night. The following day I would be leaving the Trent and Mersey Canal behind and turning on to the Macclesfield Canal for the next part of my adventure.

---

77 By a fella called Josiah Wedgewood.

Chapter 69
The Macclesfield
Canal

The Macclesfield Canal

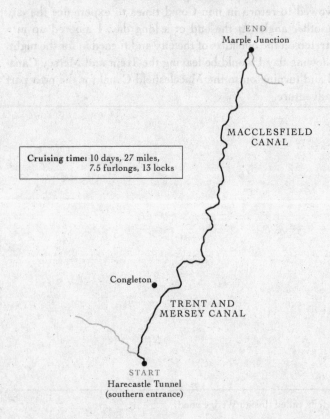

END
Marple Junction

MACCLESFIELD
CANAL

Cruising time: 10 days, 27 miles,
7.5 furlongs, 13 locks

Congleton

TRENT AND
MERSEY CANAL

START
Harecastle Tunnel
(southern entrance)

THE MACCLESFIELD CANAL

Emerging from Harecastle Tunnel, I noticed that the water had turned orange – apparently due to its iron ore content. The weather, too, seemed to turn. A coincidence, I'm sure, but with rain lashing down and a bite in the air, there was a real sense that I'd arrived "up north" upon exiting the tunnel. The canal felt vastly different. The hard industrial edges of the Trent and Mersey had been replaced by the soft curves of the Macclesfield Canal. Macclesfield has some unusual bridges. They are made from stone that has been rounded off – not sharp and angular bricks but smooth boulder-like stones. These unusual bridges are affectionately named "snake bridges" by the locals. They are designed so that horses may walk over them without letting go of the boats. These bridges are very clever in design, and handsome too.

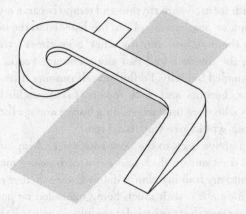

The Macclesfield Canal was a playground for me to continue running along. The canal-side vegetation came up to my shoulders in some places, and by late summer, the towpath edge was awash with orange, yellow and lilac flowers bursting through every shade of green. As the weeks went on, the blackberries too were in abundance, and I would stop my runs for a brief moment to pick and eat a particularly juicy looking one. With the grassy banks and the turnover bridges where I could spin round from one side of the canal to the other and back again, I was enjoying my runs more than ever.

The London Marathon had been rescheduled for October. After a lull in training, I was back on it, with shorter runs on weekday mornings and a long one at the weekend. By August, I was running 20 miles a week. The runs were hot and hard. Fuelling up properly had become a necessary safety requirement, and I stuffed snacks and gels into my bra and shorts while clutching a bottle of water in each hand. Occasionally I'd listen to a podcast or audiobook, but mostly I ran to a playlist I'd cultivated over the past year: an array of beat-heavy tracks, from 1980s cheese to drum and bass and techno. A playlist I'd never listen to otherwise, but one that had me running with focus, where rhythm and tempo became my only goal. I didn't think or ponder when I ran but listened to the beat and my feet hitting the floor one after the other. Sometimes I would set off away from the towpath and run along country roads, where the route was shaded but hilly. I'd find myself running through villages with quaint churches and clock towers. Locals nodded greetings, and drivers who were used to avoiding horses and cyclists along the narrow roads would give way to me too.

When I'd arrive back to the boat with sweat dripping down my forearms, I'd sit out on deck and eat a carb-heavy meal, logging my miles onto my training plan. I didn't know whether my training was in vain or not – with much being cancelled or postponed, it wasn't guaranteed that the new date would actually go ahead either. This was now part and parcel of the current world order, and I was ready to accept either outcome.

The announcement came on 7 August 2020. The marathon had gone virtual. The runners who had signed up could still do it and get medals, but we would do so remotely, downloading an app and running along our own course. I decided I would get the train back to London to do mine (if that was allowed at the time) and run along the towpath.

———————

Shortly after turning onto the Macc, I stumbled across Congleton and the most magnificent view on all sides. Turning on a bend past the town, I moored atop an aqueduct looking down on a viaduct of grand proportion. The valley below where a babbling brook echoed under the epic railway arches and fell below the canal was spectacular, and for me, evoked Brontë. Finishing my last Staffordshire oatcake out on deck, I paused and reflected on my journey. It had been two and a half months since I left London, and four and a half since we went into the first lockdown. I had travelled far slower than anticipated. With the world in stagnation, I felt I was given licence to take my time. *Why the rush?* I had thought. But there were some new considerations now. I had been relaxed with my progress, but with autumn around the corner, I knew my long days at the tiller would be compromised. I decided I needed to have a plan.

Looking down on the dramatic view below, I imagined a wild winter hunkered down on this aqueduct with tinned food and few neighbours and had this romantic vision of waking up early to write, throwing on my boots and walking in the hills with no other soul around. It was tempting. We might go into another lockdown at some point, and I didn't want to be told I couldn't move while I was stuck somewhere unsafe or unpleasant. But this spot here was beautiful. After breakfast I took out my phone and looked at winter mooring options right on top of the aqueduct.

Winter moorings are provided by the Canal and River Trust on a first come first served basis. They're released in October and can be reserved from November until March, allowing for a suspension in the 14-day moving rule during this period. Purchasing one had never been a desire of mine, but with a colder winter ahead than I'd been used to and in unfamiliar waters, I knew I needed to secure somewhere safe to stay. As tempting as it was, after much thought, I decided against Congleton. With summer nearly over, the waterways would quieten down. Holiday boaters would return their vessels to marinas, and I didn't know how winter alone in a rural setting like this might feel. I looked at the map on my phone. I had travelled so far. I just needed to get to Manchester, and then on to the Rochdale Canal, and I could make it to Todmorden in time for winter – where my brother and his family were nearby.

I looked at my bank account and the remaining redundancy money. I decided that I would purchase a winter mooring in Todmorden. Arrive in the autumn, get a job in the town over the winter months and stay until spring. If Todmorden – my first choice – was rejected, I would take it as another sign and buy a winter mooring in Congleton instead.

After a week on the aqueduct, I cruised once more along my now favourite canal. I was getting used to seeing the hills all around but continued to marvel at the splendour of them. I would find myself regularly gasping during cruises. How had I lived in this country all my life and only now appreciated its glorious hills? My previous trips "up north" had been limited to cities or to see family, and I was ashamed that my life had been so southern-centric up until this point. As I cruised along the Macclesfield Canal, the city of London with its traffic and smog was a world away, and I couldn't have been happier to be spending this precious time in such a stunning part of the world.

Chapter 70
Misogyny

The Marple Flight

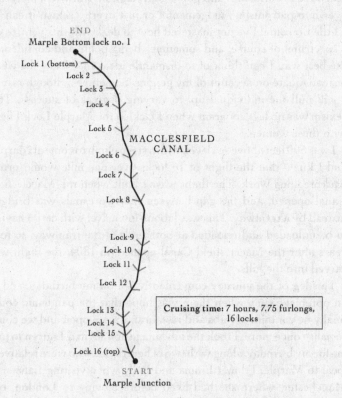

END
Marple Bottom lock no. 1

Lock 1 (bottom)

Lock 2

Lock 3

Lock 4

Lock 5

MACCLESFIELD
CANAL

Lock 6

Lock 7

Lock 8

Lock 9
Lock 10
Lock 11

Lock 12

Lock 13
Lock 14
Lock 15
Lock 16 (top)

Cruising time: *7 hours, 7.75 furlongs, 16 locks*

START
Marple Junction

ALL BOATS ARE SINKING

Perhaps my biggest frustration about living on the water (aside from the lack of bins), is the subtle microaggressions that I perceive to be unintentionally but probably laced with misogynistic undertones. Subtle as they may be, regular comments about any activity I may be engaging with are a daily occurrence that I don't accept are part and parcel for male boaters.

I do accept that intrinsically, by living on a boat on a canal, I am considered a part of the public landscape. I don't have a problem with the social, chatty element. It's wonderful and I am open and receptive to curiosities and polite conversation. But when it crosses over into patronising, judgemental or just overtly sexist, it can be a little tiresome. I've not mastered how to deal with this yet. It's on a spectrum, of course, and sometimes being polite and confident is the best way I can think of to dismantle ideas that I may be weak or inadequate on account of my gender. Sometimes, though rarely, I will pull the individual up, to varying degrees of success. This sexism was no less apparent when I tackled the Marple Lock Flight with three women.

I was 500 feet above sea level, with a steep climb to come at Marple, and I knew that the flight of 16 locks over one mile would prove backbreaking work. The flight wasn't built when the Macclesfield Canal opened, and the gap between the two canals was bridged instead by a tramway. This was labour-intensive, with cargo having to be unloaded and reloaded at both ends of the tramway, so four years after the Macclesfield Canal opened, in 1804, the flight was carved into the hills.

This leg of the journey conveniently fell on my birthday, and at an optimistic time when there was hope that the pandemic could finally be contained. Pubs and restaurants were open and we could socialise once more. I took the advantage and invited Lauryn to join me for my birthday, along with two of her friends who were relatively local to Marple. I'd met Emma and Polly when visiting Lauryn in Manchester, where she had lived before moving to London, but I had got to know them on Zoom quizzes. These quizzes were organised by Lauryn for her close friends, mostly actors, and had been running weekly since the first lockdown started. Unless I was hosting, I would come second to last almost every week. Polly is an actor. She's dry and funny with an infectious laugh, and she would finish in the middle of the quiz scoreboard. Emma, a stage manager, had gone to live at her mother's and taken a job as a postie when her theatre jobs were cancelled. She is the kindest person I think I've ever met, and I didn't know it at the time, but she would quickly become a friend for life. Emma always won the quiz.

The weather in Marple peaked at 33 degrees, with no breeze. The 16 locks would be a challenge, but I had my women with me.

"Take note of any comments," I said to my crew.

I was confident we would struggle to make the journey without one remark, and sure enough, at lock one of 16 a comment was made about my height from another boater.

"You need another few inches, love," he said as I manoeuvred into the lock, while peering over the roof of my boat.

In itself this is fairly tame, and there's a chance my gender didn't play a part at all, merely my height[78]. But I suspect, based on the regularity of these remarks whenever I'm moving the boat or using a tool or operating a lock, and the fact that they are never really uttered when I am in the company of a man, that there is a subtle level of gendered commentary going on here. During our long day, there were more examples. One was from a towpath user as Emma and Polly opened a lock gate for me.

"You shouldn't be doing that. The men should," said the dog walker.

"What men?" Polly said to the voyeur, who looked down at the boat to see me and Lauryn on the back deck, waving.

---

78 5 feet 6 inches, if you're wondering.

Other comments made during my summer voyage:

- "Are you being a damsel in distress?" (upon receiving unasked-for help from a man)
- "Come on, girl, put your back into it." (upon holding a rope)
- "You shouldn't be doing these locks on your own." (upon working a lock. I have had this one more than once)
- "He won't be having any dinner tonight, will he?" (with Will on the boat — I'm not joking)
- "When you've done chopping up your wood, do you want a go at mine?" (I'm still not joking)
- "You're very brave." (most days)
- "You're doing these locks alone? Oh dear." (with pitying eyes)

Polly and Emma ran from one lock to another, tackling them like they were toy versions with their incredible strength. I was amazed at their willingness to get stuck in. Lauryn stood on the back deck with me, taking the tiller at one point as I made a batch of homemade lemonade inside.

"You weren't kidding about the comments," said Polly. We were sitting on the towpath at the tenth lock, eating Emma's homemade vegan scones.

"I know. It can be a little exhausting," I said.

"You should get a T-shirt saying 'you wouldn't say that to a man' on it," said Lauryn.[79]

"Thank you all so much for helping," I said.

---

79 Emma has since had the T-shirt made for me.

MISOGYNY

"It's really nice to get out and actually do something," said Emma.

We finished our scones in silence. I know we were all thinking the same. That we were so grateful for this moment. For friendships old and new. For being together.

"Come on." Emma stood up. "Those last six locks aren't going to do themselves."

"Lauryn, do you want to drive?" I asked.

"Are you sure?" she said.

I nodded.

"I'll look after her," said Lauryn, walking to the boat.

"Not a 'her,'" I said, smiling. "Come on, then." I grabbed a windlass and ran up to the next lock with Emma and Polly.

The sun was searing down. It was a birthday I will never forget. I experienced more togetherness than I had ever felt on a day that can often otherwise feel quite selfish. I watched Lauryn drive *Argie* through the next six locks. I know I could have done them alone. I had done it before, and I would need to do it again. But my God was it fun (and quicker) to do them as a four.

Chapter 71
Manchester

The Ashton Canal

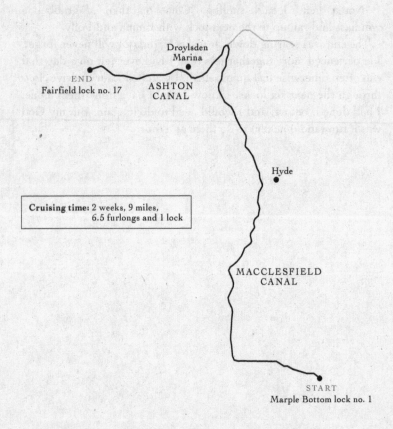

Droylsden
Marina

END
Fairfield lock no. 17

ASHTON
CANAL

Hyde

Cruising time: 2 weeks, 9 miles,
6.5 furlongs and 1 lock

MACCLESFIELD
CANAL

START
Marple Bottom lock no. 1

MANCHESTER

I had seen warnings on the Facebook boating groups about the edges of Greater Manchester: "KEEP YOUR DOORS LOCKED AT ALL TIMES" they said.

As it was considered unsafe to moor up in my next location, it would require some planning. I was told I could stop over at a marina in Droylsden to the east before tackling the epic two-day cruise through the city centre. Unlike London, Manchester is without a packed community of continuous cruisers on account of the lack of mooring rings available. I would later decide that this was a real shame. Manchester would make a great city for continuous cruisers.

I called the marina in Droylsden ahead of my arrival to ensure a spot on my first night and was given a friendly but relaxed "yeah there should be space" answer from the voice on the other end of the phone. I couldn't risk a "should be" response so decided I would find somewhere to stop before reaching the marina, and go for a run in the morning to suss out my options. I was uneasy about heading in without knowing exactly where I was aiming for, but as the greetings from locals became increasingly friendly, with assured nods and a rhetorical "How's it going?" from everyone I came across, it didn't feel unsafe to me.

At Hyde, I cruised past a boat moored up by a row of houses. It was longer than mine, 60 feet I'd say, and with a matt grey undercoat finish. It looked to be brand new. I'd been travelling behind it for a while, but the boat had stopped and was now tied up poorly against a lamp-post. I peered into the boat's cabin as I passed.

"You okay?" I said.

A man in his late thirties, 6 feet 3 inches, with tattooed arms and wearing a baseball cap, climbed out of his cabin and hoisted up his jeans.

"Something in my prop again." He was as Mancunian as they come.

"Ah, that's annoying. Good luck," I said, before cruising past. I looked back at the man. He pulled up his jeans again and bent down to retrieve the rubbish.

ALL BOATS ARE SINKING

The man and his boat caught up with me at the swing bridge just before the Ashton Canal. I tied up *Argie* and was on my way to operate the bridge as he hovered in the centre of the channel.

"Don't worry, I'll open it, and you can drive straight in," I said.

"You got a key?" he said.

"Yeah," I held up my British Waterways key.

"No, I mean an anti-vandal key." He retrieved a brass key from inside his doorway.

"What's that?" I said, looking at the thing he was holding. It looked a bit like an Allen key.

"It's to stop people misusing the locks. Extra protection from any anti-social behaviour. They're also called a handcuff key."[80]

"Ohhhhhh. I wondered what that was. I've got one somewhere. I'll get it." I had one in my boat from the previous owner but had never had reason to use it. The key would be needed along the Ashton Canal, into Manchester and beyond. I went inside, grabbed it and ran over to the bridge. I crossed the bridge to the side where the operating panel was and lifted the bridge, letting the man's boat in.

"I need to pass over your boat to go and fetch my boat. Do you mind?" I asked.

"Not at all." He smiled. That accent again.

Being a traditional narrowboat design, his didn't have much in the way of a back deck,[81] and so I climbed down onto it and squeezed myself between him and his cabin to climb back out and run and grab my boat. He cruised out from the bridge location and tied on to the landing on the other side, and we repeated the same for my boat.

We continued on in convoy. He was a faster driver than me, but I sensed his local knowledge would come in handy and decided it was in my interest to stay close behind. We cruised through the

---

80 Essentially, it's a lock on a lock.
81 Called a trad stern.

Ashton Canal, winding along through a quiet stretch. He pulled in at sundown on some mooring rings. I did the same just behind him.

"Sorry, I know I've been following you. Strength in numbers 'n' all," I said, as we both pulled our boats into position.

"Don't worry," he said. "I'm Tim."

"Nice to meet you, Tim. I'm Hannah."

"Hannah on *Argie Bargie*," he said, smiling.

We tied up our boats, chatting all the while. Before long, Tim was telling me that the boat was a recent purchase, and how he planned to cruise it down the Thames with his best friend, Tyson Fury. I hadn't heard of Tyson, but something about his name, and Tim's tattoos, gave it away.

"Is he a boxer?" I said.

"Yeah." Tim laughed.

"Oh right."

"He's having a big fight next spring, so the boat is a PR stunt for that."

"Do you do boxing yourself?" I said.

"Sometimes," he said. "You ever seen a fight?"

"No, never."

"I'll show you one sometime."

I let this hang in the air a little, unsure how to respond.

"I'm going to see how far the marina is in the morning and head there tomorrow," I said, changing the subject.

"Right, well I need to get to the other side of Manchester to get my topcoat." I could see through the windows that Tim's boat was kitted out with a wide-screen TV, marble-style kitchen surfaces and modern bar-stools. It was fancy and not at all like *Argie*. I wasn't particularly impressed by the famous boxer connection, as I think he assumed I ought to have been. But I was intrigued by Tim. And charmed.

We went inside our respective boats, and I settled in for the night. We were moored between a car park on one side and a building site on the other. It was an odd bit of the canal. I had been spoiled with woodland and farmland for so long now that it was unusual to see concrete and street lamps outside. If Tim hadn't been there, I might have felt a little vulnerable in this quiet mooring on the edge of Manchester.

I'm often asked if I feel safe on the boat. For the most part I do, but I'll take a few precautions. If an area is secluded, I'll aim to moor where there are other boats. If I'm leaving for a night, I'll try to ensure my boat is overlooked. When inside, with the doors locked and curtains shut, generally I do feel safe. The most common interference comes from people hopping onto the boat or, in the worst-case scenario, untying ropes, so sometimes if I hear a noise overnight, I will be on high alert. When I was a teenager, I remember engaging in some "boat hopping" activity in the marina in Ipswich. I've had a few incidents like this, and I know now how scary it is to wake up with someone jumping onto the boat. Teenage Hannah thought it was a laugh, but it's not.

The next morning, I awoke to find Tim and his big grey boat had left. But after his name drop the day before it didn't take me long to hunt him down on Instagram. I dropped him a message saying how nice it was to have found a buddy up in Manchester and we agreed to keep in touch.

~~~~~~

I pulled into Droylsden Marina and was greeted by two men: Pikey – tall with a long white beard and ripped chequered shirt, a cigarette dangling from his mouth, and Fred – frail and petite, holding himself up against a railing. I couldn't place their ages.

"Chuck us your rope," Pikey said.

Droylsden Marina is managed by the nearby Portland Basin Marina, a boatyard I'd passed at the turn before the Ashton. Located in a waterside housing development, the neat square of boats at Droylsden is overshadowed by new-build flats with balconies. The boats, of varying sizes and occupancy, sit close together on two sides of the square, with a spacious turning point in the middle.

It had a well-maintained toilet and shower block, laundry facilities and a book swap, gated access to the pontoons and waste disposal. Everything a boater could possibly want.

I swung round and tied up on to the only free spot.

"Do you need electricity?" Pikey said, standing at the end of my pontoon.

"Oh, I don't know. I'm not sure how long I'll be here for," I said, feeling out of place in this plush environment.

"I'll hook you up anyway. There's some left on this one."

He was pointing at the meter on the box in front of *Argie* that seemed to contain electricity and water.

"Do you have a fuckin', err…" He was trying to remember the word. "… power lead?"

"I do, but it's not going to stretch," I said.

"I've got a longer cable. I'll rewire it," said Fred, as quietly as anything.

"Are you sure? That's amazing. Thank you. Fred, was it?"

He nodded and went off to get his tools.

"Just don't talk to anyone about fuckin' being here." Pikey was wagging his cigarette-holding hand at me. "And they'll fuckin' let you stay. You'll be here all winter. Just fuckin' don't. Say. Anything."

With all the fuckings I couldn't tell if Pikey was welcoming me or not. Either way, I was happy to be in the marina. Fred rewired my plug onto his cable, and just that like I had mains electricity, which would provide a far greater supply than on *Argie*.

"Come on, let's get you a fucking coffee," Pikey said to Fred, as they walked off to the local café.

The next morning, I called Portland Basin and agreed to pay for as long as I'd end up staying. It was the end of August at this point. I'd been on the move for three months, and with the marathon and autumn round the corner, I planned to spend a few weeks in Manchester to regroup. To focus on training, job hunting and some crucial pre-winter boat maintenance.

But before all that, I had dinner booked with Tim.

Chapter 72
Not a Date

I nearly cancelled a few times. It felt weird to be dressing up and going out for dinner and I was adamant that Tim didn't think it was a date. It wasn't. He was just showing me the city. On Friday night he picked me up in his BMW with red leather seats and drove us for 30 minutes to a car park, where there was an Indian restaurant over three floors. I'd shared a live location with Caz, who knew all about my plans for the evening.

We chatted the whole way, covering big subjects – his four children, our families, religion – before the conversation turned to boxing. I had watched a fight on YouTube in preparation, the first I'd ever seen, and I had a million and one questions. Tim started teaching me all about the sport, giving me a blow-by-blow account of the most recent big fights. He was captivating, and though it was a world I knew nothing about and would otherwise have not been interested in, I found the passion and magnetism that Tim had for the subject endearing to say the least. This was his life, just as live music, the arts, hospitality and boating were mine.

Dinner was lovely, and afterwards Tim drove me to a pub where he introduced me to a group of self-proclaimed ex-gangsters. I was pinching myself. How the hell had I ended up in this situation? In a pub with a boxer and a load of ex-drug dealers.

Because he was driving, and I was in training, we had a pint and a half each[82] the whole evening. I arrived home and, having spent the

---

82 Now my perfect amount of booze.

evening avoiding looking at my phone, saw I had eight missed calls and a string of messages from the ever-diligent Caz. Oops.

"WHY ARE YOU IN A CAR?
ON THE A6010 ROAD?
TELL ME NOW OR I'M RINGING THE POLICE
I MEAN I'M LITERALLY GONNA CALL THE POLICE
YOU'RE ON HIS BOAT AREN'T YOU
Okay I'm gonna go to sleep now. I really hope you're NOT dead.
This would be awful if you were.
OKAY DON'T BE DEAD.
☺♥"

~~~~~~

Having a toilet that flushed and being hooked up to water and electricity was luxury, something akin to having a spa membership. During my time in Droylsden I would listen to the radio all day without care, and with no moving I had more time to focus on job hunting and marathon training. I got some interviews in Manchester and London. A few rejections, and a handful of offers. But nothing that felt right. One was a position down from where I'd left off, with less than half the salary. I was starting to feel like I wasn't going to get anything as inspiring as my last job. Jonathan called out of the blue asking me to return and work with him. I replied with a "thank you, but no".

Pikey's wife, Jane, who was in charge of the marina admin, stopped me one day as I was headed out for a run.

"Hannah," she said, panting as she caught up with me, "they're looking for bar staff at the Silly Country."

Silly Country was a local bar and getting a job there was now my biggest priority. I could receive an income, while still having the headspace to plough on with my other endeavours. I walked in on the same day and handed in my CV. I had an interview but never heard from them again. This job-hunting malarkey was hard.

ALL BOATS ARE SINKING

Tim and I didn't see much of each other, but we were communicating over messages. In the evenings I watched boxing videos on YouTube or read a biography from a female Muay Thai boxer that Tim had loaned me.[83] He hooked me up with Tyson's massage therapist, and I booked in a string of pre-and post-marathon sports massages at a ridiculously cheap mates rate. I had pulled my tracksuits out of my wardrobe, swapped my Dr. Martens for trainers and was embracing the athlete look and lifestyle. I was being influenced by my new boxing associates, I think it's fair to say.

Lauryn was unimpressed.

"Are you wearing a Tyson Fury baseball cap?" she said over FaceTime.

"Oh yeah, it's Tim's," I said.

She tutted.

"You know he's said some pretty horrendous things about homosexuality, right?" she said.

It had been playing on my mind. Google had revealed a side of Tyson that I didn't agree with.

Lauryn and I entered a debate about whether I should be mixing with Tyson. Not that I'd met him yet, but I vowed that I would challenge anything I heard in person, and I maintained a belief (one I still hold) that good can come from engaging in conversations with those with whom we disagree. My life in London, and with friends, was one big echo chamber. How were we to ever see growth and progression without communicating with one another? That said, I saw her point.

"I've dealt with a lot of homophobia, Hannah," she said. "I haven't the time or desire to engage."

I had respect for Lauryn in pulling me up. She was right. I had a moral duty to not just accept the frivolous side of my new encounters, but to challenge anything that wasn't right.

~~~~~~

---

83 *Born Fighter* by Ruqsana Begum. Read it, it's great.

NOT A DATE

Tim called one Friday.

"How's it going, Hannah?" he said. "Do you want to come and help me move my boat back through Manchester tomorrow?"

"Sure." I hadn't moved a boat in weeks and was delighted to join in.

"Tyson's coming too. Is that alright?"

"Sure," I said.

The next day, I met Tim in Lymm, west of Manchester. We picked up the boat and cruised along the Bridgewater Canal into the city, where we were due to pick up Tyson after an interview. One of Tyson's young sons and his trainer, Sugar Hill, who had flown over from Chicago, were coming along for the cruise too.

We sat outside a restaurant in Castlefield where hordes of people and their camera phones faced our table. Tim to my left, Sugar and Tyson's son along from Tyson, and the champ himself opposite me. I was trying to appear as relaxed as possible as I sat across from a man with four million[84] followers on Instagram; arguably one of the most sought-after sports personalities in the world.

Tim spent half the meal engaged in some work admin on his phone, leaving me to chat to Tyson. We talked about his training diet and his experience of looking after five kids during lockdown. We were of a similar age, and it was striking how different our lives had turned out. He questioned me on my boat adventure and marathon training. Tyson's charisma was palpable, even behind his blacked-out Louis Vuitton sunglasses and lockdown beard. I was drawn to his charm and intelligence and could see why he was so successful.

Tyson is a self-proclaimed man of excess, and he admitted that he enjoys making sure others have a full drink at all times, in lieu of his own ability to drink. We were having the same non-alcoholic beer (both of us being athletes, you know) and each round Tyson would order me another, without asking.

---

84 And counting

ALL BOATS ARE SINKING

"I run a bit," Tyson said, "but I'm not very fast."

"I bet you are," I said, taking a sip from my 0.0% beer.

"No, I'm not," he said. "Honestly. Eleven-minute miles. I carry a lot of weight."

Oh my God, I thought, *I can run faster than a world champion athlete*.

Tim piped up, "Tyson, would you give Hannah's brother a call?"

My brother, Matthias, it turns out, was a fan of the boxer. I had had no idea, but when I told him I was meeting Tyson, he said that he had followed his career and journey closely over the years.

"No, Tim," I said. "Don't worry, Tyson."

"Course I will..." He had his hand out ready to take the phone. His fingers were crooked from years of abuse.

I called my brother on FaceTime, and Tim took the phone.

"Hi, Matthias, it's Tim. How's it going? Listen, I've got someone here who wants to say hello."

Tim passed the phone to Tyson. I could see the reflection of my brother in his Louis Vuittons.

"Hi, Matthias," he greeted my brother in his husky voice.

"Oh my God. Oh my God," I could hear Matthias saying.

They spoke for a minute while my brother introduced the boxer to his son, my nephew, John. Tyson wished them both well. I was choked and thanked Tyson and Tim for the gesture. I couldn't wait to talk about it later with my brother.

Two women joined us at the table: Michelle, the interviewer with a boxing YouTube channel who had hosted the exclusive with Tyson, and Mel, who headed up his PR team. As they sat down, I took in their glamour. They were dressed in tight jeans, blouses and heels, with even tans, expensive handbags and pristine make-up. It wasn't long after meeting them that I realised these two women weren't just glamorous, they were also highly successful in a male-dominated industry. They were as badass as they come. I instantly warmed to them both.

Tim had told me that the last time this group had all been together was in Las Vegas the February before. They had some catching up to do. I sat back and listened as they reminisced, telling stories of their time together before the pandemic. The presence of Tyson's son broke any formality that may otherwise have been there, and weirdly, I didn't feel out of place in the group. They were respectful and curious. After lunch, we headed to Tim's boat, which had been moored outside the restaurant. The short journey to the boat took longer with Tyson stopping several times to have his photo taken with fans. I was beginning to understand the level of fame we were talking about here, as people of all ages stopped to say something to the boxer, often referencing his personal comeback story and his battle with mental health issues. He took it all in his stride, allowing a polite interaction for a minute or so per person. We finally reached Tim's boat and headed off for a cruise through the city centre, Tyson taking up position on the roof.

"I think you might get recognised there, Tyson," I said. He was a 6 foot 9 inch man standing on the roof of a narrowboat wearing his branded clothing line and holding Tim's barge pole like a staff.

"I would get recognised regardless. Might as well enjoy it," he said, clearly not afraid of the attention.

Sugar,[85] now a few bourbons in, helped me with the locks, while filming segments for his Instagram account.

"Don't drop your phone in, Sugar," I said, many times.

Tim was at the tiller and Michelle and Mel sat on the hatch above the door, while Tyson's son ran up and down the roof. I taught Tyson how to operate the locks, though he barely lifted a finger all day. I guess it wouldn't be worth the injury. He was fascinated by the lock system, asking questions all the while.

"Takes a fair bit of time, doesn't it," he said.

"It's called Canal Time," I explained.

"How many were there from London to here?"

"Mmm, about two hundred?" I said.

"And you did them all alone?" He seemed impressed.

"I had some help along the way, but mostly... yeah," I said.

---

85 First name terms. No biggy.

"You're brave." I normally get riled by this response, but hearing it from someone who has made their fame from receiving punches to the face made it a little more palatable.

As we passed a bar above the canal, Tyson shouted up and proceeded to buy a bottle of Woodford Reserve for the crew.

The locks we passed through were brilliantly varied, some with chain contraptions, some with landings that led to nowhere, locks that were flooded or underground. It was an impressive stretch as we weaved under the city and arrived at Canal Street, the LGBTQ+ district of Manchester. I thought of my conversation with Lauryn and kept an ear out for any remarks from the controversial boxer. Tyson spoke to a few fans sitting at tables above us, and whether he was thinking it or not, said nothing that might have made me (or Lauryn) uncomfortable.

I walked back to the boat after operating our sixth or seventh lock to find Tyson and Tim in conversation and looking over at me.

"Tyson thinks I've met a keeper," Tim said, referring to me.

"Does he?" I said.

"I think he should stop looking," Tyson said. I blushed. Nothing had happened between Tim and me. We were friends, though there had been a few flirtatious moments, but now, after this comment from Tyson, there was a suggestion in the air that couldn't be taken back.

Chapter 73
Marathon

Marathon route

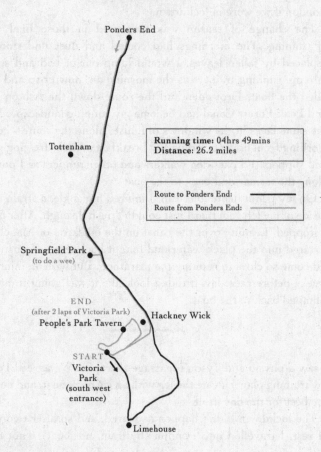

Ponders End

Tottenham

Running time: 04hrs 49mins
Distance: 26.2 miles

Route to Ponders End:
Route from Ponders End:

Springfield Park
(to do a wee)

END
(after 2 laps of Victoria Park)
People's Park Tavern

Hackney Wick

START
Victoria
Park
(south west
entrance)

Limehouse

ALL BOATS ARE SINKING

The Virtual London Marathon was fast approaching, but rumours in the press suggested we might be going into another lockdown. This would rule out the possibility of me travelling to London to run it along the towpath there, as I had planned to. In preparation for the potential of another lockdown, I asked my new Manchester associates if they would hang about that weekend to cheer me on in case I had to run the 26.2 miles along the towpath in Manchester instead. It was disappointing to think that I might not have my close friends and family around, but I couldn't travel into London if we were in lockdown.

The change of season was welcomed in those final weeks of training. The mornings had cooled and dust underfoot was replaced by fallen leaves. I would jump out of bed and straight into my running trainers as the morning air, now crisp and dewy, filled the boat. Droyslden and the route down the Ashton Canal and Peak Forest Canal had become my running landscape. I'd see the same faces in the windows of houses along the route – couples working from home or preparing breakfast in their dressing gowns and slippers. I'd pass dog walkers and other runners as I pounded along the tarmac and back to the boat.

On my penultimate long run, I injured my ankle: a strain on the inside of my left foot that I just couldn't push through. After 5 miles I stopped. Leaning over the canal on the outskirts of Manchester, I stared into the black water and fought back tears of frustration. I'd come so close to running the marathon. But with an injury two weeks before race day, it didn't look like it was going to happen. I limped back to the boat.

~~~~~~~~

I saw a physio and Tyson's massage therapist. We agreed I'd stop my training plan, elevate the leg with an ice pack on it, and hope for the best for the day itself.

The lockdown didn't happen as feared, and so after two weeks of rest, I travelled into London (by train, not boat) – not to run the official route, passing the *Cutty Sark* or running over Tower Bridge with hordes of people watching, but instead to run along a makeshift route with an app in my ear telling me how far I had left to run. My friends would be positioned along the edge of the route to pass me fuel and make sure I was okay. I also suggested to those who liked running that they might want to join me for a mile or two.

The day of the Virtual Marathon, I was a bag of nerves. I had no idea how my ankle would fare having not put weight on it for two weeks, and I just didn't know if I had it in me to complete the race. The forecast of torrential rain and strong winds were certain to make things more challenging, too.

I thought of Tyson and how he said he never gets nervous before a fight. I was channelling him as I stretched out at Victoria Park on the cold October morning. Caz was there as I limbered up. She stood a few metres away, respectfully keeping quiet as I got into the zone. I had my marathon playlist in one ear and checked in with her on timings for a fuel stop up in Ponders End.

"So, you'll lay out the bits on the floor, and I'll just grab what I need," I said to Caz for the hundredth time. I knew that if I asked her to do this, it would be done meticulously. I had a few minutes left before I was due to start when Prosecco Sarah, her husband Jamie and their now two-year-old daughter Scarlett came bounding around the corner. I wanted to run up to them and hug them all, but I knew I shouldn't. Perfectly synchronised, Sarah counted down from five and the family unzipped their hoodies to reveal three white T-shirts with slogans. Sarah's read "RUN HANNAH RUN", Jamie's "CHOOSE HANNAH" and little Scarlett's "HANNAH ROCKS". Tears welled up in my eyes.

"No, Hannah, don't cry. You have a race to run," said Sarah, wiping her own tears away. I realised that this would be an emotional day all round. As a group of friends, it was our first social outing since pre-lockdown. Sarah's reaction summed it up. We were so happy to be near each other again.

When it was time to start, Caz counted me down and cheered raucously as I headed off down the towpath alongside Victoria

Park. My ankle pain was low level but present. At the end of the park, I began my loop around the Limehouse Cut, heading up the River Lee towards Ponders End. I recognised boats along the route and spotted various locations I'd moored up at during my time in London. I ran past the spot where I'd stayed on Megan's boat after the break-up. I spotted the exact location where I'd broken my finger in Tottenham. It was all flooding back to me as I ran along the towpath that I knew so well.

Other marathon runners were out, and I saw many makeshift finish lines with friends holding signs and balloons in an attempt to recreate the traditional celebratory finish line. It was incredible to think of all the effort that had gone into this day, despite the cancellation of the main event. We greeted one another, each runner at a different stage of their race. I passed my family, who had set up camp at the Princess of Wales pub in Clapton. I couldn't help but laugh at the sight of them all in masks and Covid protection visors. It was bizarre to see them at all, let alone like that.

Just as we'd arranged, Caz was there at mile 14 in Ponders End. A line of treats was laid along the floor: water, Lucozade, paracetamol, ibuprofen, tissues, gels, sweets, a banana. I grabbed what I needed as she shouted behind me, "How's the ankle?"

I'd forgotten about it.

"It's fine!" I said.

Silly Season Will joined me at mile 14 and ran an impressive 8 miles alongside me, all while wearing a rucksack with a golfing umbrella sticking out of it and nursing a hangover.

"Only you, Will." I laughed. "Don't forget to stretch and drink lots of water," I warned as he stopped around Springfield Park, looking a little peaky.

As I ran through Tottenham past my friend Hanna and Jake's towpath-facing flat, there were posters that Hanna had made along the towpath to greet me. Jake, who had competed in many sporting challenges over the years, joined and acted as my coach for the last 8 miles, passing me fuel when he thought I needed it and giving me tips on my technique. Who had I become, I thought, as I shouted to my running partner, "How am I doing for speed?"

Other friends joined for a mile or two. Some on their own, some in pairs. They ran a few feet behind, and I listened as they caught up with one another, laughing and sharing lockdown tales after many months apart. Syd ran for 2 miles between Clapton and Hackney Wick. She was so excited to be running with me.

"You got this, Hannah!" she called from behind. "Don't think about your toenails."

"You've given me the burst of energy I needed, Syd," I said, as she peeled away. "Thank you."

"See you at the pub!"

I couldn't tell you what most of them were wearing or how they looked. I faced forward, concentrating on my step, swerving puddles and squinting in the rain. Megan's (now) partner Ben ran with me for several miles. I asked how Megan was.

"She's good. She'll be at mile twenty-two," Ben said.

I couldn't wait to see her. Things had become frosty earlier in the year, but with time apart, and so much change, I was able to see clearly that neither of us had been receptive to each other's needs in a situation that had thrown us together. I longed for us to rekindle our long and brilliant friendship.

At mile 22, Megan, the Tooting soiree lot, Jake and Sarah's husband Jamie (who was now dressed as a Stormtrooper) all ran behind me. I had 4.2 miles left to run around Victoria Park. My legs were tired, and I was drenched from head to toe. I could see a makeshift finish line that Lauryn had made for me, and a crowd of friends and family and Zeus the dog spread out, ready to cheer me on.

The runners by my side were laughing and joking.

"God, I'm knackered," Rox said at her mile 2, my 24.

As I reached the final stretch, a wide path in Victoria Park, Donna Summer's "I Feel Love" came on my playlist. Megan signalled to the rest of the runners. "Leave her now to do the last bit," she said, and they all stopped running.

ALL BOATS ARE SINKING

I ran towards my finish line, Donna still playing in my ear.

Surrounded by friends and family and covered in prosecco that Kelly and Melissa had sprayed all over me, I doubled over and crouched down on the floor. The rain was still heavy. Tears of gratitude fell down my face as my dad handed me a cheese and pickle sandwich and Lauryn placed a beer in my other hand.

"Get that down you," said my dad. I couldn't believe I'd made it. The ankle had held out. I had stopped once only to wee and completed the Virtual London Marathon in 4 hours 49 minutes. We walked the short distance to the beer garden of the People's Park Tavern. My family left and I sat with my friends, who were spread out across several tables – most of whom I hadn't seen since before the pandemic.

"You know we wouldn't all have been free for this in normal times," said Silly Season Will, looking better than when I last saw him.

"I did think that," I said, laughing.

"Well, I'm glad we were all free," he said, raising his beer to mine.

I lay my head on his shoulder and looked across at my friends, all laughing and joking in little groups, like old times. I was exhausted but couldn't have felt more content.

Chapter 74
Leaving Droylsden

After six weeks moored in Droylsden Marina, it was time to leave Manchester. Emma helped with DIY on the final few weekends when she wasn't driving around in her red van and delivering parcels. With not much of a social life nowadays, we used these sessions as a chance to catch up and had built a steadfast friendship in the process. Emma likes the boat life just enough to get on board with the various tasks and she's also a dab hand with a drill, with a level of patience and commitment to detail that I lack. This, of course, is why she's an accomplished stage manager. We would talk at length about her career, and how much she missed it. I could see it was affecting her and that these meet-ups gave her a chance to speak to someone who understood. Being with Emma also made me feel closer to Lauryn. Though I'd seen her on marathon day, it had been brief and I hadn't been particularly chatty after the run. Emma and I shared that friendship, and I couldn't wait for the three of us to be together again.

Fred, who I had met when I first arrived at the marina, was sitting like a small child on the pontoon, hunched over with his legs curved behind him. He watched as Emma and I resealed my windows on a crisp Sunday in October. Leaks are quite common on boats. The combination of steel, window seals and movement can create the smallest opening for rain to get in. With a northern winter ahead of me, I needed to bite the bullet and take out all nine of my windows, rust-treat the frames and re-affix them in position with new tape and specialist sealant. Sounds simple, but on *Argie* nothing is. Each window would take around two hours to complete. I'd been living with these leaks for longer than I care to admit and using filler to temporarily cover the cracks on a regular basis. I'd sit in my boat each time it rained, wondering which window would be the one to drip next, curse when rain poured in, grab a mixing bowl from the cupboard and say to myself, "I really must reseal my windows."

Emma led the charge and Fred, with his years of experience as a boater, sat and advised in his quiet and gentle manner. It was the perfect DIY Sunday under a warm autumn sun, as we worked a production line: Fred passing bits over and offering tips, Emma with the drill, me scraping, filling, resealing. On that first day, we completed three windows. The next weekend, another five. Finally, on the morning before my big move out of Droylsden Marina, we resealed the last window.

"Right, now we just need to see what happens when it rains," I said to my team of helpers.

"Are you leaving today?" Sean, my neighbour, poked his head out of his boat. Despite the fact that he called me chick and liked to comment on my outfit whenever he saw me, I liked him. He was a kind and sweet man, in his late 50s, I'd say. Widowed, and with a house nearby, he seemed to prefer to spend time on his boat than alone at home.

"Yup, leaving now," I said, tidying away my tools.

I'd achieved what I set out to achieve at Droylsden. I had made use of the nearby B&Q to complete some DIY jobs, stocked up on winter fuel and rested. I hadn't landed a dream job yet, but I would try to get some casual bar work once the pubs reopened up in Todmorden. But first, I had to get there.

"Which way are you headed, chick?" said Sean.

"I'm going up the Huddersfield Narrow because of the stoppage[86] on the Rochdale," I said.

Some emergency repairs were taking place at the base of the Rochdale Canal, with weekly email notices from the Canal and

---

86 A stoppage happens on a canal when planned or unplanned works take place, sometimes over the winter when waterways are quieter, and sometimes due to a fault or natural disaster, for example a landslide.

River Trust stating "further updates next week". Getting up this way was beginning to look impossible before the planned winter stoppages would have me unable to move for several months, so I decided to tackle the lesser-known Huddersfield Narrow Canal and journey the long way round to approach Todmorden from the north.

"Oooo you don't want to go up there," Sean said.

"No?" I said. "Why's that?" I rejected his negativity straight away. I'd been told enough times that a waterway was dangerous or unpleasant, and invariably I had been right to ignore the warnings. I was told Manchester was dodgy, and it had been anything but. I was told the swing bridges would make my journey up north unbearable. They hadn't.

"It's a difficult canal. It was derelict for decades," he said. "You won't be able to pull in at the locks. It's too shallow and some gates are impossible to open on your own. You'll be stuck for days trying to get through, I tell you."

"Oh, right. Well, I don't really have an option," I said.

Just then Jane walked out of her boat.

"You could always stay here for winter? The Rochdale is tricky too, you know. Terrible flooding," she said.

I had considered this, staying put in the marina. It would be comfortable and safe, with a community on hand to offer support over the coming months. Jane had told me how lovely the marina was over winter. How they all go to the pub in the evenings together and how the frozen canal pings under foot when walking across the pontoon. I could also get deliveries there, and regular supplies of coal and gas, not to mention electricity, water, showers, laundry facilities. I weighed it all up, but my heart was set.

"I know. I just want to get to Todmorden," I said, "see my brother."

"Fair enough," said Jane. She gave me some tips on pubs I could visit en route.

"I'll pop in on the way back next spring," I said to Fred, Pikey, Jane and Sean as I cruised out of the marina and headed for the Huddersfield Narrow.

Chapter 75
Lock Bottom

"The Huddersfield Narrow – not an extraneous inch."

Jasper Winn, *Water Ways*

Huddersfield Narrow

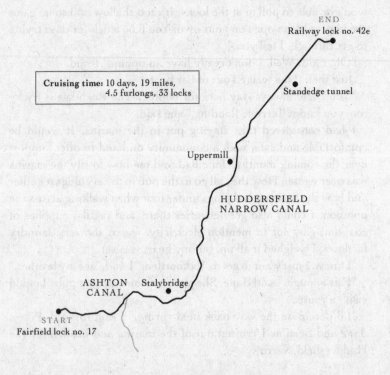

END
Railway lock no. 42e

Standedge tunnel

Cruising time: 10 days, 19 miles,
4.5 furlongs, 33 locks

Uppermill

HUDDERSFIELD
NARROW CANAL

ASHTON   Stalybridge
CANAL

START
Fairfield lock no. 17

LOCK BOTTOM

The route to Todmorden via the Huddersfield Narrow and Huddersfield Broad canals would consist of 114 locks and the longest tunnel on the UK canal network – Standedge Tunnel, a daunting prospect at 5,698 yards (3.2 miles). I would head east out of Manchester on the first Sunday after the virtual marathon. I was geared up for the move and had Emma with me to assist. Not only was she now an expert lock handler, but her positive presence on these long boat moves was much appreciated. As we set off, the autumnal air was moist with dew and the earthy smell of fallen leaves would set the tone for the next chapter in my adventure. At the first lock to the east of Portland Basin Marina, just south of Stalybridge, Emma wrestled with the lock mechanism for several minutes.

"It won't budge," she said.

I called the Canal and River Trust from my back deck to ask if they had any advice, as a woman came out from her house along the towpath.

"It's nice to see the canal getting some use," she said, putting a black rubbish bag in her wheelie bin. "I never see boats come up here."

Emma and I shared a look. Perhaps this unused canal would present further challenges after all. Another attempt and Emma managed to jiggle the mechanism free and open the paddle.

"Oh, it's okay, we're through," I said, just as someone at the Canal and River Trust answered the call. I hung up and we cruised through the lock.

"Hope they're not all like that," said Emma.

We saw only a smattering of moored boats on that first day of cruising up the Huddersfield Narrow. We saw none moving. The rising landscape on the highest canal on the UK network presented a beautiful and dramatic view of wooded land and distant hills. I would emerge from each lock to see disused mills and farmhouses marking the edge of the Pennines. Not only were the boats sparse, but towpath users were limited to a few dog walkers here and there.

ALL BOATS ARE SINKING

It wasn't like the bustling Macclesfield or the Trent and Mersey canals; the Huddersfield Narrow was deserted. Quiet and serene.

"It's such a waste that no one comes up here," I said to Emma. "It's beautiful."

"You wait until you get further up around Marsden." Emma's local knowledge about seemingly the whole of the North of England is baffling to me. Her work had stationed her in various regional theatres over the years, so she'd managed to tally up a fair bit of travel around the UK. A keen runner also, the towpath was her stomping ground, and her memory is photographic. All in all, she's like a walking map.

I repeated the "it's so beautiful" sentiment to Emma several times, shouting up to her from my back deck as she operated the locks. It was lovely to have someone to say this to, having mostly muttered it under my breath alone. We were in a routine with the moves now. Emma would stay off the boat and run up and down operating the locks, catching my rope from time to time, and mastering the gates like a pro, as I cruised in and out.

"Brrrr, it's so cold," I'd shout to Emma as she wiped sweat from her brow. I realised how strenuous the locks were only by spending so much time standing still on my back deck, watching Emma run back and forth and back and forth.

The climb was unrelenting, and the deep locks were in close succession. At single width, Emma and I whizzed through 14 on that first day up to Mossley.

"I'll get to Todmorden in no time," I said to Emma as we moored up the boat.

"That was fun," she said. "Same again next week?"

~~~~~~

I stayed put in Mossley for a week, reading, writing and enjoying walks to loosen up my post marathon legs. A week later Emma arrived.

"I've got to be at work at two p.m.," said Emma.

LOCK BOTTOM

"No problem," I said, untying my ropes at Mossley. "What have we got today… nine locks to get to Uppermill? We can easily do it."

We set off to enjoy the same routine, with me at the tiller and her operating the locks, cruising higher and higher towards the Marsden Moors. The colours were a little more vibrant, the air cooler and our spirits high. Sean had been wrong. Yes, the locks were quirky and stiff at times, and it was certainly a good idea to do this stretch with another person, but it was perfectly manageable and quite delightful.

The canal was covered in a layer of orange and yellow leaves that were densely gathered together in the water, and particularly at the locks. They slowed the boat down as we trudged through. At lock number 20 (our sixth of the day), driving out of the open gates, the boat seemed to get stuck. Emma and I stood on the gunwale either side with a large stick each, removing leaves and trying to wiggle the boat free like a tooth. It took some welly, with a few passers-by jumping on to help, too. Eventually we dislodged the boat and vowed to clear the way of leaves in the next one before entering the lock.

We carried on.

At lock number 21 at the base of the village of Uppermill, I drove the boat in as usual. It scraped along the walls inside the lock chamber. *That's weird*, I thought. *That's never happened before*. I looked up to Emma, who was looking down at me, perplexed.

"Hmmm," I said.

We continued on.

At lock 22 in Uppermill, I drove the boat in. It scraped against the side of the lock chamber again. This time my heart started to beat a little faster. It was tight. I drove in further, as *Argie* came to a halt. The boat was half in, half out the lock. I needed to cruise fully inside so we could shut the gates behind.

"It won't go in," I said to Emma who was standing above, looking down.

"What do you mean, it won't go in?" she asked.

"I'm trying, but it's jammed." I revved my engine harder. The boat inched forward but stopped again. Now it was really jammed.

I looked behind. The boat was several feet from being clear of the lock gates.

"Try again," said Emma.

I revved again. The boat didn't move. I reversed. The boat didn't move. Forward and back, again and again. Wiggle like a tooth. Nothing. I was wedged in like a cartoon cat in a mouse hole.

"Chuck us your rope," said Emma. It had started to rain.

She pulled and pulled while I revved my engine. Forward. Back. Forward. Back.

Nothing.

A dad with his child passed by.

"Would you like a hand?" he said.

"That would be great," said Emma. "You can take the other rope."

I threw him the second centre line as my phone rang. It was Tim on FaceTime. We had been in contact most days since we had met south of Manchester. Little check-ins and friendly chats; I found him very easy to talk to. Things were a little flirtatious at times. We clearly cared for each other, but I didn't see it going anywhere really. It was nice to have him as a friend, though.

"Ey up," he said.

Tim was in a room that looked like a gym. Clean walls and bright lights. A far cry from my view, stuck in a damp lock. His face, with his straight white teeth, filled the screen.

"Call you back," I said. "I'm stuck in a lock."

"You what?" he said.

"I'll call you back once I'm free." I hung up the phone.

With Emma and the passer-by holding on to the ropes above the lock, and me in the lock several yards below, I revved the engine. We were trying to get the boat fully inside the lock so we could close the gate and push the boat up from below by filling the lock with water in the usual way. But we just couldn't get it in.

"This isn't working," I said. "Let's try to reverse it again." The rain was now hammering down.

The boat wouldn't budge. It had been half an hour. Emma looked at her watch.

"I'm cold," said the man's daughter. He looked down at me in the lock.

"Don't worry, we'll be fine," I said. "Thank you for your help."

"Good luck." He threw the rope down.

Tim called again.

"What's going on?" he said.

"I'm stuck in a lock." I was laughing but it wasn't funny.

I could hear Tyson in the background. "I'll get her out."

"Do you want us to come down?" Tim said.

"I don't know," I said.

Emma looked at her watch again.

"I'll call you back, Tim."

I phoned the Canal and River Trust from inside the lock and told them I was stuck. They said they would send someone down to help. A crowd of ten or so people had assembled now and I was beginning to feel somewhat panicked.

I didn't want Emma to leave, but at this point, there clearly wasn't a lot she could do anyway. I passed her bag up as she leant down.

"Hannah, I can cancel work." Emma's eyes told me she cared. That she wasn't going to leave me if I didn't want her to.

"No, don't do that," I said. "I'll be fine. Help is on the way."

"Are you sure? Are you going to be okay?" she said.

"Well, I'm not going anywhere, am I?" We both laughed.

"Good point," said Emma.

And with that, she was gone. And I was alone on my boat, stuck in lock 22 on the Huddersfield Narrow.

I put the kettle on and paced up and down inside the boat. The view through the window was of moss-covered stone. It was surreal and bleak, like something from a horror film. And with the boat wedged, its lack of movement was disorientating. I find I have the opposite reaction now with sea legs. Not that narrowboats move like cruise ships, but the slight undulation is a more familiar and comforting home environment for me now. Without it, my boat doesn't feel like a boat.

With no sunlight able to get in and the fire having petered out, it was cold inside the lock. My kettle whistled and I laughed. A lot. What the hell was I going to do? Ten minutes passed and I heard something land on the back deck. I went outside to see a packet of Marlboro Lights and Emma's head and shoulders visible above.

"Make them last," she said.

"Thanks Emma." And she disappeared out of view again.

As I waited for the staff from the Canal and River Trust to arrive, I chain smoked on my back deck, answering questions from the crowd, with the humour I'd previously managed to retain in the presence of a friend now gone. No, this hasn't happened before. No, I don't know why. No, it isn't cold in winter. Twenty minutes later, two members of the Canal and River Trust North West team arrived, recognisable by their blue fleeces and red life jackets. Joel and Helen were sympathetic, for which I was grateful.

"You'll need more than that," I said, pointing at the windlasses in their hands.

"Pass us your ropes," said Joel, as I lassoed the ropes up to them.

We repeated the same method as before, for half an hour, trying to get my boat fully inside the lock, with the aim of closing the gates and pushing me up with the weight of the water from below. The boat didn't move.

Joel called for back-up.

"Simon knows this network like the back of his hand," he said. "Don't worry, we'll get you out."

"What happens if we don't?" I asked. It had been on my mind for an hour or so. "What happens if we can't get me out of the lock?"

He didn't answer that.

"We'll get you out," he said.

"And the other locks after this one?"

"Oh, this one is the tightest, don't worry about that," he said.

Something about this comment made me think I wasn't the first boater to have got stuck in this lock.

LOCK BOTTOM

"Why do you think it's getting stuck?" I asked, remembering how few boats I'd seen on my way up here.

"Well, these are narrow locks anyway. But they've warped over time. And by the looks of it, so has your boat."

I looked down the lock and at my boat. He was right. They both had a slight bulge in the centre. At exactly the point I was getting stuck.

Simon and another two Canal and River Trust engineers arrived, and between the five of them in their blue fleeces and red life jackets, pushing and pulling the boat by using the ropes and a large piece of timber between the lock wall and the boat itself, with me on the tiller, we finally managed to force *Argie* into the lock, scraping against the lock walls as it edged along inside. Thankfully, the scrapes occurred along the hardened black hull, rather than the blue top that I had repainted back in Stone. A few extra scrapes on the hull have never been an issue to me from an aesthetic standpoint. Finally, after some serious strength and perseverance, the group were able to close the gate behind me.

Now I needed the boat to rise up and out of the lock. Joel and Helen walked up to the top gate to release water into the lock chamber. They attached their windlasses to the paddle gear mechanisms and turned. There was the familiar clicking sound of a steel hammer hitting the toothed bar. Click click click. The water rushed in, but the boat stayed put. I looked down. I could see the water rising up around my boat, getting nearer to my through-hull penetration holes[87] on the port side. If the water went much higher, it would enter my cabin, or bilge, and the boat would sink.

I looked up to Joel and Helen.

"Stop, stop, stop," Simon said.

They turned their windlasses the other way, and the water stopped rising.

---

87 These holes on the side of hulls are where water is designed to egress from sinks, showers or bilge pumps.

At the bottom gate, the other two Canal and River Trust workers attached their windlasses to the gear mechanism, turned and lifted their paddles. The excess water emptied from the lock and into the pound below.

"Okay. Try that again," Simon said to the team, "but this time, do it very quickly."

"What? Are you sure?" I said, the fear of sinking greater than ever.

"I'm sure," he said.

Simon spoke slowly to the staff. "This time, though, we'll leave the bottom paddles open. The water will rush through under the boat and out the other side," he said. "Eventually, all this movement of water will dislodge the boat. We will flush her out. Now keep an eye on my signal and I'll tell you when to start, and when to stop."

The team got into position.

"Okay, go," said Simon.

Joel and Helen, and the two other staff on the bottom gates, cranked open the paddles with their windlasses. All at the same time. A loud cacophony of clicks. Four hammers hitting metal teeth at rapid speed. Whirlpools of water entered the chamber, this time passing through, and the water whooshed under the boat and out of the bottom gates behind me. Simon stared down into the lock, concentrating hard. Like he was looking for something in the water.

Argie didn't move.

"Okay, stop," he said.

He stepped back and inhaled through his teeth.

"Okay, let's go again." He stepped forward. I trusted Simon. I'm not sure if it's because I knew he was my only hope, but I trusted him. He'd get us out.

The team did exactly the same as before, with Simon shouting commands and then looking into the lock chamber below.

Joel shouted across the cavern. "The pound is emptying," he said, pointing to the body of water above the lock. With such a large volume of water being flushed through, the levels were lowering.

"Okay, let's try this one more time," Simon said. "But this time, we'll have two of us on the ropes."

The sun was beginning to set.

One of the team stayed on the bottom paddles, Helen and Joel on the top paddles, and Simon and another team member held onto my ropes. And me, on my boat, high on cigarettes and exhaust fumes, revving my engine and questioning how I had arrived at this place in my life.

We flushed and flushed and flushed as the two men pulled the ropes with all their might, and I revved like I've never revved before. Suddenly I felt the tiniest of movements.

"I felt it move," I said. "And again. It's moving! Keep going."

The Canal and River Trust worker on the bottom gate closed his paddles and let the water push me up from below. Eventually, after four and a half hours stuck in a lock, the boat rose up in short bursts, port side first, then starboard side, each side alternating, the movement jagged. Items inside my boat fell off the shelves and the side of *Argie* scraped against the lock walls, peeling off clumps of moss as it rose up.

Eventually the boat was bouncing again with the familiar weight of water underneath. I was free. A collective sigh of relief was shared between the six of us.

"Yes! Thank you. Thank goodness," I said to the team, who were at my eye level for the first time.

"I knew we'd get you out of there in the end," said Simon.

"I thought I'd be in there forever," I said as I waited for the team to open the top lock gates. The sun was beginning to set, and I still needed to get through a few more locks before I could find somewhere to moor up for the night. Though Joel had said this lock was the worst, I was reluctant to let them go before I was moored up safe.

"Will you stay for the next few?" I asked as I cruised out of lock 22. "I can give you head torches."

"Of course," said Joel and he and Helen assisted me through the next set of locks, thankfully with no issues.

"Am I going to have any more problems on the other side of the Standedge Tunnel?" I said to Helen and Joel. I still had 50 or so narrow locks to get through before joining the Huddersfield Broad Canal.

"No way," Joel said in the dark. "That lock twenty-two is unusually narrow. You'll be fine once you're through the tunnel."

What I didn't know at this point is that once I was through the Standedge Tunnel, a different ground team would be responsible for any issues. Canal and River Trust North West would become Canal and River Trust North East and Yorkshire. Once through, Joel and co. wouldn't have to deal with me anymore.

———

The highest, deepest and longest on the network, Standedge Tunnel is a remarkable feat of Victorian engineering. The build took 17 years, and in the early to mid-nineteenth century the bridge was used by some 40 boats a day. It is so narrow and winding that the Canal and River Trust don't allow passage without a pilot,[88] and during 2020 this meant they would cruise the boat through themselves so that social distance could be maintained between boat owner and pilot. A second Canal and River Trust volunteer would drive a van alongside the disused railway tunnel that runs parallel, shining a torch into mini tunnels that connect the two large tunnels to check in at different points along the way. Having gone through the ordeal of getting stuck in lock 22, this experience was, by comparison, a pleasure, but I could see how it would make others very nervous indeed. The boats bash about inside and the tunnel has a kink in it so there's no light at the end for most of the time inside. Passage through Standedge Tunnel took two hours in total and I eventually surfaced at Marsden, where I moored up overnight

---

88 A pilot is someone who comes on board to help when specific local knowledge is required for safe passage. They're more of a sea thing than a canal thing.

before tackling the descending flight of locks on the remainder of the Huddersfield Narrow.

I called the Canal and River Trust and booked in some volunteers to help the following day. I needed assurance that I could get through okay, and the helpers were more than willing to enjoy a day out. On the morning of the move, two retired volunteers arrived. They were energised and polite. I was jaded and nervous.

I entered the lock on the descent down from the village of Marsden towards Slaithwaite.

All was well.

The gates were shut by the helpers, and I was lowered down. No issues.

The bottom gates were opened and I drove the boat out.

I'd made it through two thirds when my boat came to a halt. It had got wedged again.

My heart sank.

The volunteers remained chipper.

"It's okay. Just give it a rev," the slightly more experienced volunteer said.

I sat down on the cushion that I'd been gifted in the summer from that kind man on the Grand Union and pulled the remaining packet of cigarettes out of my pocket. I lit up.

"No, it's not okay," I said, sighing.

I called the new team on this side of the tunnel, explained the situation afresh and went through the same process as before. Only this time, it was worse. The boat was even more stuck, and after five hours of pulling, revving, flushing; nothing. The sun was beginning to set on my second day stuck in a lock.

I climbed up the ladder to join the discussion that was being had amongst the team of helpers.

"Hannah, you can't stay here tonight," said Clare, the team's leader.

The group stood around holding their latest round of tea and looked at me. They drank from my mugs. A Wallace and Gromit mug gifted to me as a child from my parents. A *Wuthering Heights*

Penguin books mug from when I'd played Little Cathy in a stage adaptation of the book. A Happy 25th Birthday mug with a photo of Caz and me – our young and happy selves sitting around a pub table with friends. And a "Captain Hannah" mug Sarah and Jamie had gifted me when I first moved onto the boat. The mugs, familiar relics from my home below.

"I have to," I said.

"You can't, I'm afraid," said Clare. "We can't allow you to stay on the boat while it's in there."

I looked down at *Argie* and its battle scars; the paintwork scraped off the sides and the roof dirtied, with underwater lock plants flopped across it. My boat, now lifeless but for the put-put-put of the engine, was unrecognisable as the salvation it had become to me. The thing that had allowed me freedom and an opportunity to escape from the stresses of my past life.

I felt young and weak. How had it come to this? I had no job, very little money, no one around who knew or loved me. All I had was my home and it was stuck at the bottom of a lock. I looked around at the people congregating and taking photos for their Instagram accounts. I thought about their lives in this picturesque village right on the edge of the moors. The warmth and comfort available to them by being around loved ones and sleeping in their cosy houses. How, at the age of 34, had I ended up here, amongst them, but so very alone?

"This is my home." My throat was tightening. "This isn't just a holiday. I live on this."

"I'm sorry," she said.

I didn't know where to direct my frustrations. I was annoyed with myself for travelling up this canal having been warned not to by Sean. I was annoyed with the Canal and River Trust. I was annoyed at my boat. I was annoyed at the clear north/south divide and the unfair distribution of wealth and services across different parts of the UK that had no doubt played a part in the lack of maintenance of these locks. I was annoyed that I'd chosen a career path in an industry that was now under threat by a global pandemic. All of it, I was annoyed at all of it.

"Can we give it another go? Please," I said.

The team passed me my mugs back and got into position for one final attempt. Everyone seemed to find a strength from within, fuelled by tea and desperation, as we heaved and revved, and wiggled with a large plank of wood levered against my back deck and the lock wall. Six hours after I had first got stuck, we finally managed to squeeze my boat back into the lock, where we filled it up, so that I could reverse out and onto the lock landing.

With no option to go through this lock, or indeed any more ahead of me, I reversed the boat back to the winding hole (turning point) by Standedge Tunnel, turned around and moored up, ready to head through the tunnel again and back down the Huddersfield Narrow, and into Manchester once more.

"I'll call up the others down there," said Clare. "I'll ensure there's a whole team to get you through lock twenty-two. I promise."

I was too exhausted to think about the next stage, so I thanked her and went inside to relight my fire.

Chapter 76
Things People Said to Me While I Was Stuck in a Lock

- Have you tried putting Vaseline on the walls?
- I saw this on Instagram and thought I'd come down and take a look.
- Women drivers, hey.
- You were the talk of the town in the pub last night.
- I've never seen one of these locks being used before, could you hurry up so I can see?
- Are you stuck?

Chapter 77
Navvies

The term "navvy", or "navigational engineer", refers to the worker whose occupation it was to build the canal (and later railway) systems. Being a navvy was a skilled job that required engineering knowledge as well as brute strength. They built the waterway channels, packed solid banks and created towpaths. While they didn't build the locks themselves (masons did), they would be responsible for their foundations.

For the construction of Standedge Tunnel in the Pennine Hills, Welsh coal miners are thought to have been drafted in. The work would have been hard, and in brutal conditions that the miners were familiar with. The navvies would work long hours in dim light using dynamite sticks and manual tools to burrow into the rock. Markings can still be seen on the surface of the Standedge Tunnel.

It is thought that the men and women working as navvies lived alongside the canal in encampments of wooden and turf huts. Like us boaters, they were rootless people. When the railways replaced the canal network, the navvies merely transitioned across to the new transport system.

Chapter 78
Freedom

I had booked my passage back through Standedge Tunnel for a few days later. With the team on hand at Uppermill, I hoped we could get me back through together and en route to Manchester, so I could forget all about the Huddersfield Narrow and journey up to Todmorden on the (now reopened) Rochdale Canal. I'd spent two days in Marsden unable to navigate in either direction, confined to the inside of my boat, too afraid of being recognised as the woman who'd been stuck in a lock.

Tim called on the morning of the move back down.

"Listen," he said, "I'm gonna come and do this with you."

"No, please don't."

In moments of stress I have come to recognise that I have a tendency to shut down and reject help. I'd much rather get my head down and face the music alone, which means ignoring the severity of the situation and taking on the challenge with a kind of foggy internalised angst. When I had been looking down at my boat stuck in the lock at Marsden, I had felt removed from the situation before me. I'd started to feel like I was floating through each stage of the ordeal; my brain disconnected from reality.

"Hannah," Tim said, "I'm not having you do this on your own, okay?"

I was learning that Tim had a stubborn streak and wasn't going to accept a no on this.

"Okay," I said. "Thank you."

We travelled back through Standedge Tunnel, Tim asking the same set of questions to the pilot that I'd asked before, as I sat wrapped in a blanket inside my boat. We navigated through the ten

FREEDOM

locks between the south entrance of the tunnel and Uppermill and by late afternoon were back at lock 22.

There was no sign of any Canal and River Trust staff.

"Right." Tim was taking charge while I settled back into my foggy state. "We're gonna do this now and do it slowly. You're going to drive in. I'll let you down. And we'll stop if you get caught. Okay?"

"Okay," I said, with tears in my eyes.

"It's okay," said Tim.

We did just as he said, and as he released the water out of the lock, my boat slowly lowered. Halfway down and the back of the boat stopped rigid. The bow continued to drop as the stern stayed solid in position.

"Tim. Tim. Tim," I called up, as my propeller rose up and out of the water.

"It's okay," he said.

"No, it's not. I'm stuck again."

Tim didn't stop the paddles and stood watching my hopeless boat tip further. I started to feel panicked. The water continued to rush out, and *Argie* was now at a 45-degree angle, doors swinging open inside, kitchen utensils on the floor.

Tim eventually stopped the water.

It was a scene like the one from James Cameron's iconic 1990s masterpiece[89], with *Argie Bargie* nose down in the lock, its propeller high in the air, and me balanced at the back holding on to the tiller. I watched Tim run up to the top paddles and let in some water. We waited for it to push my boat back up level so we could try again. The water rose, but the boat didn't move.

"Tiiiiiimmmmm!" I shouted up from the back deck. Tim stood unmoving, ignoring my cries and continued to let in water that was whooshing in around me at speed. *This is it*, I thought, as the

---

[89] Why are you even reading a millennial's memoir if you don't know what film I'm talking about here?

voice of Paul the welder at Stanstead Abbotts boatyard came into my head: "All boats are sinking, Hannah." Was this *Argie*'s time? Was I sinking? I snapped out of my foggy state and screamed Tim's name again. As I held on tightly to the useless tiller, the water continued to enter the lock, rising further up the edges of the boat's hull. I was totally helpless as the boat remained in position. I shouted Tim's name again, my voice now hoarse. He held up his hand as if to say "wait". Suddenly the boat jolted. A small but powerful movement that shifted me from my position as well. It jolted again. Then again. One side then the other, and eventually the boat started to rise, in various wedged positions, until finally it was level with the top of the lock. Once the boat was buoyant, I was able to breathe again, though my heart was still racing.

Tim walked up and said, "Are you okay?" He was genuinely concerned.

"Just about," I said, crossing my shaking arms over my body. "I've heard too many stories of boats sinking in locks and that was just seconds from happening."

"I know," he said. "Listen." This was Tim's now-familiar introduction to an idea. "The sun's going down. Let's try again in the morning with a team and I'll bring my winch too, okay?"

I looked at Tim. He was cool and collected. I'm not sure why I trusted him so much, but I did.

"Fine," I said. "Let's try again tomorrow."

We retreated the boat back on to the lock landing, where I tied up for the night.

"See you in the morning, Hannah," said Tim. "Get some rest."

Back inside the boat, I lit my fire for the first time that day and called the Canal and River Trust. Once my "just a thought" suggestion that we grind down the lock walls had been pooh-poohed, we agreed to all meet in the morning at lock 22 to hatch a plan. I sat down, exhausted. *What if it doesn't work?* I thought. I looked at my map on the wall, at the journey so far, and began to imagine the worst; that I would be stopping here and living out my days moored outside lock 22 on the Huddersfield Narrow.

~~~~~~~

I awoke early on Saturday to find the original full team of helpers waiting by lock 22 with Tim, holding a windlass each. As I approached the group, all looking at me with helpless expressions, it was clear we held the same opinion. There was no way my boat was getting through that lock. Not today, not ever. There was only one option left: to find a spot in which to have a crane hoist my boat out of the water, onto the back of a truck, and drive it down the motorway beyond the troubled locks. Tears welled up again in my sad unemployed eyes as the figure of £1,500+ was casually dropped into the conversation.

"Don't worry," said Tim, "I know a guy who owes me a favour. He could put you on the back of his trailer."

I didn't trust that I could get insurance for a "favour", so I declined the offer.

"Or…" Tim had an idea. "Why don't we grind off your rubbing strakes?"

"My what?" I said.

"These." Tim pointed to a strip of steel on my boat just above the waterline, designed to take impact should the boat hit something. They'd received quite a battering of late. It seemed like a futile suggestion.

"They're only a couple of mil," I said, holding up my fingers to the bar.

"Could make all the difference," he said.

I smiled at Tim's glass-half-full attitude.

"It's worth a punt," he said.

At this stage I think I'd have been convinced to try my luck on a team of wild horses to get me through.

~~~~~~~

ALL BOATS ARE SINKING

Tim (whom I now owed several pints) returned the next day with his power tools and a generator and spent the morning grinding down the sides of *Argie Bargie* in the rain, while I brought him tea and looked after his cockapoo puppy Ollie inside. I stared at my walls as Tim worked outside. I was primed to use my fire extinguisher in case the insulation between wall and steel was flammable. That was the last thing I needed to happen.

The portside rubbing strake successfully removed, I started the engine and stepped off the boat to join Tim, who was staring at his handiwork. Where the bar had been, there was now exposed steel, like an open flesh wound. The rain was lashing down, and Ollie was barking inside.

"It's gotta work," Tim said under his breath.

I knew it wouldn't.

And it didn't.

The boat got stuck again.

"It's not enough," I said, as my boat remained wedged at another precarious angle inside the lock. Tim sighed and flushed me out again. Once buoyant, I reversed back on to the lock landing.

"Déjà vu," I said, tying up the boat again.

"It's okay," said Tim. "It's okay. We'll do the other side tomorrow."

I was beginning to regret letting Tim do this to my boat. Now, not only would I have to crane it out, but I'd have some welding work to pay for on top. But we'd already butchered one side – what's another?

I stood with Ollie the next morning as Tim repeated the process on the other side of my boat. He was so kind to be helping me out like this. Emma arrived.

"Ey up," she said.

Between us, we laid the rubbing strakes on my roof.

"They look like two big pole vaults mid-jump," said Emma. I was grateful to have her there.

The stage manager and the boxer stood either side of the gates and watched me drive my boat into the lock in silence.

"We'll go real slow," Tim said to Emma, shutting the gate behind me. They opened the paddles, a third of the way up. *Argie* began to descend. It nicked against the lock walls, my heart pumping a little faster each time it made contact, but it slowly continued its descent.

As the boat was lowered, I pondered. *Why am I living like this? I've lost count of all that can and does go wrong in "boat world". My boat, knackered and scarred, is a never-ending list of problems, and in a moment, it can feel like a foreign object again. One that makes me confused and angry. So why does it still fill me with joy? Is the answer within that? Do I love my boat because I experience this polarity and in overcoming challenges can appreciate the rewards more intensely? Or is it because of people like Emma and Tim? In the encounters with other humans, and our shared journey.*

The Huddersfield Narrow had brought me up against a problem that I could never have foreseen. It was stressful as anything, and yet it had been another adventure, and for that, I was and will always be grateful.

We waited until the boat was buoyant at the bottom of the lock. Emma and Tim opened the gates. Heavy and slow, like the opening sequence of *Jurassic Park*.

"Go on," Tim said.

I took a deep breath. This was exactly where I had first got stuck. Would the removal of the rubbing strakes be enough for me to get through? Tim and Emma stood with their hands on their hips. They nodded down at me. I clasped the throttle and gently pushed the lever forward. The boat inched towards the open lock gates. Water dripped from the vegetation that was growing on them. I clenched every muscle and stared intently ahead, as if my still gaze would ensure a smooth passage.

I cruised out slowly, passing Tim and Emma above, who watched me clear the lock gates. Effortlessly, I was finally out of the lock. I turned around to double check I had made it through. I had. I breathed an enormous sigh of relief and looked up to see Emma and Tim jumping up and down at the top of the lock and throwing both their arms into the air. I shouted some happy expletives up to them and joined in with the celebratory leaping.

I was free.

ALL BOATS ARE SINKING

"Tim, thank you," I said, still jumping. "Thank you. Thank you both." I was too joyous to stop the boat. They ran after me, Emma shouting, "Hey, Hannah! Where are you going!?"

I pulled in and we fell about laughing on the towpath.

"Let's get back to fucking Manchester," I said.

Chapter 79
The Worst Things
About Living on a Boat

- Lack of bins on the waterways
- Mess from the fire
- Dropping things in the water
- Being asked if I'm warm enough every day in the winter
- Battery/power issues
- Engine issues
- Running out of water
- Running out of gas [90]
- Being stuck in a lock
- Having a blocked chimney
- Having water in places it shouldn't be
- Stormy nights
- Floods
- Things getting caught in the propeller
- Rust

---

90 Yes, you landlubbers who bought up all the gas bottles for your new fancy outdoor heaters after lockdown… We couldn't get any for weeks!

Part 5

~~~~~~

Are You Winning?

Chapter 80
Tod You So

The two 10-foot strips of steel that used to be my rubbing strakes, lying upon my roof, bore evidence of my escapades up the Huddersfield Narrow. The tenants of Droylsden Marina had heard the tale from various sources within the canal community. I didn't mind if the telling had been altered as it travelled down the hills; there wasn't much more that could be exaggerated beyond the truth, I felt, and I was grateful that I didn't need to explain why they were seeing me again so soon.

"Told you it was tricky, chick," said Sean out of his side hatch window as I cruised back into my nook at Droylsden Marina two weeks after I had left.

"You didn't say I'd get stuck in a lock," I said, turning onto the pontoon.

"Well, this isn't a fucking bad place to be for winter." Pikey had his hands held out ready to catch my ropes.

"Oh, I'm still going up to Todmorden," I said. "I'll head off tomorrow."

The second UK lockdown was imminent, and I knew we would be banned from moving the boats again before long. I was still going to Todmorden for winter, but I'd need to get there quickly.

Pikey's wife Jane climbed out of Fred's boat wearing Marigolds.

"We'll help with the locks through Manchester," she said. "Won't we, Pikey?"

"I've not done those fucking locks in ten years," he said.

She looked at him.

"Oh, go on then."

"Where's Fred?" I asked them both.

335

"He's in fucking hospital," said Pikey.

Jane and Pikey were Fred's neighbours at the marina. He clearly meant a lot to them.

"We're cleaning out his fucking boat so he can get better and come home."

"Oh God, I'm sorry," I said.

I was sad about Fred. He'd been kind to me, and I was looking forward to seeing him. That evening, I messaged Tim to see if he wanted to go for a walk. He called me on FaceTime.

"Listen," he said.

"Go on, Tim."

"I really, really, really like you, Hannah. But I think I'm in danger of falling for you. And you're going up to Todminden and I don't wanna get hurt."

Pronouncing place names wrong in this part of the world would become a trend. With names like Mythonroid, Slaithwaite and Mankinholes, it really is just a punt guessing how the locals say them, and Tim's attempt at Todmorden was no exception.

I knew this conversation would have to happen at some point. He'd been great company during my time in Manchester, and I appreciated his support during Lockgate. But we were worlds apart in many ways. He was a boxer and a father of four. I was an unemployed boater. I think we were attracted to the novelty of each other's profound differences, but beyond that, it wasn't ever going to be a thing.

"I understand," I said to Tim. "Can we be friends?"

"Of course we can."[91]

Jane, Pikey and of course Emma, helped me through the Ashton Canal and Manchester city centre locks. I'd done them before with Tyson et al, so I knew what to expect, and with the expert crew of helpers, we reached the other side of Manchester, ready to make the climb up the Rochdale Canal to Todmorden.

---

91 I would later learn that Tim had met someone shortly after our cruise through Manchester with Tyson. They're married now. Good on them.

Chapter 81
Manchester
Colloquialisms

- Now then - an introduction to a thought
- How do? - a variation on "How's it going?"
- Dead good - very good
- Are you winning? - loosely speaking. How are you getting on? Is this going well for you? How are you?
- How are yer doing? - as a greeting. Absolutely never to be answered, always rhetorical.
- That's 'anging - that is ugly
- Pecking me head - annoying me
- That's dead snide - that's uncalled for
- Do one - go away / shut up / I don't agree
- Swear down - tell the truth
- Mither - can replace "annoying" or "bother" as follows
    - "Sorry to mither you."
    - "He was proper mithering me."
    - "You're being a mither."

Chapter 82
The Rochdale Canal

The Rochdale Canal

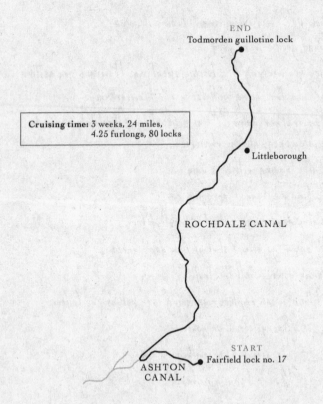

END
Todmorden guillotine lock

Cruising time: 3 weeks, 24 miles,
4.25 furlongs, 80 locks

Littleborough

ROCHDALE CANAL

START
Fairfield lock no. 17

ASHTON
CANAL

THE ROCHDALE CANAL

There was nothing quaint about the Rochdale Canal. The double locks were heavy and deep and the water shallow, with signs warning of unseen obstructions. Passing through Rochdale itself, I had to stop twice to clear rubbish from my propeller. Though the canal was wide, there was a section where the only passage was in the centre of the channel. It required immense concentration to ensure I stayed on track. More than once I became grounded, mostly to find that I was stuck on top of a shopping trolley that had been thrown into the canal.

The cityscape seemed never-ending as I rose up and out of Manchester, and the climb weaved through housing estates and along stretches overshadowed by factories and warehouses. By contrast to the brutal climb and the heavy industrial locks, the locals who stood and watched or helped me through were more friendly and inquisitive than on any other network I'd travelled through. They seemed to have no desire to rush and would interact with the warmth and intrigue that lived up to their reputation.

The urban environment continued all the way to Littleborough, where, some 30 miles and 66 locks after leaving Manchester, the landscape took a dramatic turn. After three days of cruising, I had reached the Pennines, with hills that sat directly on the edge of the canal, reflecting their heavy curves across the water, slithers of waterfalls bouncing me along as I cruised through. I passed sheep, young, but no longer lambs, grazing in the nearby hills. I stayed a few nights in Littleborough, where I moored at the base of a hill populated by alpacas, and for a few nights in Summit, named so on account of being the height of the Rochdale climb, before the canal fell again and I embarked on my final descent. My time in these locations allowed me to reacquaint myself with the countryside, breathing new life into my urban bones as I edged closer to my winter mooring.

I found my mooring just above the last lock before the town of Todmorden. It was a little rough and ready. I pulled in but struggled to locate the mooring rings where the towpath had sunk into the water. The location was set apart from a community of boaters who were moored below the lock by the Golden Lion pub. My winter mooring felt dark and cold where a wall towered over its location.[92] It didn't feel very safe and I wasn't keen on spending my winter there. I carried on cruising and tied up at the next lock landing.

The guillotine lock in Todmorden is an unusual canal structure. Unlike any lock I had seen before, it contained a big sheet of bottle green steel that lifted up and down like a... well, a guillotine. Before I entered the lock, I ran down to see if I could speak to someone on a boat there. I got the attention of a man with a white beard who was painting a canvas in the window of his wide beam. He came outside.

"Hi, I'm Hannah."

"Steve," he said with a nod.

"I've got a winter mooring above the lock, but I'd rather be down here, to be honest."

"I don't blame you," he said. Steve had a Yorkshire accent that could have come straight from a bread advert.

"I don't suppose I could ask you to move up slightly so I can squeeze in?"

"How long are you?" he asked.

"Forty-five feet."

"Ah, a wee one. Yes, that's no problem."

"Great. I'll be down shortly," I said.

I ran back up to the boat, entered the lock and operated it alone. And finally, some six months after leaving London, under a rainbow that stretched across buildings sitting along the edge of the canal, I breathed the Yorkshire air into my lungs and descended my 357th lock at the entrance to the town of Todmorden; the wonderful little town where my granny had been born some 104 years before, and which my brother and his family now called home.

Edith Pierce, my grandmother, was one of the original badass women in my life – a vicar's wife and a mother to four. It's a

---

92 The locals call this the Great Wall of Tod.

coincidence that my brother now lives there, but it's a wonderful one. Granny would have approved of the boat and of this adventure. She loved the great outdoors, and the key to her long and full life was her ability to always look forwards.

I'd visited Todmorden a handful of times and was familiar with its quirky facade. One town along from Hebden Bridge – the Crouch End of the North (or Crouch End, the Hebden Bridge of the South), Todmorden is the modest "up-and-coming" equivalent of my old London home, where cheese and craft beer shops had popped up in recent years. Word of world-famous DJs that had played above the Golden Lion in Todmorden had reached me in London, long before I'd ever visited. The town's brightly coloured shops and cafés with bunting that lay limp across their closed-up entrances due to the arrival of the second lockdown welcomed me with a warm glow. I didn't know what the winter had in store for me, but I knew I was in safe hands in this town.

As I stood on the towpath and opened the lock, I heard three pairs of feet running towards me. One small pair and two big, followed by, "Auntie Hannah!"

John ran to the canal's edge as Ellie and Matthias called after him, Matthias pushing John's younger sister Edith[93] in a buggy.

"Stay away from the edge!" said my brother.

Little John stopped in his tracks and held out a folded-up piece of paper towards me.

"This is for you," he said, grinning.

I opened up the handmade card that contained a cut out picture of Stoodley Pike, the local landmark that sits on top of a hill above Todmorden.

"It's the wizard's finger," he said, referring to the statue on the card.

"We're happy you came to see us," said the message inside the card, followed by four signatures and a picture of a boat.

---

93 Named, of course, after the OG badass woman… my grandmother.

ALL BOATS ARE SINKING

"Welcome to Todmorden," said Ellie.

"Thank you." I was moved by the card. "I can't believe I made it."

"When can you start with childcare?" said Matthias, playfully.

Perfectly on cue, Edith burst into tears.

"Don't take it personally," said Ellie. "The kids need feeding, so we should probably head back. We just wanted to say hello as you arrived. John was very excited. We're going for a walk in the park tomorrow. Do you want to join?"

"I'd love to," I said.

And with that, they were gone, and as the sun began to set, I squeezed into my new home for the next four months.

I'd done it.

Chapter 83
A Wee Dram

As is often the way with boaters, I was welcomed immediately into the fold. The others had been moored in their little cluster for several weeks before I'd arrived and had formed a bond, into which I was welcomed through daily towpath catch-ups.

"They're selling Laphroaig at twenty-five pounds a bottle," I said to Steve as I returned from Morrissons. I'd been in Todmorden for a few weeks and was getting into my rhythm with a planned weekly shop.

"You like whisky?" he said.

"Sometimes a little one before bed, but that's about it nowadays," I said.

"Well, Rose has suggested we get a firepit going this Friday before lockdown kicks in. I'll bring my whiskies and we can have a session if you like."

Steve and Rose's relationship had developed later in life and the romance between them was very much ablaze. Rose was as open and warm as Steve. She was a young at heart Yorkshire woman with a short choppy hairstyle, floral Dr. Martens and a glint in her eye that suggested she might have some tales to tell. They'd been together for eight years, and Rose and her dog had joined Steve and his dog to live together on the wide beam that backed onto my stern. It was a comfort having them as neighbours, something parental in it, as I hunkered down for my first northern winter. They'd ask if I needed anything when they headed off in their car for a fuel run. In return, I baked them (rubbish) bread, and as Christmas approached, mince pies and orangettes.

"Sure, I'll bring some snacks," I said.

ALL BOATS ARE SINKING

That Friday, Steve and Rose, Jacqui and Heidi (one down, on their pirate-themed narrowboat), Glen (who was moored opposite, an ex-teacher, now working on an ice cream van – yes, in winter) and Jimmy (as Yorkshire as they come, on his worker boat next to Glen's) stood around a fire in a metal drum, outside the Golden Lion pub. Save from Glen and I, all were dog owners. Jimmy's two spaniels darted past the flames, as Jacqui and Heidi's aged pug sat on Jacqui's lap with his tongue out. Rose and Steve's 19-year-old English sheepdog and their comparatively junior Bedlington stayed inside the wide beam.

We shared a love for boats, boat parts, boat tales, boat disasters, rivers and all things canals. And for Glen, Steve and I – whisky. We chatted like we'd been moored together for years, and before long we were dancing to music played from my phone on Rose's Bluetooth speaker. The group mocked my accent and congratulated me for my solo adventuring. I knew this was a one-off social event due to the tier system that was on its way and would bring lockdown imminently to the North of England, and I didn't hold back. As the cold December night continued on, I offered to go back to the boat and make up a batch of hot spiced cider. They looked at me like I was speaking another language.

"Trust me, you'll love it," I said.

I returned to the firepit half an hour later with a steaming saucepan of hot spiced cider, which went down as successfully as I'd hoped with the revellers. Finally, our frozen fingers and toes told us to stop with the revelry, and we retired for the night. I was spinning as I climbed into bed.

Two days later, I was able to leave my boat.

～～～～～

"Ey up." Jacqui was walking Pudding the pug along the towpath in a pram. "We were worried yesterday. Your fire wasn't lit."

A WEE DRAM

I'd hoped they hadn't noticed that I had been too hungover to light my fire the day before and so had spent all day in bed watching documentaries on my phone.

"I'm not used to drinking like that anymore," I said.

"Well, you lot got through three bottles of whisky." Rose popped her head out from under the wide beam cratch cover. Jacqui, who had taken a long drag from her vape, burst out laughing.

"We never." I'd started to pick up on the northern intonations.

"Yes, we did," said Steve, joining the debrief.

"Ah, it was fun though, wasn't it?" I said.

We stayed leaning out of our boats and on the towpath chatting to one another before the weather closed in, and we disappeared inside our homes once more. It felt special to have these kinds of interactions with my neighbours, and I was so grateful that I had found this little community. Back in London I hadn't taken the time to really get to know other boaters. This was a new thing for me, and I was finding immense satisfaction in these neighbourly interactions. Back in the boat, I threw some fuel on the fire and thought about my first winter on board. How lonely I had been. Too rushed to enjoy the boat and isolated on my own in the boatyard. I'd spent so many years on the go, and through the experience of lockdown, I was now able to stop and to take time to be with others. I think it's a northern thing too. A slower pace. The ability to pause and to listen.

Chapter 84
Hot Spiced Cider Recipe

Ingredients:

Spices – star anise, cinnamon, cloves, all spice, nutmeg
Half an orange
A dash of brandy
Brown sugar
Cider – I like Thatchers for this. Not too sweet, not too dry.

Method:

Put everything in a pan. Quantities to taste. Heat slowly
(on top of a wood burner if you have one ☺).

Chapter 85
Christmas

The fire rarely petered out, and to my joy I managed to maintain a warm living environment all day and into the night.[94] My boat was peak cosiness in that little spot opposite the Golden Lion pub in Todmorden, and with my new neighbours providing the community aspect I'd been without for so long, a waterpoint and bin facility opposite, and my brother and co. 20 minutes away, I was finding my winter up north delightful and surprisingly easy. My fears of a harsh Yorkshire winter were misplaced. I kept active by hiking in the hills and layering up with Nordic jumpers for walks into town. I was by no means a fish out of water, thriving in my new environment.

When I wasn't hiking, I was writing and baking and job hunting. I'd extended my search now to include the local area, as well as Manchester, and other canal cities like Birmingham and Liverpool. I knew I'd need to take a job soon, and while I'd said no to a few offers that didn't feel right, I was beginning to feel nervous. I pinned all my hopes on a bar job as soon as the pubs reopened. I pondered the possibility of a marina mooring on the Rochdale as I started to fall in love with Todmorden, just as my brother and Ellie had a few years earlier.

As Christmas neared, the boat reeked of cinnamon biscuits and mincemeat. By the glow of the fire, with decorations that I'd put up earlier than ever, I was feeling the joys of the festive season. For

---

94 Apart from whisky head day.

the last seven Christmases I'd been rushed off my feet at work, and now I had time to relish in rituals I'd often only laid on for others.

With the rules allowing for social bubbles, I was able to see Matthias, his wife Ellie, my nephew John and his new baby sister Edith, and spend time with them in their home. Their house, full of books, vinyl records and kids' toys, was atop a hill on the other side of town with stunning views across the valley, a basement bedroom just for me, and a bath.

"Stay whenever you want," Ellie said, as we chased John on his scooter in the park.

I didn't want to. Not because their home wasn't lovely, but because mine was. I felt the boat was so much a part of me now that I couldn't bear the thought of a night away, letting it go cold and damp.

"I'm okay, actually. Thank you, though."

I'd see my family two or three times a week, easing childcare and witnessing the children's firsts. Over my time in Todmorden, Edith would learn to speak, and John to ask questions. Many questions. Ellie and I would go for walks with the children, and our conversation would have us comparing our lockdown experiences. They were vastly different scenarios: I felt I'd lost purpose in losing my job, and with so much time with my own thoughts I was in a perpetual state of wondering what was next, while Ellie had no time for such musings, parenting two small children and working from home in the same office as my brother.

Shaking off mud from our boots in the hallway after one of our walks, Matthias took a break from screen time to say hello, tutting as I explained what I'd been up to since he last saw me.

"Ugh, what I'd do to be in your shoes," he said.

"It's not all roses," I said. "I clearly sleep a bit better than you" – Matthias was mid-yawn and I was looking at his tonsils once more – "but I haven't had a hug in months."

Matthias looked at me. We weren't a hugging pair at the best of times, least of all in the age of Covid, when hugs were reserved for parents and their children and intimate partners.

CHRISTMAS

John and I had developed a "game" called cuddle run. I'd run after him, he'd run away. Edith was more compliant, but in both cases, it was clear that their Auntie Hannah's need for human contact was not reciprocated.

The next time I saw Matthias, he gave me a hug. It was odd but appreciated.

~~~~~

Christmas was fast approaching, and I had cancelled plans to take the train to Ipswich long before the government made the same call. I wasn't comfortable seeing my parents and potentially exposing them to an infection, and with Matthias and Ellie planning to go to her parents, I'd made the decision to spend Christmas alone. It felt right, after all this time, to end the year like this. With a week to go, Boris made the call to restrict movement between tiers, and so my brother and co. wouldn't go to Ellie's parents after all.

"Come and stay on Christmas Eve," Ellie said as we walked through the park with the kids once more.

"Thank you, but I'll stay on the boat, I think, and come for lunch. I'll bring mince pies."

~~~~~

On Christmas morning, I locked up my boat at 7 a.m., pressed play on my "moochin" playlist I'd cultivated over the past year and hiked up Stoodley Pike in the dark. I'd been a few times up to the 4,265-foot hill above Todmorden, which had a monument on top like a giant sword. But I'd never been so early in the day. No other soul was up that hill on Christmas morning, and as I walked and the sun emerged from below, I was transfixed by the colours; a glow of oranges, pinks and yellows that became more vibrant every time I looked up from the ground.

The air made my cheeks ache. I was short of breath as I walked up the hill, occasionally straddling a sheer path of ice formed from the melted snow, until I reached the summit. There was a force with me up that hill that held me in profound strength and clarity. The hike marked another moment on my adventure. An acknowledgement of my ability to be surprised by what makes me happy. Being alone on Christmas morning had felt like a terrifying prospect. I'd been preoccupied of late by the thought of being behind schedule in my life. Single, jobless, childless. And Christmas often served as a reminder for all that I longed for. But I was euphoric. Euphoric to be alone. It was in this surprise, in the movement of my body, in breathing in the air, in the thought of distant family and friends, and a feeling of gratitude for my life, my health, my boat and my unwritten future that I was able to see, with all else stripped away but my presence up that hill, a sunrise and nothing more.

On returning back to the boat, I ate a smoked salmon and scrambled egg breakfast and dressed up as Santa. Astonishingly, I convinced my two-year-old nephew that I was he, delivering a truck-mounted crane to the sweet dear boy. I returned to the boat after lunch to FaceTime all the people I thought about up that hill and was in bed by 9 p.m.

Chapter 86
Boat-Themed Gifts
I've Received

- Felt pirate hat with "Captain Hannah" written on it
- "Captain Hannah" mug
- "Captain ****" mug
- Cap with "Skipper" written on the front
- "You wouldn't say that if I was a man" T-shirt
- Canal fishing book [95]
- Canal boats picture book
- Tin mugs a'plenty

---

95 From my friend Will, of course

Chapter 87
Adversities

The New Year brought snow. Lots of it. More than I'd ever seen, in fact. I would awake some mornings to discover my boat had been encased in 2-inch-thick ice. It cracked against my hull as I made my first movements of the day, like taut elastic snapping. I'd go outside to empty the ash bucket, throw a stone and watch it tap along the surface of the ice. Motion came not from the canal anymore, but from the air, where dew and chimney smoke danced in swirls around my boat. I'd lock the doors again, stick a log on the fire and put on a stove-top coffee. As the boat heated up, clumps of snow would thump off my roof and onto the ice.

When it was safe to do so, I'd layer up and climb up to Stoodley Pike. It was blizzard-like up there, with snow up to the knees. I'd lose my way on the path, and using the monument as my guide, trudge through with my focus on staying upright, stopping en route to do a snow angel. A snow angel for no one but myself. If it was too adverse, I'd traipse up the hill to my brother's home, to build a snowman with John, or jump on a sledge and head for the hill outside their home.

We were in another lockdown now, and between snow days I was looking for work. With pubs not set to open any time soon, a bar job was no longer a solution. I was running out of money. I'd been in employment one way or another since the age of 16, but I now hadn't worked in nearly a year. A job came up locally to work in a supermarket in Todmorden. I clicked on the newly posted advert. The advert disappeared as quickly as it arrived – it had been removed straight away due to oversubscription. A teaching assistant role came up – removed. Warehouse assistant – removed.

ADVERSITIES

It wasn't looking good, and it was weighing on me, like the heavy clumps of snow on my roof.

I arrived back to the boat one afternoon in the pouring rain to see two men erecting a wooden fence across the entrance to the car park a few feet from my boat, creating a barrier between the cars and the canal. I went inside to search the internet. The local Facebook group I had joined months before was a hive of activity.

A message came in from my brother, **"Come and stay at ours."**

The rain was coming, and Todmorden was on flood alert.

"I'm not sure I should leave the boat," I replied.

On the recommendation of my neighbours, I downloaded an app called Flood Aware, which was updated every half an hour to show the water level of the River Calder. If it burst its banks, the river would flood the streets of Todmorden, and the water levels on the canal would rise with it. I refreshed the screen on my new app obsessively, and over the course of the evening I saw the curve take an upward turn. The air-raid-style siren in the neighbouring town of Walsden sounded. We were surely next.

Messages came through from friends, **"You'll be alright... you're on water!"**

It was difficult to explain to non-boaters that this wouldn't necessarily ensure the safety of my home. There was still a risk to me if the water level rose. My pins could unpin and I would be swept away. The boat could be pulled onto a ledge and left at an angle as the water level subsided, which may result in the boat sinking, or if the ropes were too tight, the boat could be pulled underwater.

The feeling of threat was heightened, I'm sure, by the sound. The rain was heavy. The guillotine lock was overflowing like a waterfall as the water cascaded into the canal right next to me. The water level rose, and I threw on my raincoat and climbed onto the towpath to check my pins and ropes at regular intervals. Flooding was imminent and the town on high alert. Living in the relative safety[96]

---

96 For now

of London, I'd never really understood what "high alert" meant in areas susceptible to flooding, until now. Rushing to the shops to stock up on supplies, I walked through the sodden town and saw troops of volunteers in high vis jackets walking the streets in preparation. The chatter on social media was constant, with neighbours reaching out to one another and updates coming in from other towns nearby. There had been newly constructed defences on the River Calder, but the town was primed for the worst. Flood plans were being actioned, neighbours were sharing advice through social media, homeowners could be spotted building barricades with sandbags and the authorities had launched emergency phone lines.

The supermarkets were deserted as everyone stayed home and waited. It was incredible witnessing the community – who had been there before – come together to prepare for the worst. I did my own preparations, as pathetic as I'm sure they were. I set up my bed on my sofa, so I could be near the front door so as to move quickly if my boat became unpinned or needed adjusting to accommodate the rising water. I laid my waterproof trousers, wellies and head torch next to me.

~~~~~~~~

The rain carried on through the night and into the next day. The water level had continued to rise and I had not slept a wink. Shrubs on the towpath that I'd got used to seeing out of my window had disappeared out of view. The rain continued on. All day and into the afternoon and early evening. I continued to adjust my ropes, as did my neighbours.

"Are you okay?" said Steve as we both stood on the towpath, allowing more give in our ropes.

"I think so," I said. "According to my app, it is going to peak at six p.m."

Steve looked exhausted. None of us had slept.

"Never boring, hey," he said, returning to Rose and the dogs inside their boat.

ADVERSITIES

Then, after its peak at 6 p.m., the water level stopped rising and the canal slowly began to come down again. It was remarkable. The River Calder's defences had done the trick, and the town was saved. On Facebook, the community were thanking volunteers and applauding the success of the flood defences. They had been spared the trauma of previous years, where ground floors of shops, homes and pubs were underwater, and canal boats had drifted away and onto the towpath.

The next morning, the same two volunteers returned to remove the flood defence next to the car park.

"You were lucky," they said.

And I felt it. Lucky to be safe and secure in my home. Lucky for my neighbours. Lucky for the beautiful community of Todmorden. Their friendly chatter and apparent togetherness. The hills and the sheep. The snow. So much snow. The sunrises and the cool air on my skin. The picturesque bend of the canal where I was spending my winter, next to the Golden Lion pub.

The same routine repeated itself two more times over the next month, with thankfully the same outcome each time. The camaraderie on Facebook, the eerie silence in the streets, the waiting, the suspense and then the calm. Naively, I hadn't considered flooding as something I would need to prepare for travelling up the Rochdale Canal. Was that why the man in the marina at Bull's Junction had said I was brave to be travelling up here on my own? Maybe that was why my neighbours were so hardy and took this boating malarky all so seriously. Jane and Sean at the marina in Manchester had advised me against travelling up here for winter. So actually, I had been warned. But something in me told me not to listen, that it was something I needed to do.

Chapter 88
Dog Days

I returned to my boat one morning to see it tilted on its side. With the boats able to move again, Jimmy and his spaniels had decided to leave and were heading north towards Hebden Bridge. Despite being a veteran boater, as Jimmy had left, he had forgotten to lower the paddles on the lock below our pound. Water was fast disappearing and as the levels dropped, my boat became caught on the cill on the edge of the canal. I put my shopping down and ran to push it off, but it was too late. It was wedged in position. Jacqui had saved theirs and came to help with mine, as Rose ran towards the perpetrator with a windlass in her hand.

"Jimmy!" she shouted. "You've left the sodding paddles up!"

She disappeared towards the lock to lower the paddles.

"How are you two doing?" I said to Jacqui as we both pushed my boat off the cill.

"We're ready to go." Jacqui and Heidi were anxious to move on. "We need to get down to the main network so we can start trading again," she said.

Their pirate-themed boat relied upon seasonal footfall, and after a year off, it was more important than ever that they took advantage of the spring and summer trade.

The group was dispersing. Glen and Jimmy had left already and Rose and Steve had plans to have their wide beam craned out and put on a ferry to start a new life in Ireland.

Rose returned from the lock.

"Thanks, Rose," I said, my boat now floating again. "When are you and Steve off?"

"We can't move while he's like this." Their sheepdog Dylan's health was deteriorating. "It's too much for him. He's struggling to even get up the stairs to go outside."

I too had decided to move on, once the winter stoppages had cleared. Getting a job was now my priority, and as much as I liked Todmorden, sadly I couldn't see it happening there. My winter in the Calder Valley had been wonderful, and I was sad to say goodbye, but my neighbours were all leaving, and I knew I needed to follow suit. Something else in my brain was telling me to leave. I had experienced eight months of transience, and I wasn't ready to stop. I had to keep moving, but issues were cropping up all over the canal system, it seemed. A landslide on the Trent and Mersey had stopped passage through there, and there was a stoppage on the Macclesfield too. I'd heard tales of people getting stuck on the Rochdale for a whole year due to issues caused by flooding. This year, the stoppages were worse than usual thanks to the adverse weather, and a lack of response due to staff shortages at the Canal and River Trust. The impact of Covid, I'm sure.

It was time for us all to get off the Rochdale Canal, but one of these stoppages had been caused by a broken bridge beyond Littleborough. I knew it was unwise to leave the comfort of the town until it was fixed, only to get stuck somewhere else, without water.

All I could do was wait.

~~~~~~~

Rose wasn't herself. She stayed up most nights now with Dylan the sheepdog, who was becoming weaker and weaker by the day. I'd stopped seeing her out so much and when I did, she walked up and down the towpath with her boy, head bowed. Both tired and in pain.

We passed each other one morning.

"I can't do it, Hannah," she said. "I know I've got to. Look at him. But I can't." Rose wiped away her tears.

ALL BOATS ARE SINKING

"I'm so sorry, Rose," I said, wanting more than anything to give her a hug.

A few days later, the vet came and put Dylan to sleep. I left a bunch of roses on their roof, dropping them a message to say they were there. The towpath was quieter that night. Darker too. Knowing that so much pain was being felt on the boat next door was impossible to ignore, but there was a peace in the stillness too. I knew that with lockdown coming to an end, it marked the beginning of something for Rose and Steve. They could move to Ireland now.

The snow continued, but the days started and ended lighter with the familiar signs of spring on its way, and we all had new adventures afoot.

Chapter 89
Sent to Coventry

After a two-stage interview process, I landed a job: to help open and run a venue for music and music education in the city of Coventry, just in time for their City of Culture celebrations. I was to work from home part-time, and after a few months, go full-time. It was the perfect job for me, and I was relieved to start work again. With the part-time arrangement I could work from home to begin with, stay in Todmorden until the bridge was fixed and would have the ability to move my boat down to the Midlands on my days off throughout the spring.

I'd been to Coventry only once before and had no idea what to expect from a life there. But I remembered the beauty I'd experienced travelling through that part of England in the summer. I'd been surprised by how pretty it was, by how friendly it was. I had no connections in Coventry, but there was something that felt very right about it. It was in the unknown and would be a continuation of my adventure.

On the day I accepted the job, I bought a half bottle of champagne from Morrissons. As I poured a glass, I thought of Jonathan. I'd got a taste for champagne because of him. I'd gone on this voyage, in part, because of him. As much as I still had complicated feelings around that relationship, I was thankful.

"Cheers," I said, as I lifted my glass and took a sip.

I turned my lights off and lit a candle. A halo flickered over the canal map that I had fixed to my wall at the beginning of my journey. The map was now covered in dots. Yellow dots for my stint on the Thames when I first picked up the boat with Craig the expert skipper, blue dots for my three years in London and a red dotted line from Kensal Green in West London all the way up to Todmorden in West Yorkshire. I ran my finger along the red line up through the Grand Union Canal, along the Coventry and Birmingham and Fazeley canals, onto the Trent and Mersey, the Macclesfield, up (half of) the Huddersfield Narrow, back down and through Manchester and the Ashton Canal and finally up to the Rochdale Canal. I stood back and took it in. Under the flickering halo, the map, with tatty rips and Blu-Tack stains, looked like a beautiful and ancient relic. A piece of mine and my boat's history.

I smiled and took another sip of the champagne. *This boat has me by the heart and soul*, I thought. At times, my best friend, at other times, my greatest enemy. It is cracked and uneven, scruffy and unfinished, rusty and scratched. But it is everything I wanted it to be and more. When I see it, I can't help but smile. I stand inside and I smile. I wake up and I smile.

I looked along the length of my boat. It looked so pretty. Unrecognisable to the one I had picked up in Teddington. Since then, I had made it my own; fixed things, decorated things, filled it... with things. The boat had been my sanctuary through the most extraordinary period of my life, and it was the reason I could live so independently over the last few years.

Immediately light-headed in that one glass of bubbles kind of way, I took my jumper off. Dressed in my boxing-inspired jogging bottoms and a cropped top, I played Florence and the Machine's version of "You've Got the Love" from my phone, and I danced. I hadn't danced for so long. It felt good.

The memory of that concert in Hyde Park came flooding back. I was dancing, not alone on my boat, but with Will and Lauryn and thousands of revellers all looking up to Florence and the sky above.

I'm at Glastonbury with Megan, Peggy and Kelly in 2019 on a Sunday afternoon and we're swaying with the crowd to Kylie Minogue.

I'm at Sarah's hen do. The last song of the evening comes on. It's Donna Summer's "I Feel Love" again.

I'm at Latitude Festival. Underworld are performing, and the crowd dance with retro rave moves to "Born Slippy". Syd is to my right.

I'm 19 years old. Arms around my best friend Caz. We're singing along to Snow Patrol's "Chasing Cars" at the top of our lungs.

I'm on my boat, *Argie Bargie*, one mini bottle of champagne down, and I'm dancing to Florence and the Machine's version of "You've Got the Love".

I let the song play out.

Acknowledgements

I started writing *All Boats Are Sinking* in the summer of 2020, not really for anyone but the geese and ducks outside of my window. I left it on a laptop for a year… then I sent it to Caz. Her response and encouragement is the sole reason this book exists. Thank you, Caz O'Shaughnessy, you are my rock.

Bryony Kimmings' workshops unlocked my autobiographical voice and Tim Clare's 100-day writing challenge was a game changer. (Two big recommendations there.) I only hope the person who stole my notebook on day 95 of 100 enjoys the gems that can be found inside it! Rebecca Peyton, you have always been a huge inspiration and I hear your voice in my head most days. Mark Tovell, Euan Borland, Hanna Benihoud, Jo Dockery, Tom Langridge all read my work and gave me encouraging and useful feedback. Max told me I was a writer and I believed him; thank you, Max.

To my agent, Charlie Brotherstone, for believing in the book and me. To my editor, Debbie Chapman. Debbie, I've learned so much from you during this process, thank you for your patience and wisdom. To Rob Ward and Claire Plimmer for the gorgeous book cover and Hamish Braid for the maps and diagrams. To Lucy York, Rebecca Haydon and Imogen Palmer who worked on the manuscript, and to everyone at Summersdale.

To my family, I know it's weird that I do this stuff. I'm amazed and so grateful to you for your openness and acceptance. To my therapist, M, for all that is not here in the book, and for the financial subsidy you gave me for the majority of 2020. D, your support and love has been/is wonderful.

For my inner circle, I'm not listing you, but you're the best bunch I could ever hope for. You are all in the following WhatsApp groups and you know exactly who you are…

ALL BOATS ARE SINKING

* Mystery Chicken
* Tape Alien
* Dirty thirty holiday club
* Madness support group
* SW babes
* Tell them Dave
* Hawaii 50
* Walthsbians
* Lasagne next time
* Boaty McBoatface
* Lowlife

To all the people in this book... you've given me the best adventure.

Canalplan.uk and the Nicholson Waterways guides were two resources I used a lot while writing this book. Thank you to both. Finally, to the Canal and River Trust – I know you're up against it. Keep trying and keep looking out for boaters and their homes.

About the Author

Hannah Pierce trained as an actor before writing, producing and performing in theatre for young people and adults across the UK and abroad. She has worked a number of roles since, but a common thread of presenting live arts is always central to her career. Alongside her "real job", Hannah has written for the stage, and her one-woman show on the valiant adventures of an online dater received critical acclaim. *All Boats Are Sinking* is her first book.

Hannah looks forward to taking on her next writing project, and intends to find inspiration through her imminent foray into a little-known thing called "motherhood". She now lives in South London with one foot still firmly rooted on *Argie* – moored somewhere in the UK.

Find her on Instagram at @hannahonthewater.

Image credits

Have you enjoyed this book?

If so, why not write a review on your favourite website?

If you're interested in finding out more about our books,
find us on Facebook at **Summersdale Publishers**,
on Twitter/X at **@Summersdale** and on Instagram and
TikTok at **@summersdalebooks** and get in touch.
We'd love to hear from you!

Thanks very much for buying this Summersdale book.

www.summersdale.com